INTERACTION
BETWEEN
PARENTS
AND
CHILDREN

Sage's *Series in Interpersonal Communication* is designed to capture the breadth and depth of knowledge emanating from scientific examinations of face-to-face interaction. As such, the volumes in this series address the cognitive and overt behavior manifested by communicators as they pursue various conversational outcomes. The application of research findings to specific types of interpersonal relationships (e.g., marital, managerial) is also an important dimension of this series.

SAGE SERIES IN
INTERPERSONAL COMMUNICATION
Mark L. Knapp, Series Editor

INTERACTION BETWEEN PARENTS AND CHILDREN

LAURA STAFFORD
CHERIE L. BAYER

Sage Series

Interpersonal Communication 13

SAGE Publications
International Educational and Professional Publisher
Newbury Park   London   New Delhi

Copyright © 1993 by Sage Publications, Inc.

For information address:

 SAGE Publications, Inc.
2455 Teller Road
Newbury Park, California 91320

SAGE Publications Ltd.
6 Bonhill Street
London EC2A 4PU
United Kingdom

SAGE Publications India Pvt. Ltd.
M-32 Market
Greater Kailash I
New Delhi 110 048 India

Printed in the United States of America

Library of Congress Cataloging-in-Publication Data

Stafford, Laura.
    Interaction between parents and children / Laura
Stafford, Cherie L. Bayer.
        p.   cm.—(Sage series in interpersonal communication; 13)
    Includes bibliographical references (p.   ) and index.
    ISBN 0-8039-3474-2 (cl).—ISBN 0-8039-3475-0 (pb)
    1. Parent and child.   2. Interpersonal communication.   I. Bayer,
Cherie L.   II. Title.   III. Series: Sage series in interpersonal
communication; v. 13.
BF723.P25S63   1993
306.874—dc20   93-6478

93 94 95 96 97 10 9 8 7 6 5 4 3 2 1

Sage Production Editor: Astrid Virding

Contents

87029

Series Editor's Introduction

The interpersonal communication literature is a literature which focuses almost entirely on interacting *adults*. This book represents a welcome change from that norm by taking a close and comprehensive look at the nature of interaction between parents/caregivers and their young children. *Interaction Between Parents and Children* also comes at a time when the field of communication is giving more and more attention to the study of communication behavior across the life span. While some scholars focus on the nature of interaction during the latter stages of one's life, this book provides important insights into the nature and impact of communicative experiences during the early formative years of our life.

The questions addressed in this book are certainly key issues for scholars, but they are more than that too. Anyone who has been in a parental/caregiver role wants to know the answers to the same questions. For example: How much influence does my (the parent) behavior exert on the developing child? Is my behavior likely to be of greater influence on some aspects of the child and not others? How much and in what ways does my child influence my behavior? How much of what happens in parent-child interaction is due to heredity and how much is influenced by environmental forces? To what extent are influential early experiences subject to change later on? How and in what ways do interactions with siblings and other members of the extended family moderate or magnify the effects of direct interaction between parents and children? And how does my interaction with my spouse/partner (and others) affect my interaction with my child? These questions are central to the concerns of both scholars and parents and constitute the core of this book. The preceding questions about the mutual influence and interaction of parents/caregivers and their children have been addressed in a number of disciplines—e.g., psychology, child development, linguistics, education, communication disorders, pediatrics, and others. Stafford and Bayer have managed to sift through this complex and diverse literature, identify the areas of agreement and disagreement, and cast the conclusions in a framework for understanding human communication during this important period of development. This was a formidable undertaking and one which yields important benefits. It serves as a valuable resource for scholars throughout the academy and lays the foundation for setting an agenda for communication research in this area for the years ahead. And because of its strong interdisciplinary tone, it should serve as a vehicle for bringing scholars together to work on issues of common interest.

—MARK L. KNAPP

Acknowledgments

Sincere appreciation is expressed to a number of persons who aided in the completion of this volume. We are indebted to them for their multiple and varied contributions Considerable editorial assistance and advice was provided by Marianne Dainton. Brant Burleson served as a source of input and feedback many times over the course of this project. The direction of the anonymous reviewers is also acknowledged and appreciated. Numerous colleagues commented on specific portions of the manuscript; although too many to name, their input is greatly appreciated. Preparation of the final manuscript was speeded by the efforts and insightful comments of Lynn Talerico and Pat Strohl.

Finally, we express our gratitude to the series editor, Mark Knapp, for his guidance and counsel in this endeavor. His patience appears infinite. Laura Stafford also thanks both her families of origin and procreation for their support.

Overview

This volume focuses on the interpersonal communication of parents and their children. To even begin to summarize what is known about this topic is akin to assembling a monumental jigsaw puzzle. Research about parent-child communication may be found in every division of the social and behavioral sciences. The domains of language acquisition, development of communication, cognitive development, and socialization are among pieces of this puzzle. Once assembled, these literatures provide a wealth of information about the processes by which parents and children communicate. That is not to say the subject matter has been exhausted. Indeed, many pieces of the puzzle are missing. These missing pieces are the provocative issues and questions driving many programs of research today.

In the chapters that follow, the reader will discover that the research literature is vast, multidisciplinary, and sometimes contradictory. Absolute claims about parent-child communication are difficult to make. Consequently, the potential for scholarly examination of the communication of parents and their children is enormous.

THE PURPOSE

This book endeavors to offer an interdisciplinary integration of recent Western (primarily American) research on parent-child interaction in the "traditional family structure." This focus allows us to meet our goal to compile the most robust conclusions possible from the extant research. Despite the importance of understanding co-cultural and cross-cultural variations in parenting practices, the fundamental data base on which to draw such conclusions does not yet exist. The vast majority of research has been conducted by white middle-class researchers on white middle-class families. Moreover, the task would simply become unmanageable to synthesize from all cultures all potential patterns of parent-child interaction, despite the relatively limited literature base. Hence, it is within this constraint our conclusions are offered.

The purposes of attempting an interdisciplinary integration of literature on parent-child interaction are to illustrate the surprising amount of convergence among disciplines and, we hope, to encourage interdisciplinary awareness, if not collaboration. Given the diverse methodologies evidenced in the literatures, another goal is to encourage dialogue across such boundaries. "Communication across methodological boundaries is often difficult. Although such communication has occurred and resulted in valuable contributions over the years, it is the exception rather than the rule" (Vuchinich, Vuchinich, & Coughlin, 1992, p. 89). Thus it is our intent that this volume function as a research heuristic and a vehicle for conversation between theorists, researchers, and practitioners. The lack of interaction among these groups slows the progress of all.

To accomplish these goals, the tripartite framework proposed by Peterson and Rollins (1987) in their extensive review and synthesis of research about parent-child relations is employed. This framework is derived from theoretical and/or research assumptions concerning the direction of influence between parent and child. Broadly categorized, there are three different views about "who affects whom" in the parent-child dyad and family system. These three views are labeled *unidirectional, bidirectional,* and *systemic.* This volume will illustrate how issues of personal agency shift within each framework but, moreover, how such theoretical notions have been formulated to reflect the development of the child. Research on three topics, widely considered important child variables, is reviewed from each of the three frameworks.

The child variables examined in this volume are *self-control, self-concept,* and *communication competencies* (i.e., language and communication). These were selected on the basis of four criteria: (1) their historical tradition, (2) their currency as evidenced by the number of contemporary empirical studies employing these concepts, (3) their integral relationship to socialization, and perhaps most significant, (4) their importance to today's scholars and practitioners.

Reviewing the same three topics from each of the frameworks organizes the research in terms of the underlying assumptions about the nature of interaction. Such a scheme allows interdisciplinary integration of the literature drawn on. It also serves another important purpose; an historical overview of research on parent-child socialization emerges. The Western historical trend in research methodology has been a move from unidirectional approaches to bidirectional approaches to systemic approaches. This project is necessarily selective in its scope. The reader is not presented a comprehensive review of research about the communicative behaviors of parents and their children. Instead, this book focuses on the issues and selected topics that pertain to interpersonal interaction. Our strategy is to offer concise summaries, point to seminal works, and highlight research exemplars.

OPERATIONAL DEFINITION OF COMMUNICATION

Given that a communication perspective is taken, we must explain what we mean by *interpersonal communication.* The communication discipline is itself eclectic in character. Little consensus exists among its students as to the necessary components of *human communication.* Following Cappella (1987), we view the central and defining feature of interpersonal communication as mutual influence in dyadic interaction: "For interpersonal communication to occur each person must affect the other's observable behavior patterns relative to their typical or baseline patterns" (p. 189). This definition provides the minimal basis for any communication approach to the study of parent-child interactive behavior. It places the communication researcher's focus squarely on mutual influence and observable behavior. Cappella refers to inquiry into the nature of mutual influence and overt behavior as *second-order questions.* Second-order questions are the heart of interpersonal communication, as they focus on the interaction patterns of persons. Evidence related to these questions is examined here as interpersonal communication between parents and children.

We have also touched on topics beyond those of observable behavior, again following Cappella (1987), who notes that communication as interaction necessarily includes phenomena beyond observable behavior. Cappella discussed *first-order questions* as those concerned with factors affecting encoding and decoding processes. An example of a first-order question would be belief systems. Parental beliefs, expectations, and perceptions of the child, for example, influence parent-child interaction. The same holds true for the belief systems of the child. Hence, questions concerning how such belief systems are associated with the manner in which people send and receive messages are quite relevant to the research on parent-child communication.

Some of the literature reviewed reflects Cappella's *third-order questions,* that is, the association between communication patterns (second-order questions) and relationship states and/or outcomes. Third-order questions concern how the observable patterns of interaction are related to consequences for relationships between the interactants and/or the individuals. To illustrate one of many possible third-order questions, the observable reciprocity between mother and child in the Western culture has been argued to be critical for the child's development of communication competencies.

In sum, this framework links the patterns of interpersonal communication with individuals' perceptions, cognitions, and social relationships. It allows scholars to explain and understand the comprehensive picture of interpersonal communication.

A PREVIEW: WHAT THIS BOOK IS

The book is organized into ten chapters. The first three chapters are prefatory. They address fundamental issues and controversies related to parent-child communication. Definitions and issues concerning the three selected child variables are also discussed.

Chapter 1 raises several central issues in developmental theory and research. The issues are basic. Yet they have no easy answers, even after decades of investigative effort. For example, the debate about the relationship of hereditary/genetic factors and environmental influences on communicative behavior is on-going. A review of basic issues is necessary because theories, research, and practice are founded on explicit or, more often, implicit assumptions concerning such issues. Chapter 2 reviews the basics of theories that are the historical roots for many current approaches to the study of the interaction between children and parents. These two chapters, in combination, should assist critical evaluation of the material contained in the remainder of the book. Chapter 3 offers definitions of the three selected variables that serve as examples throughout this text. As indicated earlier, these three variables are self-control, self-concept, and communication and language. Selected issues pertaining to these variables will also be considered.

The heart of this volume is found in Chapters 4 through 9. These chapters are organized thematically by unidirectional, bidirectional, and systemic perspectives on theory and research (Peterson & Rollins, 1987). Chapters 4 and 5 are concerned with findings from research conducted in the unidirectional (social mold) tradition. Such research is driven by the assumption that parental characteristics or caregiving styles influence causally the cognitive, affective, and behavioral development of the child. Social mold approaches thus view the child as a more or less passive entity. The child is molded by his or her parents. The earliest hypotheses in this tradition were derived from psychoanalytic theory. An example is the infamous relationship proposed between toilet training experiences and personality development. Generally, such proposals have lacked strong support in empirical investigations (Rathus, 1990). Subsequent unidirectional research investigated hypotheses driven by theories that integrated psychoanalytic tenets with learning theory (e.g., Miller & Dollard, 1962). A progression of other eclectic approaches followed (e.g., Ainsworth & Bell, 1970; Baumrind, 1967; Coopersmith, 1967). As will become apparent, pure unidirectional orientations seldom actually exist. Even unidirectional researchers recognize child factors as playing some part in parenting, particularly when noting that parents adapt their behavior in response to the development of the child. For those interested in communication phenomena, the social mold approach has been expressed in the question, "How does the communication of the parent impact the child?" Various antecedent conditions of parental communication, dimensions of parenting, and research findings with respect to this question are examined in Chapters 4 and 5.

Chapters 6 and 7 focus on bidirectional models. These models represent the interaction of parents and children as patterns of reciprocal and interdependent behaviors. This perspective emerged when Bell (1968) questioned the tendency of researchers to interpret correlational findings uncritically as evidence for parents effecting changes in children's behavior. Bell demonstrated how such results could just as easily be interpreted as child effects on parental behavior. Thus the scope of inquiry is expanded for bidirectional researchers to two questions. First, in what ways does the child influence parental communication? Second, in what ways are parent-child communicative behaviors mutually reciprocal?

Numerous examples of child behaviors that significantly influence caregivers have been empirically observed. The question today is not *if* children's behavior influences adults, but *how* and *to what degree* it does (Belsky, 1990). Claims that children exercise greater influence over parents than parents do over children are being explored (see review by Bell & Chapman, 1986).

The other bidirectional question asked from a communication perspective focuses on reciprocal interaction; it seeks to describe and explain patterns of parent-child behaviors (e.g., Bruner, 1983; Kaye & Charney, 1980; Street, 1982). Chapters 6 and 7 summarize selected research findings pertinent to bidirectional processes.

Chapters 8 and 9 chronicle the progress toward a systemic perspective. This is the final organizing domain in Peterson and Rollins's (1987) analytic framework. Unlike the other two perspectives, systems perspectives are not usually concerned with the relative strength of influence exerted by the various members of the system. Rather, systems perspectives assume that "all members of a given social network (or family) can influence each other simultaneously" (Peterson & Rollins, 1987, p. 494). All members of the family, and others outside the immediate family, are considered agents of socialization.

There is a paucity of communication research examining the family as a system. This is unexpected, because many concepts and axioms of interpersonal communication theory originated in systems perspective research (e.g., Haley, 1963; Watzlawick, Beavin, & Jackson, 1967). One reason for the relative lack of information about the system is that scholars of the family tend to study the family one dyad at a time, rather than as a unit (Peterson & Rollins, 1987). For example, psychologists have traditionally concentrated on the parent-child dyad, particularly the mother and child. In contrast, the marital pair has been the province of sociologists. Systemic perspectives urge researchers to study the family as an entity. Theorists also consider the larger system within which the family functions. This larger system includes, at a minimum, extended networks, the culture, and society.

A true systems approach for research on the parent-child system should include peers, teachers, and all other members and environmental factors (e.g., political, educational, and economic) impinging on it. To limit the scope of Chapters 8 and 9, however, the focus is on associations between mothers and fathers, the marital relationship, and siblings, with the child variables.

Finally, in Chapter 10, the Epilogue offers a recap of the three frameworks, a broad synthesis, and will identify concerns about and limitations of the present literature.

PARING "EVERYTHING": WHAT THIS BOOK IS NOT

It is difficult to imagine any aspect of children's social and emotional development that is not influenced, to some degree, by communicative interaction with parents. Thus we must be cautious in our enthusiasm for including everything in the scope of parent-child communication. There are other texts focused solely on language (see Lindfors, 1987), social development (see Grusec & Lytton, 1988), cognitive development (see Flavell, 1985), moral development (see Damon, 1988), and human development (see Berk, 1991). Issues related to these topics will emerge in our discussion, but no attempt has been made to synthesize these vast literatures. Excellent up-to-date reviews are available, and many of these will be noted for the reader's reference.

Second, no attempt is made to offer in-depth coverage or a critique of numerous theories relevant to parent-child communication, nor do we discuss all of the theories or perspectives mentioned in the entire volume. A basic review of several foundational theories will be offered. Such a review reveals the diverse theoretical roots of the many literatures on parent-child interaction. The theories selected are those directly tied to both major controversies and the bulk of research on parent-child interaction. There is no consensus that one or another of them is the most fundamental or significant; rather each presents a different perspective for the researcher to consider on various problems. In fact, many "grand theories" that have undergirded much research in the past are no longer sufficient (Markus & Nurius, 1984). The theories highlighted herein have been extended, revised, and/or reinterpreted with major and minor splits from the originals. Also, at times eclectic theoretical approaches that are virtually unrelated to these basic theories emerge. These also provide useful conceptualizations for research. Thus some of the subsequent chapters may give the reader a feeling that theories have run rampant, precisely for the reason that they have done exactly that in recent years. Yet the astute reader will notice allusions to the issues addressed by these theories throughout the volume. Research from numerous orientations has uncovered rich and unexpected connections between dimensions of actual parent behavior and certain characteristics of children (Skinner, 1991). A single theoretical account for such converging findings has not been developed. This does not diminish the importance of the findings, nor does this diminish the importance of theory. Such statements simply reflect how differing theoretical orientations often arrive at the same place. The same holds true regardless of research method invoked. Bailey (1987) asserted:

> In the past there has often been altogether too much chauvinism and dogmatism in social research, with adherents of a particular method claiming a superior method for social research and condemning all others. It is my view that such rivalry is detrimental to the development of social research and the pursuit of

knowledge. The truth of the matter is that each approach has its strengths and weaknesses. Conversely, there are times when each particular method is inappropriate. The tendency to tout one method over others can prevent researchers from seeing the essential complementarity of these various methods. (p. 10)

What corpus of conclusions on parent-child interpersonal interaction can be drawn? This is our aim. The reader will find more commonality in research findings across disparate orientations than one might expect. Of course, there is never total convergence; areas of dissension will be noted as well.

CONCLUSION

Although the focus is on parent-child interaction and selected child variables traditionally studied as *outcomes,* this volume is not intended to serve as an advice manual on how to promote optimal development. Our intent is to provide a guide to some issues and diverse literature bases confronting anyone studying interpersonal communication between parents and children, rather than to serve as a comprehensive and exhaustive synthesis of all issues and topics in this domain. We consider research within three primary historical paradigms. In unidirectional approaches, children are passive agents, shaped by others. In bidirectional approaches, children are active agents in their own socialization; children socialize parents. In systemic approaches, children are part of the family system, and family processes have consequences for all family members. We simply highlight those consequences for the child.

Our strategy has been to keep the focus primarily on interaction. Only three variables (self-control, self-concept, and communication competencies) are discussed in any detail. This has been done in an effort to pare "everything" to a manageable body of literature. These exemplar variables allow the similarity in issues, findings, and problems across disciplines to emerge within each overarching theoretical framework. Each two-chapter section linked to one perspective stands almost separate from those sections on the remaining two perspectives. As a result, a clearer picture of each perspective is drawn.

The goal is to provide an overview and draw what generalizations seem robust from each of the three frameworks, given the current state of knowledge. We aspire to demonstrate that many generalizations emerge regardless of discipline, theory, or method invoked. Many disciplines study interaction and communication. The focus of the communication discipline is on inter-action, hence this discipline seems an appropriate meeting ground for inter-disciplinary efforts. A communication perspective on the study of parents and children lends logical coherence to research findings obtained across disciplines.

In sum, we hope to promote further interdisciplinary integration well be-yond the scope here. This need for collaboration has long been recognized, and "integrative work should be pursued because it can lead to more valid scientific conclusions" (Vuchinich et al., 1992, p. 89). In addition, we hope to foster dialogue between theorists, researchers, and practitioners. Above all, we hope to stimulate further substantive research into the communication between children and parents.

1

Continuing Controversies About Children and Their Development Relevant to Parent-Child Interaction

INTRODUCTION

To understand human communication, it is necessary at the outset to appreciate its complexities. Consider, for example, a conversation between two well-acquainted adults. Note that:

1. Most, if not all, utterances are novel constructions. That is, conversations are not based on the exchange of memorized stock phrases but rather on expressions constructed spontaneously.
2. Each speaker's turn at talk is accompanied by nonverbal cues. These may vary in quality and/or intensity of expression in an infinite number of combinations.
3. Interaction occurs in physical settings, which may change—subtly or dramatically—from day to day.
4. The possibility of repetition is negated by the fact that historical time never repeats.
5. Above all, individuals themselves are ever changing.

In sum, each communicative interaction is unique. As such, weaving a theoretical web to account for even the most ordinary communication event among adults presents a Sisyphean task. This web is considerably more intricate when one of the actors is a developing child.

To date, interpersonal communication scholars have focused almost exclusively on the behavior of relatively mature actors. Children largely have been neglected. Ironically, in consequence, nearly all theoretical accounts of children's communicative development and parent-child communication have been formulated by scholars in disciplines other than communication (but see e.g., Applegate, Burke, Burleson, Delia, & Kline, 1985). Regardless of origin, however, such accounts have contributed greatly to our understanding of parent-child communication. They have also produced controversies over a number of critical issues. Seeking answers to the questions raised by these issues undoubtedly will influence research and theorizing in the years ahead.

Given the communication discipline's primary focus on adult and young adult behavior, typical students of human communication may be somewhat unfamiliar with the issues unique to the study of children. Children's development is simultaneously visible and obscured, continuous and discontinuous, dramatic and subtle, and it occurs in multiple domains (e.g., physical, cognitive, social, and emotional). All of these characteristics, and likely many more, may be observed to impact children's communicative development. In an amazingly short period of time, children develop conversational pragmatics, discover strategic uses of nonverbal gestures, and acquire the fundamentals of their native language. By age 5, children possess a near adultlike command of many communicative skills. Such skills normally continue to be refined and elaborated at least through adolescence. But individual achievements alone cannot fully explain communication development. It is also a social process. The task of this chapter is to survey basic controversies in the study of children, particularly those relevant to parent-child interaction. The four controversies to be examined are broadly categorized as addressing:

a. Cultural constructions of "the child";
b. Roles of heredity and environment;
c. Processes and paths of development;
d. Outcomes of earlier versus later experience.

This scheme consciously departs from the typical organizing framework employed by developmental scholars (e.g., Grusec & Lytton, 1988; Salkind, 1985), because the intent here is to inform rather than to provide a basis for theoretical critique. Also, it will soon become apparent that separation of the issues outlined above, no matter on whose authority, is somewhat artificial. Clear lines of demarcation simply do not exist.

THE CONTROVERSIES

"What is the nature of human beings?" poses both the ultimate philosophical question and the starting point for inquiry into parent-child communication. It is not simply an academic exercise to be concerned with whether humans are inherently good, blank slates, or innately evil or whether they have free will or are determined by their environment, and so forth. Such values underlie scholars' investigations and the advice given by practitioners. In addition, the lay theories of parents are as important in a pragmatic sense as formal theories resulting from tussles with such issues are in a scientific sense. Thus this survey begins with the essential issue in the study of human behavior, that of the nature of *the child*.

What Is *The Child*?

Perspectives on children are cultural inventions: beliefs about the nature, development, and socialization of children constructed and sustained in the service of a society's beliefs about human nature, the social order, and the cosmos.

Borstelmann (1983, p. 1)

Members of Western cultures view childhood as a special period of life, something to be valued and respected. It was not always this way. Historical reviews paint a picture of children being treated cruelly: ignored, abandoned, or worse. For example, in ancient Rome infanticide was a father's prerogative (although it was not generally exercised). John Calvin, in the 16th century, decreed the death penalty for juveniles who were chronically disobedient to their parents (Maccoby, 1980). Children were often treated as miniature adults and expected to act as such. Maccoby (1980) contended that by today's standards most of the children in Europe and America were subject to extreme child abuse. Borstelmann (1983) moderated this bleak picture by cautioning the reader to consider what life was like for adults during the same historical periods. Children may not have been singled out for harsh treatment. Rather, he argued that children were caught in the same unmerciful situation and struggle for survival endured by adults.

These explanations for the treatment of children do not, however, explain societal beliefs about the child. Such treatment of children may be seen to reflect culturally held puritanical notions about the child's evil essence. Parents of earlier times seemed to be preoccupied with breaking the child's sinful will via austere discipline; displays of affection were thought harmful for the child (Maccoby, 1980). Paradoxically, this strict manner of child rearing was a result of the growing scholarly attention to parenting and pedagogy. The general consensus at the time was of the need to train children with severe discipline.

Not all agreed. Most notably during the Age of Enlightenment, Jean-Jacques Rousseau championed the claim that childhood was a unique stage of life and children's behavior was perfectly appropriate for this stage. Despite his writings, however, children's essential differences from adults were not widely acknowledged until the 19th century.

Specific conceptions of the nature of the child have evolved from ancient Greece to more modern times. Yet there are important commonalities among most views:

1. Children are the future of the society.
2. Early childhood experience is related to adult character.
3. Caregivers' behavior relates to socialization goals.
4. Discipline of children and expression of affection are both recognized as important parental behaviors.

These points emerge from prescientific views of Plato and Aristotle, and the modern-day conceptions stemming from Judeo-Christian doctrine and the writings of John Locke and Rousseau.

ANCIENT GREECE

In general, children were objects of adult affection and held a secure place within the family. Vigorous physical play was encouraged to develop the body. The goal of socialization, according to philosophers Plato and Aristotle, was to prepare persons to govern the state.

In his efforts to establish a meritocracy, Plato called for state intervention in child rearing. Children of both sexes would thus be afforded equal opportunity to develop their natural abilities in a setting isolated from corrupting influences of society. Self-control in children would develop from the example of firm control demonstrated and exercised by their teachers. But balance between affection and control was important; excesses such as spoiling or tyranny were to be avoided. The former would give rise to "peevish, easily upset children," the latter to children "sullen, spiritless, servile" in nature.

Plato's student, Aristotle, implicitly acknowledged a concern for fostering natural differences among children, but he disagreed on where this should occur. Reasoning that different environments were likely to serve children's individualized needs better than a monolithic, state-operated system, Aristotle advocated rearing children in the home. Aristotle was also concerned with individual liberty and privacy. Preserving the sanctity of the family was central to achieving this larger goal. However, Aristotle did argue for the most capable boys to be placed into the care of the state for training. The seeds of individualism were sown in ancient Greece, although they lay relatively dormant for many centuries. Plato's attention to children's individual abilities and emphasis on balance in adult caregiving behavior and Aristotle's endorsement of the family are notions that have endured to the present. Aristotle might also be considered the first life-span developmentalist. He referred to three stages of life (youth, prime, and elderly) and identified cognitive and behavioral characteristics for each stage. For example, during the stage of youth, Aristotle commented that one knows all and acts impulsively.

MODERN INFLUENCES

Contemporary Western cultural images of the child are multidimensional and tend to cycle into and out of prominence across time (Borstelmann, 1983). Nevertheless, these images find their roots in one of three distinct views of the child's nature at birth: (1) innately evil, (2) blank slate, and (3) innately good. These originate, respectively, from the tenets of Christianity, the empirical views of Locke, and the humanistic philosophy of Rousseau.

The innately evil child was conceived from the Judeo-Christian view of children born in original sin. In the Old Testament, children are characterized as self-willed and prone to mischief, lacking in understanding, and generally in need of discipline. Punishment was thus legitimized. The puritanical expression "Spare the rod, spoil the child" originated from such a view.

Yet there was a measure of ambivalence in the way children were regarded in the Old Testament. They were also seen as a gift from God and thus a source of family honor. This paradoxical view of children was exacerbated in the writings of the New Testament. There, children were symbolized as the hope of regeneration. Described as unspoiled, trusting, and therefore more able to receive God, children were depicted as models for adults of the desired religious attitude.

The origins of parental inconsistency seem to stem from this Judeo-Christian construction of the child. The unresolved paradox of the Judeo-Christian view set the stage for "an antipathy . . . between parental control of and affection for the child that has persisted to the present day" (Borstelmann, 1983, p. 36). In general, however, the innate sinfulness of children preoccupied parents adhering to Judeo-Christian views.

Whereas the Judeo-Christian view focused mainly on the evil child, Locke, the father of British empiricism, offered a sharply contrasting view.

Locke (1690/1959) invoked the powerful metaphor of the blank slate, or *tabula rasa,* in characterizing the essential nature and potential of children. All that a child becomes is a function of his or her experiences. This claim implies a view of infants as neither antisocial nor prosocial but asocial. Child rearing thus is a weighty responsibility for parents. In Locke's view, children's rationality and individualism would be fostered by parents strategically using incentives and disincentives to mold behavior. Locke (1693/1964) encouraged parents to exercise reasonable authority and to use deliberately environmental contingencies to achieve explicit goals. He further stressed the importance of parents serving as, and providing, good role models.

Locke's writings provided the foundation for American behaviorism, which is built on associationism, reinforcement, modeling, and imitation. In essence, he was the first to articulate the social mold perspective. Locke was also concerned with parental expression of affection. He provided a sensitive developmental analysis of the relationship between parent and child and suggested that the liaison should be founded on authority early in life but, as the child matured, move toward a relationship based on egalitarianism and friendship. It has been only relatively recently that texts have considered the implications of such power shifts and endorsed them to parents (e.g., Jensen & Kingston, 1986).

The third distinct view, that of the child as innately good, was offered by Rousseau (1762/1911). Rousseau characterized the child as active, exploring, and innately well motivated, corruptible only by a corrupted adult society. A doctrine of *romantic naturalism* emerged from Rousseau's memorable phrases such as "Reverse the usual practice and you will almost always do right" and "Never punish him, for he does not know what it is to do wrong" (quoted in Kessen, 1965, p. 80). The implication of romantic naturalism was that leaving the child to his or her own devices was the best route to social and moral development. From this point of view, the parenting task was not nearly so demanding. Parents were encouraged to let nature be the teacher. Given an innately good child, the child's expressive freedom was to be encouraged. Rousseauean parents seemingly were licensed to be permissive, even indulgent.

Parenthetically, it should be noted that the doctrine of romantic naturalism was built on selected Rousseauean phrases taken out of context from *Emile, or on Education* (1762/1911) (Borstelmann, 1983; Kessen, 1965). Rousseau did not mean to imply that children should be raised in a laissez-faire fashion but rather under conditions of "well-regulated liberty." Our concern is not with setting the record straight but rather to point out that romantic naturalism is alive and well today in some best-selling parenting manuals (e.g., Gordon, 1970).

IMPLICATIONS

The essential nature of human beings has mystified philosophers, theologians, and scientists for millennia. The preceding section has examined the pervasive themes in cultural conceptions of the child, from the Greek philosophers' consideration of their unique individual abilities and how these might best be developed to the three disparate views in modern conceptions.

The practical importance of considering adult conceptions of children is linked to the assumption that the quality and quantity of parent-child interactions can be predicted from the views held by parents (Bochner & Eisenberg, 1987; Sigel, 1985). Given the reasonableness of this claim, it is surprising that the reflexive nature of belief systems and behavior is understudied. But then, the relationships are quite complex. Although sporadically reported, studies examining parental belief systems and child outcomes have supported the theorized relationship (Collins & Gunnar, 1990; see also review by Murphey, 1992).

However, the current weight of the evidence is somewhat insufficient to guide professionals such as parent educators or family counselors. Although talking about interpersonal communication in general, not parent-child interaction specifically, Cappella (1987) has questioned whether intervention is better directed toward beliefs about relationships or toward patterns of interactions within the relationship. The question at hand is, "Which would induce beneficial changes in the relationship?" The state of knowledge at this time does not allow the question to be answered.

The issue of parental beliefs impacting patterns of interaction is an important one. For those who would conduct these needed investigations, two points are worth stressing. First, the concept of the child is part of a theory's substructure. Because of its concealed nature, the assumed image merits both acknowledgment and close scrutiny as the theory's heuristic and explanatory merits are evaluated. In addition, these assumptions constrain, to a greater or lesser degree, what researchers choose to look for among communication phenomena, thus further shaping theoretical explanations. It would serve us well to remember that:

> Social scientists have often failed to consider that they too, like parents and their advisors, seek to capture, contain, and control "the child" in the service of their particular ideologies. "The child" is always, however, a cultural invention, a

powerful symbol of how adults view themselves and the world in which they
live. (Borstelmann, 1983, p. 11)

The Role of Heredity and Environment

There are two sharply contrasted doctrines of development. One emphasizes
heredity and the powerlessness of environment. The other exalts environment
and makes it the architect of the growing organism. The former doctrine traces
the makeup of the individual to all determining unit characters of genes. Even
complex psychological characteristics are attributed to these original packets of
chromosomal material. The alternative doctrine suggests that even physical
characteristics are molded by the conditions of development; and that mental
characteristics, including capacity, talent and temperament are ultimately the
result of training and conditioning.

Gesell (1928; quoted in Kessen, 1965, p. 212)

The nature-nurture controversy on where development is determined is of
relatively recent vintage. We have seen that Rousseau emphasized children's
inborn motivations, whereas Locke exalted environmental interaction. Neither philosopher, however, discounted a considerable and important role for
the other factor. Unfortunately, the same cannot be said for the social and
behavioral scientists of the 20th century. Protestations of Skinner (1963,
1987) aside, the explanation of human behavior in a simple environmental
stimulus-response paradigm, although certainly parsimonious, has proven
neither sufficient nor satisfactory. Behavior is multiply determined. To omit
consideration of any reasonable contributing factor is to risk misunderstand-
ing the communicative process. In considering the nature-nurture issue,
there are three key points:

1. The behavior of children and parents has origins in the domains of both heredity
   and environment.
2. The individual's genetic program unfolds in the environment; thus research
   addressing the nature-nurture issue should address both the range of behavioral
   possibilities and their expression.
3. There are multiple constituents of *nature* and *nurture*.

In the late 19th and early 20th centuries, two disparate research agendas
emerged. British scientists focused on genetic determinants whereas mainstream American researchers addressed the environmental antecedents
(Grusec & Lytton, 1988). This scholarly segregation contributed to the widespread dissemination of two (mis)conceptions: (1) that the gene-behavior

pathway was independent of the environment-behavior pathway and (2) that the linkage between genes and behavior, and environment and behavior was relatively close and direct (Gottlieb, 1983).

According to McClearn (1964), the so-called nature-nurture controversy erupted when Watson (1924), the father of American behaviorism, rejected the claim that behavior could be influenced by one's genetic makeup and issued his infamous boast:

> Give me a dozen healthy infants, well formed, and my own special world to bring them up in, and I'll guarantee to take any one of them at random and train him [*sic*] to be any type of specialist I might select: a doctor, lawyer, artist, merchant, chief, and even a beggarman and thief, regardless of his talents, penchants, tendencies, abilities, and vocation of his ancestors. (p. 104)

The vehemency of the proponents of behaviorism, and their emphasis on environmental contingencies to the exclusion of all else, became the lightning rod for nativists' critiques. The most strident response was issued by Chomsky (1965) in his review of Skinner's *Verbal Behavior* (1957). Unfortunately, the behaviorist-nativist debate stifled the more tenable view that behavioral variability was most likely a function of interaction of an individual's genetic and/or biological makeup and the environment (Anastasi, 1958; Gesell, 1928). More often than not, lip service, instead of research effort, was paid to Anastasi's (1958) call for examination of how heredity and environment impact development. Even today "there probably is no issue more violently debated" than what is learned and what is innate (McConnell, 1989, p. 342).

Understanding how nature and nurture interact has taken the form of comparative studies of twins (e.g., Lytton, Watts, & Dunn, 1988) and adopted children (e.g., Thompson & Plomin, 1988). The result is a view decidedly more based in the interaction of nature and nurture than the total reliance on one or the other.

Thus far, the question of nature and nurture in the development and expression of human behavior has been discussed as though there were clear-cut distinctions. Actually, these terms have been used quite loosely. There is no single view of what aspects belong to *nature* and what belongs to *nurture*.

The content of nurture was specified quite nicely in the writings of Locke and Rousseau (see "Modern Influences," above). These philosophers were far less precise about what the nature of human beings entailed. Darwin (1859), however, was infinitely more specific. He positively placed *Homo sapiens* within the phylogenetic sequence of biological organisms. His work spearheaded the debates on the nature of the human species and dominated the study of the family for the last half of the 19th century (Hutter, 1985).

And as Mendel's principles of genetic inheritance became more widely known, scientific understanding of humans' biological nature became a necessary complement to the work of the philosophers (McClearn, 1964). Identification of variables and their categorization into nature and nurture are still far from uniform or precise. For example, *nature* can engender physiological, biochemical, anatomical, ecological, or evolutionary dimensions, and various combinations of these. Another approach is to lump considerably more diffuse sets of phenomena under each label. Cappella (1991) located "social, cultural, and environmental forces impinging on the organism" in the nurture category and associated "biological, genetic, and evolutionary forces" with nature (p. 4). Digging into the nature-nurture question often proves to be far more complicated compared with its surface appearance. Just as the interaction hypothesis may be the most reasonable, it is more useful to consider nature and nurture as multidimensional.

> In looking for biological sources of ultimate causation for patterns of human interaction, one is not easily brought to a position of biological determinism. Rather, I think that one comes to appreciate the intricate relationship between social and biological behavior and the common biological bases that we all share as human primates in that most human of activities, communication. (Cappella, 1991, p. 28)

In general, communication scholars have been detached from the nature-nurture controversy. According to Cappella (1991), a normative, singular focus by communication scholars on social and cultural (i.e., environmental) factors has obscured examination of potential biological or genetic mediators of behavior.

Why should communication scholars confront these issues? First, consider the research ramifications. The social mold view owes its existence to a singular focus on environmental influences. Ascribing all outcomes to parental actions often led to researchers making inflated claims touting the family's influence on children's personality and intellectual development (Bochner & Eisenberg, 1987). Of course, the opposite and more objectionable position for most social scientists would be to focus solely on the gene-behavior relationship. Rather, "An individual's genotype (i.e., genetic composition) is best viewed developmentally as setting limits to, or circumscribing, behavior variation rather than establishing a blueprint from which behavior expression invariably and inexorably flows" (Gottlieb, 1983, p. 2).

Second, recognizing that there are biological, as well as social, origins of behavior balances our understanding of human communication (Cappella, 1991). It seems reasonable that there are biological influences that are universal among members of the species but also unique to individuals. Undoubtedly, the same can be said with respect to social influences. Parents' behavior does affect development, but within the constraints of genetics (Clarke-Stewart, 1988). Eventually, all possibilities must be considered for a full accounting of human interactive behavior.

Processes and Paths of Development

The central tenet of a developmental approach is to observe, describe, and explain change over time. Understandably then, there is tremendous diversity in developmental research. As a starting point for considering the controversies surrounding processes of development, it will be useful to identify two important commonalities. First, developmental approaches share an interest in studying the human being as he or she changes over time. Second, the perspective rests on the assumption of Werner's (1957) orthogenetic principle: "Wherever development occurs, it proceeds from a state of relative globality and lack of differentiation to states of increasing differentiation, articulation, and hierarchic integration" (p. 126).

Beyond these commonalities, theoretical explanations vary widely in addressing a number of critical issues.

1. *What develops?* That is, what aspects of the individual as a biological being situated in time and space are changing?
2. *How does it develop?* How can the process be described? Is development quantitative, qualitative, or both? Is it continuous or discontinuous? Is the process systematically related to the individual's chronological age? Is it integrated with and dependent on developments in other domains? Or is development simply a collection of parallel processes?
3. *What is normal development?* What are the implications when deviations from the norms are observed? What are the implications for parents and educators to foster this?

The complexity of each of these seemingly simple questions becomes apparent as each is examined in the following sections.

WHAT DEVELOPS?

The quick answer is, of course, everything. The human infant progresses through a dramatic, yet lengthy, sequence of change in every imaginable aspect. The emergence of the life-span perspective has informed considerably the study of development but has not yet significantly affected the focus and direction of communication research (but see Nussbaum, 1989). Communication studies necessarily cut across disciplines because, as has been previously noted, communicative behavior is multiply determined. The essential point here is for the communication researcher to integrate the psychological, physiological, social, and cultural as a foundation for research. Then the question shifts from what can be related to communication, to what bears a significant relation to communicative behavior.

HOW DOES IT DEVELOP?

At present, most theories that are developmental in their approach address a limited range of phenomena and are relatively informal in nature. To ask the question of how something develops draws one once again into the nature-nurture controversy. In this respect, theoretical accounts of processes are founded on one of two basic models. First is the maturation model, which depicts the unfolding of the genetic program of the individual. Maturation includes changes accompanying growth and the passage of time. The second model emphasizes organismic responses to environmental stimuli. Learning is seen as the result of experience rather than the unfolding of innate mechanisms. It would be reasonable to suggest that, conterminous with the change in attitudes regarding the nature-nurture issue, future theoretical accounts will also lean toward interactionist explanations for observed behavior.

For many years, developmental research has relied on explanatory models that are simplistically described as *ages*-and-*stages*. These two components were inextricably linked via Gesell's work in the first half of the 20th century on maturation and related individual developmental achievements.

Actually, there are different implications for each component. First, consider age. Chronological age offers many advantages for research and practice, such as measurement accuracy and convenience. It is easy enough to develop statistical norms for behavior given a certain age. Perhaps the biggest drawback to the use of age as an explanatory variable is that development is a process. Age may be only a descriptive index of development not an explanation for it. Other variables, such as social class, cognitive development, or emotional development, may be involved in explanations for the relationships of variables under study. Chronological age may be associated only tangentially with these variables.

The second component, stages, deals with the "shape" of development. The earlier theories dichotomized shape, examining it as either (1) continuous, consisting of relatively smooth sequences depending on a consistent series of underlying laws or antecedents, or (2) discontinuous, change as independent and qualitatively different stages characterized by distinct properties. The behaviorist approach is the paradigm case for continuous change. Freud's psychoanalytic theory is a classic discontinuous approach. The ages-and-stages model is probably both simplistic and outmoded. While the concept of stages has served a valuable function in organizing data and has promoted clarity of theoretical explanation, there has been a good deal of debate over whether or not development occurs in stages. Empirical studies, particularly those addressing hypotheses derived from Piagetian theory, have not obtained convincing evidence for stages as abrupt, qualitative changes governed by different sets of laws (Flavell, 1982). But at the same time, development is not solely continuous. Thus Kagan (1971) has suggested that researchers might better consider the shape of developmental processes along a continuum of continuity and discontinuity.

The question of why development proceeds as it does raises in itself another long-running controversy. That is, should the explanations for development be law governed or can the "why" question be addressed by positing a more rulelike explanation that incorporates conditions accounting for individual differences? Traditionally, laws are viewed as generalizations that do not accommodate individual differences in explaining behavior, whereas rules can explain apparent deviations. Dealing with these questions is largely a matter of scholarly preference and philosophical view. However, the rich descriptions of humans' behavior offered by interpretive, or rules, explanations have been an increasingly popular approach to research (see Rizzo, Corsaro, & Bates, 1992).

WHAT IS NORMAL DEVELOPMENT?

Normative development is often considered the baseline for comparison as researchers proceed in their work. However, as Walsh (1982) noted, what constitutes normalcy has not been established consistently. Although several views of normality have been noted (see Offer & Sabshin, 1974), three are most common: (1) normality as health, (2) normality as utopia, and (3) normality as statistical norm.

Normality as health is the view that a family, or all of its members, is normal if there is an absence of dysfunctions such as emotional disturbances, drug abuse, and so forth. In the view of normality as utopia, functioning at the optimum level has been considered normal. In this case, a continuum may be drawn with average or asymptomatic families in the midrange and severely dysfunctional families at the low end of a continuum. Walsh (1982) noted that *normal* can also be viewed as simply the average, that is, the typical pattern or statistical norm. This is the concept of normality most often demonstrated in the literature, in which researchers define a child or family as normal if it falls within the statistical midrange. From this view, the outliers, by definition, are abnormal; optimal families are as "abnormal" as dysfunctional ones.

Undoubtedly, how one defines what is normal has implications for research questions, policy, and practice, as well as parental expectations and practices. Research findings might easily be misinterpreted unless one understands the particular conceptualization employed by researchers.

The social mold perspective reflects the pervasive, albeit implicit, assumption in the literature on child development that there is *a* good or right way to parent. The quest has been to find the optimal parenting behaviors that will, cross-situationally, result in optimal child outcomes. Parents are also caught in this trap; witness the plethora of popular parenting books and manuals, magazines, and parenting skills training programs. The presumption of many scholars that there is one right way to parent was built on a model of white middle- to upper-class parenting. This bias has, however, devalued parenting styles of various ethnic groups and minorities that may be just as beneficial for children. The trend today is toward the position that there may be multiple paths to normal, or optimal, development (Parke & Asher, 1983). Yet as will be discussed in the Epilogue, not all researchers have shifted away from the one right (white middle-class) way to parent. Problems of researcher ethnocentrism merit consideration in determinations of normal family interaction.

Outcomes of Earlier Versus Later Experience

The last controversy to be examined concerns at what point, if ever, childhood experience is related to adult outcomes. Implicitly or explicitly, most theoretical perspectives deal with the issue of the "formativeness" of early experience. One stance is a strongly deterministic one, leading to a view that parents' socialization strategies and their consequences for children are molding, cumulative, and relatively immutable. The contrasting perspective stresses a greater degree of human choice or free will. The implication of the second view is that although child outcomes at certain points in the socialization process may be seen as direct consequences of parents' communication, such developmental achievements are not fixed for life (Belsky, 1990).

In seeking answers to this debate, however, philosophical questions are raised. In particular, the determinism versus free will debate goes directly to the ontological question concerning the degree to which humans have free choice. This debate, like the nature-nurture controversy, has often been heated. Consider, first, the definitions of each term provided in the *Dictionary of Behavioral Science* (Wolman, 1989):

> Determinism. The doctrine that all phenomena, including behavior, are effects of preceding causes. Thus, with knowledge of relevant antecedent conditions, the subsequent events can be predicted. (p. 91)

> Free will. The philosophical and religious doctrine that attributes the cause of behavior to volition and independent decisions of the person rather than to external determinants. (p. 139)

The debate seems to stem from *implications* of the deterministic model. Critics claim that this model, which focuses on explaining cause and-effect relationships among variables to predict future behavior, denies by implication human ability to choose. Therefore, how can individuals either accept credit for their achievements or be held responsible for their negative actions? In effect, determinism has been critiqued as *predeterminism*, a view of human nature that reduces humans to pawns of the environment.

Obviously, this is related to the controversial issue of the active or passive nature of the child in relationship to the outside world. Do children play an active role in selecting experiences they desire to investigate and understand? Do children have control over their own environment? Do children even have choices? Or are children (pre)determined by the occurrences in their environment? Are children molded by experiences as they passively react to rewards and punishments, virtually independent of their own choices?

The central question raised is how active are children in influencing their own outcomes or to what extent are children passive vessels simply to be filled by the parent and environment? Perhaps a more tenable answer is in the middle of these extremes. Today, very few scholars seem to be predeterminists (à la Skinner) or teleologists (who assert that persons are always active and planning). Rather most scholars describe themselves as "soft" determinists. From this position, behavior is seen as constrained by the environment at times, but at other times and in other situations, behavior is the exercise of one's free will.

The notion that every *thing* a person is can be traced to antecedents in one's genetic makeup and/or social experience is remarkably pervasive in American society. The notion has been long perpetuated by theorists and writers of texts and popular books on parenting. The search for antecedents of adult behavior in childhood experiences has generated a great deal of research.

However, claims that early experiences carry much, if any, weight past middle childhood and adolescence have been challenged. Some argue that little association, of virtually any kind, has been found between adult characteristics and parenting and early family life (Halverson, 1988; McCrae & Costa, 1988a, 1988b; Rowe, 1990). The studies using retrospective techniques to assess the now-adult remembrances of childhood interactions with parents are notable exceptions. However, such evidence is often granted little credence due to methodological problems (Halverson, 1988). Yet, Kohlberg, Ricks, and Snarey (1984), based on their extensive review of studies of child development, contend that the idea of early interaction determining the path for the rest of one's life is "a myth" (p. 93).

> It would doubtless seem incredible to many readers that variables such as social class, educational opportunities, religious training, and parent love and discipline have no substantive influence. . . . But imagine for a moment that this is correct, what will it mean? (McCrae & Costa, 1988a, p. 448)

Indeed, what would it mean? How *would* the study of parent-child interaction change? How would intervention change?

Early experience is not totally discounted. Even Rowe (1990), one of the most outspoken of the critics, pointed out that extremely abusive or neglectful parenting practices probably do have long-term repercussions. How extreme does the interaction between a child and a parent have to be before it retains a formative influence? Rowe asks, What is the threshold at which parenting carries long-term effects? As of yet, this question lacks answer.

The dispute over the formativeness of parent-child interaction is of utmost theoretical importance. If consequences of parent-child interaction are related only in the short term, entire disciplines of study are constructing nothing more than a parenting manual aimed at helping parents survive the early years or, perhaps at best, recording social history à la Gergen (1973).

In sum, crucial questions for scholars concerned with the interaction between parents and children include the following: Are the socialization practices of parents important beyond childhood? If so, to what extent? And how alterable or unalterable might such effects be?

SUMMARY AND CONCLUSIONS

In this chapter, issues pertaining to parent-child interaction were reviewed. These included the nature of the child, the role of heredity and environment, the paths of development, and the formativeness of early experience. All of these issues are still the focus of vigorous debate; points of controversy were brought to attention within these broad issues.

The importance of the issues discussed in this chapter both reflect and impact researchers' questions and theoretical explanations as well as practitioners' advice and everyday parenting practices. Perhaps methodological, statistical, and theoretical advances will resolve these issues, but it seems unlikely that it may happen any time in the near future. Across disciplines, however, many scholars are promoting more middle-ground, interactive positions on these controversies. For example, neither heredity nor environment is privileged, but the effects of both are being acknowledged and/or explicitly studied.

In sum, the key point is to recognize that theorists hold not-always acknowledged assumptions concerning such timeless issues as those highlighted here. Understanding implications of the explicit and implicit assumptions one makes to develop theory, conduct research, or advise parents is paramount.

2

Theoretical Orientations

INTRODUCTION

Before delving into the literature concerning parent-child interaction, some of the historically significant theoretical orientations that stimulated the research are delineated. Theories are considered within four major categories: personality theories, learning theories, humanistic theories, and structuralist theories. Two broad perspectives are also summarized: symbolic interactionism and systems theory.

The purpose of this chapter is prefatory. The information here sketches some of the seminal ideas that have influenced the study of interaction between children and parents. Mention of most of these theories will be scattered throughout later chapters. It is recommended that those desiring in-depth discussion consult the original sources or any of the many excellent secondary sources analyzing these theoretical views.

THEORETICAL APPROACHES

Personality Theories

Personality is "the dynamic organization within the individual of the psychophysical systems that determines his [sic] characteristic behavior and thought" (Allport, 1961, p. 28). There are two major views of personality. The first is the person-oriented approach; personality develops as a result of socialization. The question is how people become whole functioning individuals (McConnell, 1989). The second focus, the trait-oriented approach, considers the personality of an individual as an innate temperament. Thus questions center on the unfolding of this personality with maturation.

PERSON-ORIENTED VIEWS

The person-oriented approach is most congruent with the question, "What early experiences influence adult personality?" These theorists accord a significant formative role to the past, yet also believe individuals have some control in their lives. That is, humans of all ages are seen as active decision makers.

Freud's (e.g., 1938) psychoanalytic theory is the paradigm example of this branch of personality theory. With biological maturation as the underlying mechanism, Freud claimed that personality emerged from the interaction of the child's innate internal motivations (i.e., libidinal drives) and socialization experiences. Moreover, personality was proposed to be set by age 5.

Personality was theorized to develop through three dimensions: id, ego, and superego. The unconscious id is governed by the pleasure principle; children's sexual and aggressive drives must be satisfied immediately. The ego develops out of the id and enables self-preservation by serving as the agent of rational control of inborn instincts and of realistic expression of emotion. The superego is the product of socialization and enables one to act in morally acceptable ways.

Before Freud's work, people with "disturbances" were often thought to be possessed by evil spirits. Freud helped dispel such superstitions through his view that adult dysfunction could be traced back to early experience. In particular, parental responses to the child's behavioral expression of libidinal drives often exacerbated the child's internal turmoil. Frustration or overindulgence of libidinal drives particular to any stage were thus to be avoided; otherwise, fixation might occur. However, early experiences, although quite important, did not necessarily carve personality in stone. Personality could be altered, most likely as an adult (often in psychoanalysis).

Another legacy of Freud's work is the concept of ages and stages; stages of personality development were defined not only in terms of the underlying libidinal drives of the child but also in terms of the age of onset and offset. Yet Freud's account of what happens when during childhood has not been supported by empirical research (e.g., Parisi, 1987).

Psychoanalytic theory is a significant root for the study of parent-child interaction. Its strengths lie in Freud's conceptualization of development in a useful way (i.e., through the notion of stages), and its enduring contribution remains the notion of unconscious motivation. Criticism has been leveled at the theory's narrow focus on libidinal drives and emotion to the omission of other factors influencing behavior (e.g., cognition).

Many theorists have built significantly on Freud's work. In contrast to Freud's preoccupation with early life, Erikson and Adler viewed personality development from a life-span perspective. Erikson's (1950) psychosocial theory incorporated much of Freud's original thought but also focused on personality development as a function of interaction with members of the social community. Adler (1927, 1923/1955) adopted a more humanistic approach, viewing individuals as predominantly in control of their destinies. Adlerian approaches to parenting tend to stress children's experiencing the consequences of their actions; as such, external environment is highlighted and the role of internal drives is downplayed.

In sum, person-oriented theories are similar in that children and adults are described as active beings, nature and nurture interact, and early experiences are seen as malleable. Theories in this category vary in the degree to which early experiences are viewed as formative and the extent to which internal drives (the essence of nature) or external environment (nurture) influence personality development.

TRAIT-ORIENTED VIEWS

Although some researchers differentiate the constructs of traits and temperament, others use them interchangeably. Such will be the case here. The critical question is, "How do combinations of innate temperaments manifest themselves in both thought and behavior?" The earliest temperament theorist was the physician Galen (about A.D. 1000), who believed that traits were biological. Research on temperament waned for many years, but in the 20th century, Galen's search for traits that endure across the life of the individual has been revived.

Trait theorists ground their research in three assumptions: (1) innateness of personality traits, (2) structuralist tenets, and (3) the continuous nature of development. First, quite simply, traits are thought to be inherited. Second, structuralism is the notion that mental processes and behavior can be understood by examining combinations of their structure (e.g., Wundt, 1897/1902). Thus (innate) personality is thought to be understood in terms of its structure. Finally, continuity in the manifestation of traits is given prime consideration. Because traits are innate and based on combinations of mental structures, researchers should be able to record the gradual unfolding of the traits already within the individual. Hence radical changes in personality are not thought to occur through the life span.

One of the traits first studied was intelligence, but research failed to provide evidence of continuity in infant intelligence and other cognitive processes. On the other hand, emotional temperaments are more readily explained by innateness and continuity (Buss & Plomin, 1984). Longitudinal studies of twins have lent substantial evidence to the enduring nature of emotional temperaments. Finally, research suggests that combinations of innate traits (i.e., temperaments) predict how people respond to their environment. However, the weight accorded nature and nurture in explaining development and behavior from a trait orientation does vary from theorist to theorist. Some believe unequivocally that nature determines personality. Others contend that nature may set limits but it is nurture that enhances or constrains children in reaching those limits. Some trait-oriented theorists take the position that one can learn to reform inherited tendencies. Today, most trait scholars accord some role to environmental influences, as Wundt (1897/1902) did in his seminal work. He claimed that ultimately cognitive structure depended on the integration of the innate workings of the mind and experience in the environment. Trait explanations became increasingly interactionist from the 1960s through the 1980s.

In sum, trait scholars generally stress nature over nurture in the development of personality and argue for continuity of development in terms of the endurance of traits. The important point is that research attention is drawn to the effect of infants' temperaments on interaction between parents and children and hence the effect of children on their own development. Given that traits were initially considered to be innate, they were little explored by those unidirectional researchers interested in parental influences on the child. As bidirectional and systemic perspectives have emerged, child traits have received increased notice. These are now thought of as compelling forces in parents' interaction with children.

Learning Theories

Despite the influence and contributions of personality theories to the study of child *development,* parent-child *interaction* has been examined primarily from frameworks grounded in learning theories. The major categories of behaviorist and social-learning theories are considered.

BEHAVIORISM

Behaviorism revolutionized psychology; covert operations of persons' minds were put aside for the analysis of observable behavior. The reaction to the emphasis on mind was led by Watson (1924), who is considered the father of American behaviorism. Locke's empiricism was foundational for behaviorism, as were the theories of Darwin (1859) and Pavlov (1927).

Adaptive learning and behavior were the hallmarks of behaviorist research and theory development. Environmental stimuli and associated organismic responses were of primary interest; in essence, learning was reduced to one basic process. The underlying philosophical position was positivistic; people learn "things," "real" objects in their environment. Strict rigor in experimentation was introduced, and answers were sought to several central questions: "What is the stimulus?" "What does the organism attend to?" "What reinforcement of behavior contingent on the stimulus would determine whether or not the behavior would be learned or extinguished?"

The agenda of the behaviorism movement was captured in Watson's claim that the selection of experiences would shape a child into whatever kind of person one wished to create. This is clearly a radical stance on the nature-nurture issue: Nurture accounted for all. Thus parenting is of paramount importance. Parents' selection of experiences for the child and reinforcement of desired responses molded the child. It should be noted that the basic learning process was continuous. Behaviorists did not believe that learning was built necessarily on prior learning, nor did it necessarily occur in specific sequences. Rather children's acquisition of adult habits depended on the order in which they were exposed to these behaviors.

Perhaps the most influential, and comprehensive, learning theory is that developed by Skinner. It extended to many aspects of development, including language learning. As the title *Verbal Behavior* (Skinner, 1957) implies, language is behavior learned via reinforcement. Neither cognitions nor self-control are necessary to change behavior or acquire new behaviors (Skinner, 1987). Skinner became a lightning rod for criticism, not only from Chomsky (see Chapter 1) but from many others. He was the one to advocate that psychology was properly a science of behavior only and should focus solely on the contingencies of reinforcement (Skinner, 1963). Thus it should not be surprising that his convictions were challenged on the grounds of tunnel vision. Specifically, he has been faulted for his conception of humans as passive and lacking choice. In addition, Skinner almost completely ignored potential genetic influences on behavior. At best he saw inherited factors as simply priming individuals to respond in an operant reinforcement manner.

The simplicity of the behaviorist model, one of stimulus-response-reinforcement (S-R-R), is both its strength and weakness. Clearly it allowed for well-controlled experimental research. Such simplicity also lent itself to popularization in parenting books. These parenting manuals give parents a checklist of specific techniques to mold the child's environment and behavior. However, critics note that the model is inadequate for explaining the complexity or creativity of human behavior. For example, it is not necessary for children to have heard sentences to create them. The theory tends to fall apart for explaining language and communication development. Nor, critics charge, can behaviorists adequately account for empirical evidence that directly refutes the theory.

Behaviorism is the (radical) prototype of the unidirectional perspective for parent-child research. Its theme is to describe and explain how a child's behavior is shaped through interaction with parents.

SOCIAL-LEARNING THEORIES

As pure behaviorism waned in popularity, numerous social-learning theories emerged. These *neobehaviorist* theories start with the basic stimulus-response component then incorporate to varying degrees the mediating factor of the child's cognitive processes. Some social-learning theories see a weak role for cognition, whereas others posit a quite strong role. The plural *theories* serves to emphasize this diversity of views. Perhaps the most influential of these is Bandura's (e.g., 1969, 1977) social-learning theory. Modeling and imitation are seen as central forces in behavioral development as are the reciprocal influences of cognition, behavior, and environment (Bandura, 1986).

A number of social interactionist approaches are also subsumed within the category of social-learning theories. These represent the shift from theories stressing either innate structure or environmental influences to theories built on the interaction of the internal and external domains. The central tenet of social interactionist views is that children learn through active interaction in the environment, the crucial aspect of which is the adult who serves as the child's guide and aide (e.g., Bruner, 1983). The influence among these individuals is also seen as reciprocal. From this research perspective, questions about the child's active participation in developmental processes and parental influence are pursued.

In sum, social-learning theories mark a transition from theories viewing the child as a passive-reactive entity to a view of the child as active and interactive. Both internal and environmental factors must be taken into account. Significant roles are attributed to both the child and the parent. These models are decidedly more complex than the behaviorist model; understanding the interaction of the individual and environment and the child's cognitive operations in responding to the environment are emphasized.

Critics contend that social-learning theorists place too much emphasis on social influences and too little on biological ones. Also, development across the life span is generally not considered. Another point of criticism centers on the ambiguities of social-learning theory. There is no single social-learning theory; formulations vary widely in the factors considered and relative weights given each. The individual theories have less in common than the theories falling within most other general categories of theory. According to the critics, it is more appropriate to consider social-learning theories as individual and eclectic perspectives.

Humanistic Orientations

Humanistic theories of human development and action emerged out of Gestalt psychology. Humanistic psychologists ground their work in the assumptions of free will, the active nature of human beings, and the critical functions of perceptions of persons and situations. Maslow (1954), well-known for his needs theory, believed humanistic theories took the best of psychoanalysis and behaviorism and elaborated on them to form a more holistic explanation of activities of humans.

Perhaps the most influential of the humanistic theorists was Rogers (1961). His central thesis was that individuals are free to choose and control their actions even though these are driven by human needs. Rogers provided specific guidelines for "creating" an optimal, "fully functioning individual." Such guidelines have been incorporated into popular parenting manuals (e.g., Gordon, 1970) and have been used in Rogerian therapy. The focus is on aiding an individual to understand his or her feelings; from greater knowledge of self, one gains the ability to guide one's own behavior. This development of self-control in children rests largely on considering children's perceptions and their interpretations of parental actions. The aim of Rogerian approaches in general is to enable persons to reject external controls to someday become all they can be (i.e., achieve optimal development).

Humanism is underrepresented in the social sciences, because many researchers do not see this perspective as scientific. However, others claim that there is no intrinsic conflict between *science* and *humanism*. Humanistic scholars tackle many of the same issues as do social scientists. Yet, mostly because of the lack of research from a humanistic orientation (not the controversy over what is and is not science), this perspective will not surface much in this volume, with one important exception.

That exception is Kelly (1955), whose personal construct theory has been adapted to social scientific research. His propositions have been foundational for a constructivist theory of communication (Delia, O'Keefe, & O'Keefe, 1982). Kelly argued that personality and socialization occur via the way persons mentally organize their own experiences. Although humans seek to understand, predict, and control events in their lives, people may construct or interpret the same events differently. Having organized experiences into their own unique personal constructs, individuals then rely on these construals to guide subsequent actions. Of particular interest here, and like other humanist theoreticians, Kelly saw persons as active and human development as continuous in the sense that experiences accumulate in cognitive representations. Children do not have innate personalities but rather develop constructs from their perception of events; such constructs can conceivably be revised with further experiences.

In summary, the central tenet of humanistic theories is the belief in free choice. Given this, individuals possess the ability to overcome any negative influence of early experiences. In addition, humanism stresses optimal development as normal, quite a contrast to Freud, who viewed normalcy as the absence of pathology.

Humanistic theories have been applied more in therapy than in social scientific research. Humanist scholarship has been challenged as not really explicating complete and testable theories. Moreover, little data have been collected to assess their claims, aside from research based on personal construct theory (see Neimeyer & Neimeyer, 1990).

Structuralist Theories

As noted earlier, structuralism is the contention that human behavior and mental activity are functions of various structures. The assumption driving structuralist research is that such frames can be "discovered" through a scientific method. Both nativist theories and cognitive theories stress the discovery of underlying structure. The former assumes that such structures are present at birth, the latter that structures are constructed over time from biological rudiments.

NATIVISM

The nativistic perspective, in its pure form, proposes some sort of innate prewiring as an explanation for development. It thus stands in direct opposition to behaviorist assumptions. After lying relatively dormant for several years, nativism is alive and well (see e.g., Carey & Gelman, 1991, on the resurgence of nativism). Although the nativist stance is most apparent in language acquisition research, nativistic assumptions have also been adopted in other aspects of developmental research (e.g., the development of emotions, Izard & Malatesta, 1987).

The paradigm exemplar of nativism is Chomsky's theory of language as developing, for the most part, independently of the environment. Chomsky (1957) maintained that the linguistic development of children cannot be explained by simple exposure to, and reinforcement by, adult speech as claimed by behaviorists. Rather adult speech was seen as garbled, filled with disfluencies, and ungrammatical. Such input to the child was thought to be too confusing and too unsystematic to account for language acquisition as it actually occurred. Therefore, language development was explained by Chomsky as an unfolding of internal cognitions with maturation.

It was never proposed that the environment was completely unimportant; children do learn the language of their own community. But the nativist stance concerning the child was decidedly more active than the behaviorist view. Children were thought to be able to abstract systemic rules from the confusing input around them and thus develop competence in their native language. This ability was possible because the child was innately endowed with a brain structure for language development, the language acquisition device (LAD; e.g., Chomsky, 1965).

For the most part, criticisms of the nativist approach have been strident. The first point of critique is directly tied to the nature versus nurture debate. The strong emphasis on innate structure as an explanation for development excluded a significant role for environmental influences. Clearly this perspective accords a minor role to parents and minimizes their influences on their offspring. More specifically, Chomsky's theory has been criticized for separating language from thought. Although language was posited to be innately prewired, other cognitive activities were not. Chomsky's isolation of language as a distinctly unique form of cognition has been highly contended.

Despite such criticisms, there is little question that Chomsky greatly influenced the study of language development and provided an influential heuristic for the study of parent-child interaction. Although conceptualizations of the LAD have changed, principles of this approach are still adopted by some linguists. Moreover, his theory represents the epitome of innatists' positions. Thus it serves to illustrate nativistic orientations in general.

COGNITIVE THEORIES

Cognitive theories are largely concerned with the maturation of theorized cognitive structures within the individual. The maturation process is assumed to progress through sequential stages, such that later development depends on earlier achievement. The writings of Piaget (e.g., 1983) are both the seminal outline for and paradigm exemplar of cognitive structural theories. The standard account of Piaget's theory stresses the development of cognitive structure through a sequence of stages involving the adaptive processes of accommodation and assimilation.

Piaget grounds his theory in two laws. His *law of activity* assumes that it is natural for humans to act on their environment. The *law of interest* states that individuals will be attracted to things that are novel and will seek to understand them.

Much has been made of the fact that Piaget was trained in the biological sciences, and rightly so. His work builds on the assumption of two inherited tendencies: organization and adaptation. The tendency toward organization assumes that biological systems (e.g., digestive and muscular) are organized in hierarchies. Human rationality, that is, cognition, was seen no differently by Piaget; logical operations systematize and combine experiences into coherent systems and processes. Adaptation, the second tendency, alludes to the plasticity of biological organisms. Typically, all beings must adjust to the environment. Thus, in essence, the genetic program unfolds in the environment, but it is subject to external constraints or enhancements. In short, Piaget too is an interactional theorist.

The motivational construct in Piaget's theory is equilibration, or the individual's efforts to achieve psychological balance through organizing the environment in cognition. Adaptation occurs through the joint processes of assimilation and accommodation. When information is processed in terms of existing cognitive structures, assimilation is operating. This is typically seen when children encounter a new object, but use it in a familiar way. Accommodation is the process through which cognitive structure is modified to incorporate new information. Thinking (and action) shifts to accommodate the new experience.

Like Freud did for personality development, Piaget outlined an invariant sequence of stages in cognitive development. The child's early representation depends on schemata developed through sensory and motor activity (ages 0-2). The preoperational stage (ages 2-7) is the period during which the child gradually masters a different dimension of experience, based in symbolic representation, reversibility, and conservation. Concrete operations (ages 7-11) is the period in which logic and reasoning are applied by children to the manipulation of objects. Children's ability to deal with abstract concepts and relationships represented symbolically was seen as limited during this period but typically emerged after age 11 (formal operations). Piaget held that all children must progress through these same stages, in this order. Yet development was not necessarily seen as a smooth or gradual process. It could occur in leaps at times and rather slowly at other points.

Piaget (1959) built on this basic scheme to propose that the development of communication was critically related to a shift in cognitive abilities, allowing the child to move from egocentric thought to increasingly consider the perspectives of others. Although this notion is highly individualistic, Piaget did acknowledge the contribution of social forces to the progression through stages of communication development.

Rather than being a historical artifact, Piaget is highly influential in current research and theory on problems in socialization and communicative development. The theory is broad in scope, integrative, and heuristic. Not surprisingly, it has been foundational for many other theories dealing with more limited domains of cognitive activity (e.g., moral development; Kohlberg, 1969). Piaget has sensitized scholars, practitioners, and parents to the fact that children think differently at different ages. In the latter case, parents may find that they teach the same things over again at different levels. For example, family rules accepted by the young child may no longer be accepted by the adolescent and must be defended by parents.

Yet Piaget's theory has been much criticized. In many ways, it lacks formal completeness. For example, some constructs are not well defined. Moreover, the theory does not specify what behaviors should be expected at various stages of cognitive development. Other than the general motivating principle of equilibration, the child's motives for activity are ignored (Flavell, 1982). And, being normative in its outline, Piaget's theory does little to account for the fact of individual differences. A considerable amount of empirical research has neither fully supported nor entirely disproven Piaget's basic claims.

Overarching Perspectives

Attention will now turn to two broad and far-reaching perspectives: symbolic interactionism and systems theory. These are presented in the same section because it is questionable to claim that either is a unified theory. Perhaps they are better considered orientations, as each encompasses a broad range of views and many theories.

SYMBOLIC INTERACTIONISM

Symbolic interactionism is a distinctive approach and not easily compared with any of those previously mentioned. It explains behavior as a function of "the meanings of ideas in the mind and not by instincts, forces, libidinal energy, needs, drives, or a built in profit motive" (Burr, Leigh, Day, & Constantine, 1979, p. 67). This distinguishes symbolic interactionism from psychoanalytic theory and also from behaviorism, which completely ignores mental processes. Unlike social-learning theory, symbolic interactionism places little importance on reinforcement. This perspective emerged from the work of many sociologists, including Cooley (1902, 1909), Dewey (1922), and Blumer (1969). Even though Blumer is credited with coining the term *symbolic interactionism,* when one thinks of symbolic interactionism, one first recalls the work of Mead (1934). Baldwin's (1986) synthesis of Mead's work and symbolic interactionism is highly recommended. The emphasis in symbolic interactionism is the interrelationship between the individual and society; each is a product of the other. Cooley (1909) was one of the first scholars to underscore the relationship between personality development of the individual and family life (Hutter, 1985). Although seemingly simplistic now, this was actually quite a novel turn in the sociology of that time.

A critical aspect of symbolic interactionism is that humans live in a symbolic as well as a physical environment. Thus, to understand humans, one studies the *mentalistic symbols* and values that influence their interaction within social groups. That is, a dialectical process occurs between individuals and society because the symbols to which humans respond emerge, in turn, from the shared interaction of individuals. People decide what actions to take during their interactions with others on the basis of the symbols used and beliefs about symbol meanings.

In regard to interaction between parents and children specifically, parent-child interactions form mutually shared expectations and norms. Although theoretically parents and children engage in mutual influence, in truncated representations of symbolic interactionism and associated research designs, parents become the socializers and the child the socializee. Such a *parental power* stance is reminiscent of some social mold research (Peterson & Rollins, 1987). For example, many formulations of self-concept and self-esteem implicitly or explicitly are grounded in symbolic interactionism. What is often misleading about these studies is that in the process of adapting theory to a research design, the active component of the child tends to be forgotten.

The emphasis on mental processes makes it clear that in symbolic interactionism, the function of perceptions and meanings is paramount. For example, even though parents generally hold the role of socializers, the power of a parent is a function of the child's perception of the parent-child relationship (Smith, 1988). Thus one may conclude that because parental power is "perceptual," symbolic interactionism is a social mold approach. In fact, symbolic interactionism shares many more similarities with bidirectional and broad systems approaches than with unidirectional stances. All three views recognize the mutual influence between individuals, whereas unidirectional views do not.

In sum, symbolic interactionism approaches have been a driving force in family theory for well over 50 years. Burgess (1926) is credited with the first application of principles of symbolic interactionism to the study of the family (Hutter, 1985). Unfortunately, as pointed out by Hutter (1985), symbolic interactionists who have studied the family have failed to take the larger context into account. One of Mead's original concerns, the macrolevel aspects of the family (e.g., institutional factors like the political and economic environment), has been virtually ignored by present-day scholars of the family. The primary criticism of symbolic interactionism is the inability to translate most of its tenets into quantitative research. Hence despite years of theorizing, symbolic interactionism has generated relatively little empirical research. Critics state that because it has few testable hypotheses, it is impossible to provide evidence for or against basic assumptions of symbolic interactionism. In consequence, as many contend that theories must be capable of being disproven, symbolic interactionism fails to constitute a theory. This perspective has also been critiqued for its general failure to take emotions into account, rather favoring a highly rational view of humankind. Finally, some insist that symbolic interactionism is more philosophic in nature than scientific and thus consider it nonscientific, like humanistic views.

SYSTEMS APPROACHES

General systems theory can be traced to von Bertalanffy (1962) and has been invoked for the explanation of numerous and diverse phenomena. One set of laws is posited to govern all systems. These systems (whether human, mechanical, and so on) are composed of objects, attributes, relationships, and environments. *Objects* are the parts of the system and may be concrete physical entities (e.g., persons) or abstractions (e.g., perceptions and beliefs). *Attributes* are properties of a system, such as openness. *Relationships* refers to the interconnectedness of the objects. Finally, no system exists in isolation. Systems are contained in *environments* but also have reflexive relationships with them. They are affected by and also affect social, cultural, and physical milieus.

Application of general systems theory to the study of human behaviors is built on the tenet that general laws of all systems can be applied to humans. Yet, the gravity of such *laws* has not been uniformly endorsed by many systems scholars (e.g., Fisher, 1978). More accepted is the principle of interdependent components mutually and simultaneously influencing all other systems components. Indeed, the critical assumption of systems conceptualizations of human behavior is that all members of a social network influence each other (see Monge, 1977, for a theoretical statement of systems theory directly related to human communication).

Systems approaches have numerous guiding assumptions. Five concepts most applicable to family interaction are reviewed here. These interrelated concepts are (1) wholeness, organization, and circularity, (2) interdependence of system elements, (3) subsystems, (4) boundaries between and inter-actions among subsystems, and (5) homeostasis and change.

First, wholeness implies that no one element of the system can be under-stood in isolation from other system elements. No matter how chaotic inter-action in a family may first appear, organization exists in the interaction among individuals; patterns of interaction can be unearthed. Each individual's behavior influences each other individual's behavior in a circu-lar, as opposed to a linear, association. Thus the starting point and direction of cause and effect are irrelevant.

As noted above, the concept of interdependence is key in all system con-ceptualizations. Because the family is a holistic entity, the parent-child dyad cannot be understood without considering the numerous other facets of the complete family system. Furthermore,

> Interdependence implies that no family member is totally in control, inaccessi-ble, or unmoved by the actions of other family members. Although one or more individuals may be accorded more power in the family unit, all individuals are affected by the actions of others. (Yerby, Buerkel-Rothfuss, & Bochner, 1990, p. 10)

But interdependence between parents and children appears to have a par-adox in the notion of *boundaries*. Boundaries index structural properties of organization and can best be thought of as lines of differentiation between subsystems. Each family system is composed of numerous *subsystems:* a spousal subsystem and a subsystem between each parent and child, among the siblings, and so forth. Subsystems define many family roles and func-tions. For example, in functional families the marital subsystem is the strong-est coalition. When the boundaries between the subsystems become too permeable and are inappropriately crossed, such as when a parent-child sub-system is stronger than the marital subsystem, some type of dysfunction is usually apparent (P. Minuchin, 1985; S. Minuchin, 1974).

Finally, the concepts of *homeostasis* and *change* are relevant. Families resist change and strive to maintain the status quo; system members cling to current patterns of interaction. Changes are stressful, whether they are nor-mal life-course changes or unexpected events. Nonetheless, families do change. Families transform in response to each member's development as well as to the development of the constituent dyads (e.g., marital, sibling, and so forth). In addition, events that occur with the passage of time, such as the birth of a new member, an accident in the family, and so forth, modify family interaction patterns.

More complete explanations of family systemic concepts are found in Bochner and Eisenberg (1987), Minuchin (1985, 1988), and Yerby et al. (1990). Beyond the immediate family, models based on ecological theory and relationship perspectives encourage explorations of social networks as well (e.g., Belsky, 1984; Bronfenbrenner, 1986; Hinde & Stevenson-Hinde, 1987). Systems perspectives serve as Peterson and Rollins's (1987) third organizing framework for this text, hence, Chapters 8 and 9 will concentrate extensively on this framework. Therefore, further consideration of key issues and criticisms of systems perspectives will be reserved for those chapters.

SUMMARY AND CONCLUSIONS

Positions most influential in the study of parent-child interaction have been reviewed. Traces of each will be apparent as the book progresses. However, comprehensive theoretical reviews are left to texts designed for that purpose.

Each of these orientations has either left its legacy in current theories or is itself a current driving force in research. As various topics of parent-child interaction are considered in the following chapters, the influence of each of these traditions will become readily apparent, although not all theories and theorists are relevant to all three paradigms and variables.

It should become apparent throughout subsequent chapters that the study of parent-child interaction has progressed beyond narrowly focused theoretical approaches to understanding influences on the child. This general shift to more comprehensive orientations acknowledges and embraces multiple approaches to understanding the child. Awareness is growing across disciplines of the inordinate number of facets of human life that must be considered in the study of parent-child interaction.

3

What the Child Becomes: Three Selected Variables

INTRODUCTION

Three elements directly related to the communication of parents with their children are examined in this book: (1) self-control, concentrating particularly on compliance; (2) self-concept, specifically self-esteem and locus of control; and (3) communicative competencies, or language and communication. Studies related to each construct will be reviewed as they reflect the assumptions of a particular organizing framework (i.e., unidirectional, bidirectional, and systems). Within each section, research results will be integrated to form a comprehensive picture of what is known across disciplines about self-control, self-concept, and language and communication. What is known is distilled from research mainly on white middle-class Americans but also at times from research on similar Western cultures. Most of the conceptions, beliefs, and practices related to the variables discussed here all vary pending cultural and co-cultural contexts (Shweder & LeVine, 1984; see also the Epilogue). The reader is cautioned to keep this in mind.

It is common to hear the variables considered here referred to as *outcome* variables. This likely reflects the fact that researchers originally studied them as outcomes of parental or environmental influences (i.e., from the social mold tradition). These outcomes have also been the focus of research from bidirectional and systemic orientations. Although they are still considered cornerstones of socialization, these variables are no longer seen as simple outcomes (Grusec & Lytton, 1988). Some bidirectional perspectives assume a cause-and-effect relationship but reverse the direction of causality. The child affects the parents. Other bidirectional perspectives propose processes of and associations between parent and child messages that are mutually influential. That is, the central interest is in reciprocity. Finally, systems approaches are concerned with process, not outcomes. Total concentration on process emphasizes the ways in which all members of a system influence, and are influenced by, each other.

The reader is cautioned about an inherent problem with terminology in systems perspectives. Terms such as *associated* and *related* must not be read to imply causal relationships. Within a systems paradigm, these terms are meant to be taken literally: elements are "associated" or "linked"; they are not related in a linear causal manner. What might appear to be a seemingly contradictory point is that although outcomes and cause and effect are not theoretically relevant, systems theorists interested in child development are naturally concerned with how systemic processes affect the child. The phrase *consequences for the child* is often used. One must appreciate the fact that these researchers do not claim that other family members are not affected or that family members are the "cause" of child outcomes. Systems researchers direct their attention to the consequences for the child rather than to those experienced by other family members.

In this chapter, each of the three focal variables are defined and core issues raised. Although self-control, self-concept, and communication are considered individually, they are difficult to tease apart. For example, the constructs of self-concept and self-control have been identified as part of a larger domain, the *self-system* (Gunnar & Sroufe, 1991; Harter, 1983). Only recently have self-control and self-concept been considered interdependent processes (Markus & Nurius, 1984). Language and self are also intertwined. For Mead (1934), language is the cardinal catalyst in the genesis of self. Difficult as it is to separate self-control, self-concept, and language and communication, they are important components of the socialization process, "a lifelong process through which a human being becomes—and continues to be—a more or less adequately functioning and contributing member of a particular society (or any social group)" (Goodman, 1985a, p. 66).

SELF-CONTROL

Issues of Definition and Scope

The essence of self-control is the ability to control one's inner processes and behavior outputs voluntarily (McConnell, 1989). It thus involves impulse control, delayed gratification, the engagement of prosocial behaviors, and similar aspects (Harter, 1983). Self-control includes cognitive, emotional, and behavioral elements (see e.g., Labouvie-Vief, Hakim-Larson, DeVoe, & Schoeberlein, 1989) as well as moral development and moral conscience. Moreover, ego development is often considered to be related to, if not part of, a progression of moral development.

Three aspects of self-control are considered here: (1) compliance, (2) internalization, and (3) moral conscience. Attention is devoted primarily to compliance due to its probable relationship to internalization and conscience and the probable link between the communication of children and parents to compliance. Before proceeding, however, the use of terms should be clarified. First, a distinction is drawn between the concepts of compliance and internalization. *Compliance* refers to the extent to which the child obeys directives given by caregivers (Lepper, 1983). Compliance is "an immediate and appropriate response by the child to an adult's request" (Honig, 1985). To oversimplify somewhat, compliant behavior generally occurs because a parent "said so." In total compliance, the child conforms to, or adapts behaviors in accordance with, adult wishes. Compliance can also come from identification (Kelman, 1958). In this instance a child obeys because the child wants to be liked by the person issuing the directive. This process has been labeled the "good boy, good girl" stage by Kohlberg (1969, 1976) and conformity by Loevinger (1966).

In contrast, *internalization* refers to the child's taking as part of himself or herself the values and beliefs of the society as guiding principles (Aronfreed, 1969). There are many concepts similar to internalization (e.g., self-regulation, see Kopp, 1982).

The significance of internalization for socialization is hardly underrated. Both cross-culturally and throughout the course of civilizations, external control of a child's actions is replaced by internally driven personal control. Such a progression has been construed "as the most efficient means of ensuring the social and moral order is upheld" (Harter, 1983, p. 339). Researchers explore "the degree to which behaviors are externally initiated and controlled versus self-initiated and managed" (Grolnick & Ryan, 1989, p. 149). Certain paradigms, however, place little stock in self-control. Behaviorists, in general, do not explicitly acknowledge or discuss any aspect of a child's self-control.

A developed moral conscience is a step beyond internalization. Interestingly, current conceptions of morality can be traced to Plato. Moral socialization has been proposed to depend on affective or emotional components, cognitive development, and behavioral components (Brody & Shaffer, 1982). For example, Freud was concerned with morality and stressed unconscious struggles. Maslow (1954) posited that needs were the driving factor of moral behavior. A strong Piagetian influence is evident in Kohlberg's (1969) prominent theory of the development of moral behavior. He considered a moral conscience as a cognitive reasoning system. Other scholars stress different and/or additional dimensions. Loevinger's (1976) concept of ego development is quite similar, although not isomorphic, to Kohlberg's (1969) moral development (Harter, 1983). Whereas theories of morality often highlight rational thinking, theories of ego development often stress the development of autonomy and individual values. However, both general concepts emphasize autonomous decision making on the basis of internal guidance, beyond societal or parental values. The nature and process of ego development highlights key aspects of development of self-control. Ego development emerges as a research concern in studies of adolescents. The process has been described using hierarchical models with levels based on ways of viewing and understanding "the social world" (see Loevinger, 1976). Researchers typically examine the maturation of a set of related functions (e.g., cognition and interpersonal skill). In essence, ego development refers to individuation, or autonomy, and independence, which according to Ryan and Lynch (1989), are fostered by attachment to parents, not detachment: "Teenagers who are attached to parents thus will experience them as emotionally accepting and supportive of independence and autonomy despite periodic struggles" (p. 341). From this stance, attachment is not some "regressive bond from which the teenager must free him or herself" (p. 341).

Ego development also illustrates the interrelationship of self-control with self-concept. For example, ego development is considered to be a fundamental component of self-concept and is highly associated with adolescent self-esteem (Erikson, 1959). In addition, aspects of parent-child communication during early adolescence appear to be associated with adolescent ego development (see e.g., Cooper, Grotevant, & Condon, 1983).

As a child progresses through adolescence into young adulthood, blind or unquestioning obedience to authority is generally seen as undesirable (Peterson, Rollins, & Thomas, 1985). The internalization of parental and societal values and the development of a moral belief system so that "good" decisions can be made are considered preferable. Indeed, Kohlberg (1969) described moral conscience as reasoning that inoculates one from uncritical acceptance of societal rules (see Quinn, 1987, for a compatible humanistic insight into morality). Thus morality or moral conscience is ultimately a self-chosen ethical principle (Kohlberg, 1969, 1976). Such positions assume that persons have some degree of free will. Compliance, internalization, and moral development appear to be integrally and (many contend) hierarchically related components of self-control. It has been proposed that obeying compliance requests promotes internalization, which is then predictive of the later development of a moral conscience. In other words, compliance has been proposed to be a rudiment of or, by some, essential to internalization and moral development (Kochanska, 1991; Kohlberg, 1969, 1976). Given this stance, processes of seeking and gaining compliance are of great interest.

Unless one takes a nativist stance that morality is an unfolding of a natural maturational process, communication is one of the primary modes through which compliance (and ultimately internalization, and moral reasoning) is achieved. Both Cooley (1902) and Mead (1934) claimed the origin of self-control emerged from social interaction and the child's internalization of the evaluations of others. In turn, self-control directs one's behavior when external consequences are not present. Moreover, Mead (1934) clearly maintained one's self-concept was foundational to the development of morality.

From a unidirectional research orientation, the key variables in this process are the communication tactics of parents seeking to gain children's compliance (for an overview from a communication perspective of the theoretical underpinnings of compliance gaining, see Garko, 1990). Interpersonal power is at the core of compliance gaining (Berger, 1985). So too is the fact of culture. For example, Bronfenbrenner (1986) proposed that as the average level of stability and structure in the society or culture decreases, the ideal ratio of control to freedom set by parents increases.

Child compliance has also been explained as bidirectional and systemic processes. From a bidirectional perspective, compliance is seen as a mutual process. Children play quite an active role in compliance. Social-learning theories emphasize a child's free will and choice in compliance and thus are highly relevant to bidirectional approaches to noncompliance. Mediating child factors include temperament (Kaler & Kopp, 1990) and comprehension (Kochanska, 1991). In addition, child compliance (or lack thereof) has been related to effects on parents. Finally, systems theorists discuss compliance and noncompliance as functions of the communicative interaction of the entire family, with influences and consequences from, and on, all family members. Findings from studies from the three frameworks will be discussed in upcoming chapters.

Research from all orientations shows a link between early compliance-gaining efforts, internalization, and later moral development. These associations, although well documented, remain unexplained (Gunnar & Sroufe, 1991). Such strong, yet unaccounted for, connections beg for continued research on the communication between children and parents in regard to self-control. These links also carry strong implications for the advice offered by practitioners.

ADDITIONAL ISSUES

The study of children's compliance further illustrates the various positions on the controversies outlined in Chapter 1. The study of compliance-gaining efforts immediately raises questions about the underlying conceptions of the child. The conception of the child as a blank slate, innately good, or innately evil is potentially linked to compliance strategies. Indeed, Higgins (1991) noted that others' expectations and perceptions of the child are influential factors in the development of compliance, internalization, and subsequent moral development.

For example, from the assumptions of unidirectional orientations, if the child is believed to be innately evil, the child must be brought into line by adult efforts. The result is likely the use of relatively controlling compliance tactics. Even more benevolent views of the nature of the child do not reduce the emphasis unidirectional researchers place on examining the effects of parental tactics. Socialization is still a one-way street. From bidirectional approaches, compliance is necessary both for a child's safety as well as for teaching societal guidelines. These must be balanced with the development of autonomy. The stance taken toward children from bidirectional orientations has been predominantly that children are predisposed to comply; they are innately good. Bidirectional researchers study the child's active role in choosing whether or not to comply (see Chapter 7) and the potential benefits from the choice of noncompliance (e.g., the development of autonomy or reasoning skills). There is no single conception of the child from a systems perspective. A systems researcher would examine compliance as multiply determined and contingent on numerous interrelated factors in the family system.

How the roles of heredity and environment in shaping the child are understood influence how compliance-gaining research is conducted and how theory is translated into practice. And parental beliefs in this respect also need to be considered by researchers. Parents who emphasize the role of heredity may see different children as uniquely individual due to their genetic inheritance. To illustrate, a mother who believes one child is simply stubborn and ill-willed by nature will likely invoke different strategies than she will with the child's sibling who "inherited" a more cheerful disposition. Indeed, research has documented that parents do not attempt to gain compliance from or discipline all their offspring in the same manner (e.g., McHale & Pawletko, 1992; Smetana, 1989).

Positions adopted by researchers, as well as parental beliefs regarding determinism and free will are also relevant in the study of self-control. Parents who have little belief in their ability to control aspects of their own world and fates likely use different child-rearing practices from parents who place more emphasis on their own abilities to influence their lives, and hence the lives of their children (McKinney & Peterson, 1987).

The progression from compliance to moral conscience raises the issue of the continuous versus discontinuous nature of such development. Scholars studying moral development tend to agree that the development of compliance, internalization, and a moral conscience are at least somewhat overlapping processes in the child's early years (Lytton, 1980). It has been argued that when children shift from simple compliance to internalization: "Children are motivated to have their self-concept attributes match their self-guide attributes, not in order to display features that others will like or admire, but in order to be the right kind of person, . . . a 'good' person" (Higgins, 1991, p. 134). This shift is critical as it has been posited as the onset of true self-control. This change also has been proposed to be the point at which morality begins (Hoffman, 1983). Yet it is unclear whether these overlapping processes represent a continuous, gradual development such that moral development is a simple extension of internalization, which in turn is a simple extension of compliance. Or, at some point in time, is there an abrupt qualitative change?

A blended perspective of continuity and discontinuity is now emerging to explain ego development (Grotevant & Cooper, 1986). Ego development is considered to have elements of a continuous process in the maintenance of attachment to parents. Yet ego development also exhibits features of a discontinuous process in that the relationships between the child and the adult change significantly. Basically, adolescence is considered to be a time of renegotiation of roles between parents and children.

As in all areas of socialization, the active versus passive nature of the child is debated. The question raised is how active the child is in evaluating and/or accepting parental control attempts. Most scholars concur that initially the parent has greater power in the dyad, but the question remains as to what extent child compliance is a result of passive reaction to that power versus the child's willingness and active decision to follow adult wishes. Likewise, the child is now being seen as having an influence over his or her own autonomy and hence ego development (Eisenberg, 1992). Issues of the formativeness of early experience are of interest as well. To illustrate, recall the concern of the humanists on "becoming," or optimal development. Much therapy is aimed at helping the adult acquire a state of optimal self-control not successfully acquired during childhood.

Conclusion

Internalization of societal norms, values, and beliefs is a fundamental aspect of socialization. Compliance is the first step toward that end, yet it is distinct from internalization. For the individual child, the development of a moral conscience (and self-concept) appear to follow compliance closely. Attitudes about the nature of children in general, and the nature of one child specifically, likely mediate choices of compliance attempts and investigations undertaken. Researchers and practitioners must remember that parental beliefs about their ability to influence children should also be instrumental in the choice of strategies. Finally, how active the child is in choosing to comply is a substantive issue and deserves further consideration. The progression from compliance to internalization to moral conscience is yet to be well understood.

Finally, keep in mind that the development of compliance is linked to the development of autonomy (via moral development and ego development). These are mutual developmental processes. This poses an interesting question for communication scholars. How can parental concerns for immediate compliance be juxtaposed with the child's need for developing independence and autonomy? Research addressing such issues will be considered in later chapters.

SELF-CONCEPT

Issues of Definition and Scope

Parental roles in the development of the child's concept of self are often considered to be paramount. Of course, unless a pure unidirectional stance is taken, the child plays a considerable role in this process, too. Most explanations of the emergence of self-concept share one underlying assumption; in some way, shape, or form, communication is the medium through which one's sense of self emerges. Given the emphasis on communication in the development of self-concept, attention of those interested in parent-child interaction is logically warranted.

The reader may be aware that the terms *self, self-concept,* and *self-esteem* have been used rather loosely. *Self* has been conceived of as a construct, a schema, and a theory (Eder, 1988). Often *self* serves more as a prefix than as a construct (Harter, 1983). Terms such as those just mentioned—as well as *self-recognition, self-control, self-image, self-theory, self-perception, self-awareness, self-appraisal,* and *self-efficacy,* to name but a few—are often bounced about in the literature. Thorough reviews of the literature on the development of self-concept also often include the constructs of locus of control and ego development. It is challenging to disentangle and, at the same time, find some coherence in the research of such diverse yet integrally related constructs. Several reviews have managed do to so with clarity but not necessarily with consensus (see, e.g., Damon, 1983; Gunnar & Sroufe, 1991; Harter, 1983).

Self-esteem is part of a broader construct, the development of a sense of self. Numerous books and articles review developmental perspectives, historical approaches, and various theoretical stances taken in the study of self (see e.g., Gunnar & Sroufe, 1991; Stern, 1985). Research on the development of the rudiments of sense of self will not be summarized here. This is not meant to overlook the tremendous amount of work on the development of self. As Chien (1944) remarked, however, "everyone, with the possible exception of infants, some philosophers and psychopaths, is aware of one's self" (quoted in Franks, 1985, p. 29). This discussion begins at the point at which the rudiments of self have been acquired. It is the self in relationship to others, the social self, that is examined here.

More specifically, research on perception of self— that is, self-concept— is considered. Two aspects of self-concept (self-esteem and locus of control) are covered. Self-esteem is especially highlighted because it is considered a superordinate construct within this general domain of research and also because it is the evaluative component of self-concept. In addition, locus of control merits inclusion as many believe it to be a core feature of self-esteem.

Self-esteem is seldom clearly defined (Harter, 1983). Perhaps the best known definition of self-esteem is James's (1890) formula:

$$\text{Self-Esteem} = \text{Successes} \div \text{Pretensions}$$

As a ratio of one's accomplishments to one's potentials, this affect-based conception of self-esteem remains quite viable. For example, studies on self-esteem quite often cite Coopersmith (1967). Self-esteem, in his conceptualization, is "the evaluation which the individual makes and customarily maintains with regard to himself [*sic*]; it expresses an attitude of approval or disapproval . . . self-esteem is a personal judgement of worthiness" (p. 5).

Such definitions are still somewhat vague. Distinguishing self-esteem from other "self" constructs is made somewhat easier by seeing them as hierarchically related (Harter, 1983). Self-esteem references how one feels about one's worth across various life domains (e.g., academic, physical, socioemotional, social aspects). Some theorists pursue investigations of domain-specific self-esteem, whereas others explore the more global construct. For example, Rosenberg (1965, 1979) has focused on a global, unidimensional construct of self-esteem that involves the evaluative feelings of self-worth individuals possess. Subcomponents of self-esteem and related constructs often studied include one's sense of control, worthiness, competence, and acceptance (Coopersmith, 1967; Epstein, 1981). The importance of various dimensions and domains is recognized. Nevertheless, it is this global, affective component of self-esteem that demands scrutiny. The reason is simple from the standpoint of communication research; self-esteem is frequently believed to be both a consequence and an antecedent of communicative behaviors (Berger & Metzger, 1984).

While personal control is sometimes seen as merely a component of self-esteem, other theorists make stronger claims. A feeling of control may form the core of self-esteem and thus be a necessary prerequisite for the development of self-esteem (Damon, 1983). Control is discussed here as locus of control. Locus of control refers to the extent to which one accepts personal responsibility for himself or herself (Chandler, Wolf, Cook, & Dugovics, 1980). Very generally, internal locus of control is a basic belief that one has a fair degree of personal control over one's self and one's environment. An external locus of control makes reference to an individual's belief that fate, luck, or other people have control (Chapman, Skinner, & Baltes, 1990). Locus of control was originally theorized to be a global construct (see Rotter, 1966). Recently though, it has been argued that people may possess an internal locus of control, an external locus, or both (see Lefcourt, 1976; Miller, Lefcourt, Holmes, Ware, & Saleh, 1986). Such controversies aside, internality and externality of locus of control are primary dimensions. At a very early age, and at some fundamental level, a basic sense of control over one's self and one's environment is necessary.

ADDITIONAL ISSUES

Not surprisingly, the study of self-concept raises once again the timeless issues outlined in Chapter 1. Perhaps the most intriguing are the formativeness of early experience and the child's role in the process of developing his or her self-concept. Most studies of self-concept still take a primarily unidirectional orientation, placing heavy emphasis on the role of adults as formative agents. The basic sense of self is often felt to be set in place early and remain relatively stable throughout the course of one's life. Locus of control is also often presumed to be set at a young age (Crandall, Katkovisky, & Crandall, 1965). However others, although viewing self as relatively stable, hold that sense of self can be altered (e.g., Freud). James (1890) contended more strongly that the child was instrumental in forming and altering sense of self. Moreover, according to most theories, self-esteem should be somewhat flexible. Thus the formativeness of early experience is a point of clear contention.

A second significant issue concerns the assumptions related to the active versus passive nature of the child. Much of the theory and research on self-esteem emphasizes the influences of others. Social mold frameworks search for a blueprint to construct the maximal self-concept. Trait theorists underscore the passive nature of the child and are more likely to claim that temperaments are genetic. Social interactionists, in addition to highlighting the influence of significant others, also see the child as an active agent in the process of forming self-concept.

James (1890) claimed that one could change his or her self-concept through self-effort. This early conceptualization of self-esteem has not been entirely forgotten. In fact, as will be shown in upcoming chapters, the child is being rediscovered as an active agent in the formation of self-esteem *and* of others' self-esteem. Hence, bidirectional stances on self-esteem were present quite early. Systems views of self-concept are most widely known from the work of Satir (1988) in which all family members play roles that likewise are associated with all other family members' roles. Given that systems scholars believe that every aspect in the system affects every other aspect, it seems that self-concept is considered in flux.

This is inherently tied to the continuity discontinuity debate. Does the child's self-esteem change during adolescence, as symbolic interactionists have sometimes said, due to the roles of significant others changing from parents to peers? Or is the development of self-esteem relatively continuous? This is an important yet unresolved issue for scholars interested in studying the relationship between communication and self-concept during adolescence.

Finally, the universal versus culturally bound nature of the self and self-concept should be considered. It has been proposed that *self* is defined differently across various cultures (see e.g., Rosaldo, 1984).

Conclusion

Self-esteem has probably been studied more than any other aspect of self. In all likelihood, this is due to the proposals about numerous correlates and consequences of self-esteem. Self-esteem apparently corresponds with mental health, life satisfaction, happiness, academic achievement, ego development, and locus of control. Inverse relations with depression, anxiety, and maladjustment have been established (see Damon, 1983). Self-esteem is also intimately tied to the psychological well-being of adolescents (see review by

Rosenberg, 1985). Likewise, an internal locus of control correlates with academic abilities, mental health, less debilitative anxiety, less emotional maladjustment, greater persistence, greater ability to evaluate and use information from the environment, and of course, higher self-esteem (e.g., Chapman et al., 1990; Gordon, Nowicki, & Wichern, 1981).

In sum, self-concept warrants attention because of the fundamental role attributed to interpersonal communication in its formation, self-concept's close interrelationship with socialization, and its pragmatic importance as illustrated by the many personal attributes and indices of mental and social health with which self-esteem and locus of control are correlated.

COMMUNICATION COMPETENCIES

Issues of Definition and Scope

The third area to be covered is communication competencies (language and communication). "No one denies that language occurs as—or, simply, is—perhaps the central fact of interpersonal social action" (Silverstein, 1991, p. 143). Language is an essential element of culture (Goodman, 1985b) and it is through communication that children (and adults) are socialized into a culture. The development of communication is intimately intertwined with socialization. As the child acquires the ability to understand language and communicate symbolically, socialization proceeds more efficiently. Competence in the social world outside the family context furthermore depends largely on development and mastery of language and pragmatic conversational skills.

The tremendous effort devoted to the study of language and communication reflects the awesome complexity of the subject matter. It is perplexing and intriguing as to how language and communication emerge. Consider the following quotations:

> While still unable to tie their shoelaces, most three-year-olds are quite happily using language to ask and answer questions, express fears, doubts, and opinions, make friends with others, and generally make their mark on the world about them. (Foster, 1990, p. 1)

> That children should be able to acquire such an extraordinarily complex, versatile, and sophisticated behavior system with such apparent ease and speed seems indeed amazing, and it is therefore hardly surprising that speculation continues as to how this task is accomplished. (Schaffer, 1989, p. 1)

The vast amount of research generated within social science is also of fairly recent vintage, although the emergence of language has long intrigued philosophers (Rice, 1989). The study of children's communication competencies, somewhat ironically, is extremely new to the discipline of communication.

At one time, the domain was relatively limited to grammar. Communication development is now under investigation, as opposed to strictly language development. In many ways this expansion has "opened Pandora's box, creating more questions and issues to be addressed" (Shatz, 1983, p. 879). Recall that *communication* and *language* are ambiguous terms. Terms such as *language, language use, pragmatics, communication, communication skills, conversation, interpersonal interaction, social interaction,* and so forth, abound. There is little conceptual clarification and much conceptual overlap and confusion.

Hymes's (1972) concept of communication competence lends some guidance through this quagmire. Hymes's somewhat generic term *communication competence* is adopted herein. Knowledge of one's language in addition to being able to use it appropriately and effectively in a given setting (communication) are separable, yet interrelated components of communicative competence.

Language is a comparatively easy realm to identify; the usual components are phonology, lexicon, semantics, morphology, and syntax (Foster, 1990). The traditional linguistic approach closely equates language with grammar. Semantics is relevant to language research but has not been examined as vigorously as grammar. Language research is no longer limited to the traditional components. Numerous additional elements are now considered open for study under the rubric of language. Yet, despite this expanded scope, the word *language* remains closely equated with "structural interests of sentence grammarians" (Jacobs, 1986, p. 313).

The second part of communicative competence, communication, is more difficult to define or narrow in scope. Hymes (1972) simply referred to communication as the social use of language. Yet social uses (or skills) still leaves the scope muddled. For example, pragmatics, often defined as the use of language, is now increasingly studied as communication. Discourse knowledge, illocutionary knowledge, and social rule use; gaining and holding an audience; the ability to persuade or comfort peers; and conversation are all considered part and parcel of communication. So are numerous other elements. Clearly, the scope of *communication* is not clear.

Nor is there any definitive demarcation between communication and language. Jacobs (1986) noted that "the concepts of language and communica-

tion, although intimately related, have never really been happily married"
(p. 313). Questions of meaning, coherence, and function, for example, are
salient to both language and communication scholars. However, although
these scholars ask many of the same questions, they seldom use each others'
work. Communication scholars readily admit that the study of the use of
language to create messages to perform social actions (e.g., speech acts) is
highly relevant to their field, yet "a detailed understanding of the organization of linguistic forms and functions" has generally been bypassed (p. 313).
Scholars of language have been equally reticent to integrate theories of language structure with the work of communication scholars. The potential
meeting ground for these apparently reluctant partners is the study of conversation. (Also see Jacobs, 1985.)

Recently, studies of the conversation of parents and children have begun
to accumulate. Howe (1981) synthesized work by scholars who had begun
to explore this area. She concluded from the evidence available at that time
"that the children who engaged in the theoretically most helpful conversations developed [language] most rapidly" (p. 19). Not surprisingly, *conversation* has become fair game for language scholars (Snow, 1991).

Many fields are beginning to appreciate the interrelationship of language
and communication and consequently have directed research attention to
conversation. Hence, instead of restricting the forthcoming discussion to just
the structure or the social use of language, studies that explore interaction
will be highlighted. Conversation is the aspect of interaction between parents
and children that most closely parallels the definition of interpersonal communication adopted in the Overview; thus literature relevant to parent-child
conversation will receive central attention.

ADDITIONAL ISSUES

There is more agreement among scholars concerning the relationships of
parent-child interaction to self-concept or to compliance than is found
among scholars of language and communication. Beyond the raging nature-
nurture controversy, there is little consensus even as to what constitutes the
fundamental issues (Rice, 1989).

Understanding of communication-related issues requires a brief outline of
the historical context in which such issues have emerged. In the study of
language acquisition, theoretical development occurred in response to the
explanation forwarded by Skinner. Recall from Chapter 2 that behaviorism
viewed language as no different from any other "learned habit." From this
approach the child was a passive beneficiary of language. Chomsky's response gave impetus to what is considered as the traditional linguistic ap-

proach. Language acquisition was seen as a process of deducing and discovering regularities of grammar. Most who adhere to this approach contend that language is an innate characteristic of humans (Bohannon & Warren-Leubecker, 1989). In such theories, the child is not inactive. Acting like a little professor and language processor, the child figures out the rules to language. Yet language is still also an unfolding of the child's innate dispositions as the child cognitively matures.

If the behaviorist and nativist perspectives are considered the radical elements at either end of a theoretical continuum, then the interactionist approach may be thought of as a moderate compromise. This approach recognizes, and often accepts, the more powerful arguments from both camps.

Social interactionists by no means share a unified position on the role of the environment, but they are in agreement that the environment plays a stronger role than innate devices (Shatz, 1981). Although most social interactionists adopt some innatist tenets, not all do. Consider, for example, Moerk's (1989) position: "Interactions are sufficient to enable the child to acquire language skills. No innate knowledge or language-specific processes are relied upon" (p. 21). Moerk even argued for a more bidirectional stance for input, that is, children and their environment constitute a dynamic system. A slightly different version of a social interactionist approach stresses cognition and is sometimes equated with psycholinguistics. The primary assumption of cognitive-interaction perspectives is that language development, for the most part, depends on and is concurrent with nonlinguistic components of cognitive development. À la Piaget, language is one of many abilities resulting from cognitive maturation.

As should now be recognized, the debate centers on the familiar nature-nurture controversy. Because strict behaviorist notions of language acquisition have virtually been abandoned, the two schools now engaged in vigorous debates are the nativist and the social interactionist.

According to Howe (1981), efforts to document the position that adult speech to children has unique properties that are helpful to the development of language and that adult speech is neither garbled nor disfluent began in an effort to discover language input that could aid children's language acquisition. Demonstration of this claim would "help emphasize the active role that children play in the general [language] learning process" (Howe, 1981, p. v). In other words, such investigations were undertaken so that innatist positions could be challenged.

Hence early research into the nature-nurture debate focused on the documentation of *motherese* (see Snow & Ferguson, 1977). Motherese (also known as baby talk, or BT) is a distinct form of speech used by adults when talking to young children. It is clearly different from the style used by adults to address older children and adults (Ferguson, 1977). According to Snow (1977b), BT is generally characterized as simple (in that utterances are shorter and syntactically less complex) and redundant. In addition, BT contains many questions and imperatives, few past tenses, and few disfluencies. It is also relatively high pitched with exaggerated intonation patterns.

That motherese exists, at least in many Western cultures, is now well documented. It should be noted that research is not on how mothers talk, but rather the speech style adults adopt when talking with and to young children. Fatherese is basically the same as motherese (Lewis & Gregory, 1987). However, fathers may not engage in motherese as extensively as mothers (Snow, Perlmann, & Nathan, 1987).

The accumulated evidence of motherese would logically appear to support the idea that maternal input must serve some facilitative function and thus refute innatists' positions. Yet even Snow (1979), one of the strongest supporters of the role of motherese in language acquisition, commented that "demonstration of the availability of simplified, redundant, linguistic input to language learning provides no basis for concluding that such input is necessary or even helpful to normal language acquisition" (p. 157).

In regard to nature versus nurture then, there is no clear consensus. Within each school, the relative contributions of the environment and innate abilities of the child depend on what aspect of language input and language learning one is discussing. Certain components of language and communication appear less susceptible to environmental influences than others (Miller, 1990). However, both stances appear to be moving toward a position of an active child.

Other issues in the study of language and communication include the processes and paths of optimal development. As noted, there may be many paths to normal ranges of language development. This will be addressed more explicitly in later chapters. In addition, the continuity-discontinuity of development is considered. On this issue, many scholars agree. Development of communicative abilities appears to be continuous. In regard to the origin of speech, "the bulk of recent evidence . . . favors the continuity hypothesis, namely, that during infancy and childhood, behavioral development unfolds in a smooth or continuous fashion with age rather than exhibiting sharp discontinuities" (Kent & Hodge, 1991, p. 25; see also Cappella, 1991). However, there are those who maintain the position of a discontinuous transition (see Haslett, 1987).

To concentrate on interaction, neither the vast amount of work on language and communication development that centers around the description and documentation of what develops when (ages) nor the order in which aspects appear is considered in this volume. Numerous authors present the development of language and communication with a lesser emphasis on interaction. Brown's (1973) volume outlining stages of language, particularly semantics, should not be overlooked. See Foster (1990) for insightful reviews of the development of prelinguistic communication, language, and communication. The early functions of language have been outlined by Halliday (1973). Dore (1978) presented a classic piece on the acquisition of speech acts. A pragmatic focus is also taken by Dimitracopoulou (1990). Relative to a specific social skill, the development of persuasive abilities have been documented by Delia, Kline, and Burleson (1979) and Haslett (1987). A developmental approach to conversation is offered by Wells and Gutfreund (1987). Ingram (1991) outlined phonological development. Although many of these sources cover additional topics as well, they serve as a starting point for those interested in the question, "What develops when?"

Conclusion

According to Schaffer (1989), the renewed interest of scholars of child language and communication development has followed two predominant trends. Two of these loosely follow the framework offered by Peterson and Rollins (1987). Although seldom labeled as such by language scholars, one trend closely parallels unidirectional orientations, the other bidirectional ones. From a unidirectional orientation, efforts are aimed at determining which characteristics of adult speech serve to aid communication competencies. Unidirectional researchers ask, "What is the optimal path to language development?"

The second trend is a focus on "the *interaction* of adult and child rather than on either one individual or the other: Its focus is on the dyad and its aim is to elucidate the interpersonal processes that form the background to the initial appearance and further development of language" (Schaffer, 1989, p. 2). This parallels bidirectional orientations. Also consistent with bidirectional approaches are research efforts aimed at explaining how the child influences parental speech. The discussion of such research shall be undertaken in Chapter 7.

Although not specifically discussed by Schaffer as a major trend, a third orientation implicit in his writing resembles systemic approaches. Schaffer alluded to the role of others in the language environment. Furthermore, he admonished researchers' preoccupation with the mother and hence the failure to incorporate other facets of the child's environment. Some scholars are now considering additional environmental aspects such as other family members and elements of a larger system outside the immediate family. Systemic orientations are discussed in Chapters 8 and 9.

SUMMARY AND CONCLUSIONS

This chapter outlined three concepts that are intertwined with socialization: self-control, self-concept, and communication competencies. The view of these constructs used herein has been put forth. Within each section, selected points of contention in the study of each variable have been highlighted. Across the three variables, issues that consistently re-emerge are nature versus nurture, the continuity versus discontinuity of development, and the active versus passive nature of the child.

Self-control, self-concept, and communication competencies will serve as the exemplar variables due to interest in these variables across numerous disciplines, their inherent ties to socialization processes, and most important, their fundamental interrelationships with parent-child interaction.

By discussing these three constructs as exemplars of parent-child interaction research across the three overarching frames of unidirectional, bidirectional, and system orientations, the reader will acquire an understanding of the similarity in historical trends across disciplines and topics. Also, a richer understanding of the remarkable convergence among disciplines in regard to important aspects of parent-child communication should become apparent. It is hoped that demonstration of this convergence and the issues wherein convergence is lacking, as well as the questions still to be answered, will serve to stimulate interdisciplinary dialogue and collaboration and dialogue between practitioners, theorists, and researchers.

4

The Child as Clay:
An Overview of the
Unidirectional Approach

INTRODUCTION

We have hinted at and offered glimpses of the three perspectives organizing this book. This chapter introduces the unidirectional approach. First, its basic premises are outlined. Parental personality characteristics thought to be directly influential on parenting and hence child outcomes are then considered with a concentration on Schaefer's (1959) model. Two distinct descriptions of parenting styles, one classic and the other more contemporary, are then reviewed. Both may be seen as reflecting parental personality, but each highlights differences in message use in interaction with children.

THE UNIDIRECTIONAL APPROACH

The unidirectional approach has been referred to as the social mold perspective and has served as the basis of socialization research for many de cades (Peterson & Rollins, 1987). Radical behaviorism exemplifies the strongest sense of the unidirectional perspective. Today variants of social learning theory are more likely to be employed in unidirectional research. In addition, symbolic interactionism has been applied as a unidirectional approach, albeit incorrectly.

The unidirectional approach generally assumes the child to be a passive entity. Parents are seen as molding children, as if they were a lump of clay. Thus this view recalls Locke's concept of the child as a *tabula rasa*. A person-oriented as opposed to a trait-oriented stance is usually (although not always) taken. Little attention is given most innate or biological determinants, overall maturation aside. This perspective may expand to include any external influence on the socialization of the child, such as culture, social class, ethnicity, family history, and other members of the kin network. Discussion here is limited to parental characteristics and communication.

The central tenet of the unidirectional view is that parenting input somehow influences the child's development. The characteristics of the child are direct outcomes of parenting characteristics and communication patterns. In other words, the assumption is one of linear cause and effect. Given this, the unidirectional quest has been to discover the "right" way to parent, or how to "cause" optimal development.

Privileging parenting as a powerful causal force in children's development is not simply an assumption. It reflects certain facts of life. First, the parent-child relationship is usually biological in origin and its long-term continuance is obliged by social convention. Second, as Maccoby and Martin (1983) asserted:

> The parent comes to the relationship as a well-formed person who already has a language, preestablished friendships, a vast fund of knowledge and skills, and well-developed tastes and interests. Although these things are influenced by the arrival of the child, to a substantial degree they remain stable. (p. 2)

Thus parents are seen as somewhat fixed entities with greater power and social competence. Therefore, when there is accommodating to do, it is most likely the child who bends to parental influence and demands.

PARENTAL PERSONALITY

Much of social mold research has focused on the broad input variable of parental personality (recall Allport's definition of personality in Chapter 2). Theoretically, personality figures prominently as a predictor of parental communicative behavior. Research relating personality to interaction reflects Cappella's (1987) first-order questions concerning encoding and decoding processes. Parents' inner beliefs, values, and goals are assumed to be operationalized by their behaviors. Moreover, child-rearing patterns exhibit considerable stability over the course of children's development (e.g., Roberts, Block, & Block, 1984). Thus theorists suggest that understanding the relationship between personality traits and enacted behavior is necessary for fully understanding the dynamics of communication between parents and children (e.g., Hinde & Stevenson-Hinde, 1986).

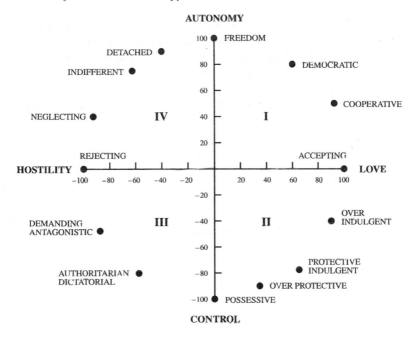

Figure 4.1. Hypothetical circumplex model of parenting styles.
SOURCE: Schaefer (1959, p. 232).

Classic studies of mothers have suggested that their behaviors may be factored into two primary enduring dispositions toward parenting (Baldwin, 1948; Becker, 1964; Sears, Maccoby, & Levin, 1957; Symonds, 1939). In the earliest study, Symonds (1939) described *dominance-submission* as a factor of mothers' tendency to control children's behavior. The second dimension, *acceptance-rejection,* referred to mothers' affective disposition toward children.

The early descriptive research was replicated and refined by Schaefer's (1959) factor-analytic study of maternal behaviors assessed in parent-child interaction via interviews and behavioral observations. From these analyses, a hypothetical circumplex model, organized around two bipolar dimensions, autonomy-control and hostility-love, was proposed (Figure 4.1).

Maternal behavior along the autonomy-control axis varies from allowing the child almost complete independence to the parent totally controlling the child's activities. Along the orthogonal axis, mothers' actions were arrayed from highly nurturing, child-centered behavior, to hostile behavior and noninvolvement with the child.

These primary factors interact to form four quadrants, each of which describes a unique pattern of parenting behavior. For quadrant I (autonomy-love), maternal behaviors were those that endorsed and facilitated children's sense of individuality and independence while simultaneously expressing affection and support. Quadrant II (control-love) contains "a complex and conflicted set of parental attitudes and behaviors" (Maccoby & Martin, 1983, p. 45). It is a pattern of positive involvement but possessive maternal behavior. In contrast, *hostile control* and *hostile irritability* characterized the array of maternal behaviors in quadrant III (control-hostility). The styles in quadrant IV (autonomy-hostility) were labeled *rejecting, neglecting, indifferent,* and *detached.* Lack of involvement, ranging from keeping children at a distance to abrupt dismissal of children's attempts to initiate interaction, appears to be the primary behavioral criterion of this quadrant (Maccoby & Martin, 1983).

Schaefer's model has provided a basis for comparing and integrating findings of individual studies of parental behavior. In addition, researchers have assumed functional continuity in parental behavior across time and have used this general model to correlate parental behavior with child outcomes at later points in development (see reviews by Maccoby & Martin, 1983; Peterson & Rollins, 1987; Rollins & Thomas, 1979). While the aggregates of parental behaviors comprising the warmth and control dimensions tend to vary with children's developmental level, invariably the qualities of these behaviors still can be divided into two categories. This is acknowledged by some authors' use of more general labels such as parental *responsiveness* (for warmth) and *demandingness* (for control) (Maccoby & Martin, 1983).

There are significant limitations to this model. First, its empirical basis is data drawn from the assessment of *maternal* behavior. Thus it may not be a *parenting* model so much as a *mothering* model. As will be discussed later, there are differences in the typical interaction styles of mothers and fathers with their children. Second, this model only characterizes maternal behavior with respect to older children. Researchers have not reached consensus on primary dimensions of maternal behavior with infants (Schaefer, 1989). Third, parenting is more complex than this model implies. Situational and temporal factors that influence parental actions are not accommodated by this model. The implication is that parental style is "set," or that parents will act in the same manner toward all of their children, at all times, in all situations. Evidence clearly shows that this is not the case. For example, parents may be better able to tolerate children's exuberant behavior in different settings and/or at certain times compared with other settings and times.

The last limitation may be the most important for communication researchers; this model does not readily guide analysis of specific communication messages and patterns (Burleson, 1983). That is, although the warmth-control model has been useful for organizing literature and drawing generalizations, it is less useful for analyzing parents' messages. What constitutes a "warm" message and a "controlling" message is unclear. Some concepts bear the same label, but the fact that they have different constitutive and/or operational definitions is often obscured. Furthermore, because concepts ranging from molecular to molar levels of analysis have been gathered under the warmth and control dimensions, generating research hypotheses from this model is problematic for communication studies.

Communication Styles of Parents

The problem as to the definition of warmth and control for analyzing parents' stable patterns of behavior is redressed to varying degrees in the models discussed below. Two approaches are reviewed: First, Baumrind's model of parental competence and, second, the emerging constructivist work on the reflection-enhancing quality of parental communication.

BAUMRIND'S TAXONOMY

Baumrind's examination of parenting styles is an eclectic approach not readily traced to a particular historical theory. Her work appears to be based on the rejection of previous theories, as opposed to the adoption of any one theory. She did not see psychoanalytic, humanistic, or behaviorist theories as terribly valuable in understanding parent-child interactions and their effects on children. Her goal was to examine "a synthesis" of factors such as permissiveness and control (Baumrind, 1966, p. 888). Note she did not refer to parental personalities per se but rather to attitudes and behaviors (Baumrind & Black, 1967). Applying a bottom-up approach, she searched for and interpreted several types. Yet unquestionably, she too was a unidirectional researcher. She clearly defended one of the types as being a better route to development than the others.

The Baumrind taxonomy emerged from an intensive, multimethod analysis of parent-child interaction. She observed and evaluated mothers and fathers as they and their 3- and 4-year-old children engaged in structured tasks. Data were collected in both home and laboratory settings. Parents were also interviewed. Dimensions assessed were parental control, parental maturity demands, parent-child communication, and parental nurturance.

Parental control was defined as parent behavior in service of child socialization. This was measured as parents' ability to enforce directives, consistency, ability to withstand nuisance behaviors (e.g., whining, pleading, and crying), and use of incentive and reinforcement, either positive or negative.

Included as *maturity demand* variables were ratings of parents' ability to teach the child skills necessary for intellectual, social, and emotional independence and allowing the child to make independent decisions. Baumrind isolated *communication* behaviors by examining patterns of offering reason with directives, engaging in and encouraging debate over contentious issues, and disclosing the source of power. Also included were measures of verbal ease and spontaneity, and directive clarity. The final dimension of the study was *nurturance*. This was defined as the "caretaking function." Upon closer examination of its component variables, it appears to be a measure of parental affect. Baumrind (1967) studied in the home or laboratory environment the variables "satisfies child," "supports child," and "uses positive incentive and reinforcement" and the ratings "attentiveness to child," "warmth in the form of support," "reassurance and nurturance," "absence of (parental) hostile behavior," and "solicitousness in the form of time spent with the child and involvement with child's performance and pleasure" (pp. 57-58).

The analysis of child and parental behavior revealed three distinct interaction styles: authoritative (pattern 1), permissive (pattern 2), and authoritarian (pattern 3).

Authoritative Style. Pattern 1 parents communicated facts and cognitive insights to their children better than other parents and were far more willing to accept a child's argument as a reason for retracting a directive. These parents were good arguers, more often using reason to gain compliance and also to encourage verbal give and take in reaching agreement with the child. These parents were not cowed by nuisance behaviors; they appeared able to resist child coercion. Authoritative parents were responsive to child-initiated interaction in a manner and to a degree that was generally satisfying for the child.

Significant differences emerged for support behaviors and use of positive incentives between this group of parents and the authoritarian parents (see below). The authoritative-type parents affirmed children's bids for support and attention and used more positive than negative reinforcements. In addition, authoritative parents had significantly higher scores for expression of affection and parent-child rapport and scored higher on all variables comprising the warmth dimension.

Baumrind (1967) commented, "Parents of Pattern 1 children balanced high nurturance with high control and high demands with clear communication about what was required of the child" (p. 80).

The constitutive definition of the authoritative parent describes this parent as one who endeavors:

to direct the child's activities but in a rational issue-oriented manner. She [*sic*] encourages verbal give and take, and shares with the child the reasoning behind her policy. She values both expressive and instrumental attributes, both autonomous self-will and disciplined conformity. Therefore, she exerts firm control at points of parent-child divergence, but does not hem the child in with restrictions. She recognizes her own special rights as an adult, but also the child's individual interests and special ways. The authoritative parent affirms the child's present qualities, but also sets standards for future conduct. She uses reason as well as power to achieve her objectives. She does not base her decisions on group consensus or the individual child's desires; but also, does not regard herself as infallible, or divinely inspired. (Baumrind, 1968, p. 261)

Children of the authoritative parents were highly ranked on subjective mood measures, self-reliance, and approach tendency or self-control. These children were described as being realistic, competent, and content.

Permissive Style. Permissive parents were the lowest on the control and maturity demand dimensions and intermediate for nurturance among the three patterns. The households of permissive parents were comparatively chaotic. Family activity was uncoordinated and rule enforcement lax. Both parents reported that they felt less control over their children. These parents also held the most conflicted attitudes toward child discipline.

Whereas permissive parents may be seen as generally responsive to their children, they are simultaneously undemanding. Low demands on maturity combined with some reticence to offer reasons and engage in discourse were associated with this style. These parents were least likely to offer factual information or to provide interpretations to children. However, in parent initiated control sequences, permissive parents were most likely to be coercive. They relied on guilt or diversion tactics. Concurrently, these parents were most likely to give in to pleading or complaining from the child.

Displays of affect by permissive parents were not significantly different from authoritative parents. Permissive mothers more often withdrew love and used ridicule as negative sanctions.

The Permissive prototype parent is one who attempts:

to behave in an acceptant and affirmative manner towards the child's impulses, desires, and actions. She [*sic*] consults with him [*sic*] about policy decisions and gives explanations for family rules. She makes few demands for household responsibility and orderly behavior. She presents herself to the child as a resource for him to use as he wishes, not as an active agent responsible for shaping or altering his ongoing or future behavior. She allows the child to regulate his own activities as much as possible, avoids the exercise of control, and does not encourage him to obey externally defined standards. She attempts to use reason but not overt power to accomplish her ends. (Baumrind, 1968, p. 256)

Children of permissive parents had low rankings for self-reliance and self-control or approach tendency. Characterized as relatively immature, these children were described as tending to regress when hurt, as impetuous, and as pursuing activities aimlessly.

Authoritarian Style. Assertion of parental power is the primary factor distinguishing this style (pattern 3) from the other two styles. These parents were highly demanding, yet simultaneously unresponsive to children's needs and desires. Parental verbal messages were unilateral and tended to be negative in affect.

Authoritarian parents often did not offer reasons when they issued directives, were the least likely to encourage verbal responses, and were also highly unlikely to change their position in face of children's arguments. Authoritarian parents were intermediate to the other parent types in the degree to which they were coerced by nuisance behaviors.

Of the three patterns, the authoritarian pattern was lowest for nurturance. Specifically, these parents were least likely to engage in interactions resulting in satisfying child outcomes. Authoritarian parents were generally indifferent to children's bids for support and attention and were the least likely to use positive reinforcement. Expression of affect was lowest for this pattern. Mothers showed less approval, empathy, and sympathy, and there was less evidence of a loving relationship. In fact, mothers reported using scare tactics to control their children. Particularly striking is the extreme lack of rapport between authoritarian parents and children.

The definition of the Authoritarian style depicts a parent who attempts:

> to shape, control and evaluate the behavior and attitudes of the child in accordance with a set of standard of conduct, usually an absolute standard, theologically motivated and formulated by a higher authority. She [*sic*] values obedience as a virtue and favors punitive, forceful measures to curb self-will at points where the child's actions or beliefs conflict with what she thinks is right conduct. She believes in inculcating such instrumental values as respect for authority, respect for work, and respect for the preservation of order and traditional structure. She does not encourage verbal give and take, believing that the child should accept her word for what is right. (Baumrind, 1968, p. 261)

Baumrind (1967) observed that children of authoritarian parents ranked low for peer affiliation and subjective mood and lower on the approach dimension relative to children of authoritative parents. These children were also described as passively hostile, disaffiliative, dysphoric, vulnerable to stress, and as doing "more careful work."

Before closing, a brief note is required about a fourth style, *neglecting*, reported in Baumrind's (1971) follow-up study. This style would find its counterpart in quadrant IV of Schaefer's model (see Figure 4.1). Baumrind (1971) observed that this disproportionately small group of parents was neglecting only by comparison to the other "highly nurturant, involved" parents (p. 70). Perhaps most significant, children of neglecting parents were not distinguishable by a unique pattern of scores on various child behavior assessments. Because of these points of ambiguity, researchers adopting Baumrind's framework generally focus on her three primary styles.

Summary. Using a somewhat different theoretical perspective and research methods, Baumrind's observations converge with and extend earlier studies on parental socialization styles. As noted, the parental styles interpreted correspond to three quadrants of the Schaefer model. Baumrind's taxonomy was verified in a later study with a larger sample of parents and children (see Baumrind, 1971). Testimony to the strength of this work is that it continues to be utilized widely in socialization research (e.g., Buri, Louiselle, Misukanis, & Mueller, 1988; Dornbusch, Ritter, Leiderman, Roberts, & Fraleigh, 1987; Greenberger & Goldberg, 1989; Kochanska, Kuczynski, & Radke-Yarrow, 1989). Baumrind's work has not significantly influenced communication research, however, which is surprising when one considers her detailed assessment of parental communication behaviors of the various parental types.

CONSTRUCTIVISM

Constructivism utilizes the concept of reflection-enhancing communication for the study of parent-child interaction (Applegate et al., 1985; Applegate, Burleson, & Delia, 1992). "Reflection-enhancing messages encourage recipients to consider the causes and consequences of their own and others' actions. These messages also encourage recipients to see how actions both grow out of and create psychological and affective states" (Applegate et al., 1992, p. 3). Individual differences in parents' messages are evaluated along this dimension. Then, these qualitative differences are studied relative to the development of communication skills in children. Wide variation in the reflection-enhancing quality of parents' messages has been observed and appears to be predictive of important child outcomes (e.g., person-centered communication skills and status among peers).

The model used in the research on reflection-enhancing communication illustrates the proposed relationships (Figure 4.2). As is clearly evident, this research model is "a unidirectional one in which influence flows from the parent to

Complexity of Parental Social Cognition	→	Complexity of Parental Reflection-Enhancing Communication	→	Complexity of Child's Social Cognition	→	Complexity of Child's Person-Centered Communication

Figure 4.2. Constructivist model of communication development in children as a function of parental reflection-enhancing communication.
SOURCE: Applegate et al. (1992, p. 13). Reprinted by permission from Lawrence Erlbaum.

child" (Applegate et al., 1992, p. 11). Although the path is directional, the linkage between parental talk and children's communication is seen as mediated by the child's knowledge of other persons and social situations. Here, parental talk does not function primarily as a model for children's simple imitation (as behaviorists would propose). Instead, these researchers contend that "sustained exposure to these more complex forms of behavior will have their primary influence on the child's interpersonal cognitive structures rather than directly on behavior" (Applegate et al., 1992, p. 8). In a nutshell, parental messages impart a logic about other persons and social life. It is this body of social knowledge that children rely on to guide their interactions with other persons.

These claims are derived from the theoretical perspective well known in the communication discipline as constructivism. The label makes specific reference to the perspective's use of key tenets and core concepts in personal construct theory (Kelly, 1955; also see Chapter 2). As the term *constructivism* is common in the developmental literature, the reader should be careful to distinguish this particular approach from others similarly labeled.

The general constructivist perspective on human communication is not easily reduced to brief description. Interested readers are referred to Delia et al. (1982) and Burleson (1987) for expanded overviews. Constructivist researchers in communication have focused on the relationship of social cognition and strategic message production; that is, how individual differences in social knowledge relate to the choice and use of messages to achieve goals. The following discussion highlights the two central concepts: interpersonal construct complexity and person-centered communication.

Interpersonal Construct Complexity. In brief, constructivists claim that the more well developed one's social-cognitive abilities are, the more able one will be to produce messages adapted to another person. Person-adapted messages should increase the likelihood that one's goals will be achieved through communication with other persons.

To explain social-cognitive development, constructivism starts from the assumption that persons actively interpret their everyday experiences. Following Kelly's (1955) views, these interpreted experiences are represented cognitively in personal constructs. Personal constructs become "references" for construing, or making sense of, events and persons in the social world. As persons' experiences accumulate, these core elements increase in number and change qualitatively. Personal constructs become organized into systems related to specific domains of one's experience. The system considered pivotal for communication studies is the interpersonal construct system. By definition, it is the set of "constructs used in the interpretation, evaluation, and anticipation of people and their thoughts and behavior" (Burleson, 1987, p. 307). Construct systems become more complex in organization and content, particularly during childhood and adolescence (see Delia et al., 1979). More constructs are added (increasing differentiation). Also, constructs become less concrete and more abstract in their representation of experience, and are increasingly integrated with other constructs in a system.

Person-Centered Messages. In the constructivists' theoretical conception, the interpersonal construct system is the basis for understanding and responding to other persons. Their claim of the functional relationship of this knowledge base to communication is a strong one. First, constructivists see the process of communication as being organized by communicator goals. Thus complex knowledge of other persons will enable one to achieve one's goals. Put another way, one's ability to engage in appropriate and effective strategic discourse depends crucially on one's base of social knowledge. Complicating matters however, constructivists suggest that communicators often pursue multiple goals. For example, one might try to persuade one's spouse to carry out the trash, simultaneously trying to avoid a dispute that could disrupt the relationship. Complex social knowledge aids the pursuit of multiple goals in communication.

The theoretical link of social-cognitive abilities to communicative behavior is provided by insights from the sociolinguistic theory of Bernstein (1974), the work of developmental theorists (particularly Piaget, 1959; Werner, 1957), and symbolic interactionism (in particular the Chicago school grounded in Mead, 1934). These theorists suggest that societies and individuals develop means to orient to others' perspectives and in turn coordinate individual actions in interpersonal interaction. Such resources are intimately related to social knowledge.

The primary concern here relates to language resources and how conceptions of social life are expressed symbolically. Bernstein (1974) identified two diametrically opposed cultural conceptions of individuals, social roles, and social processes (e.g., communication), and argued that these are expressed in everyday life via language. One view is of a *position-centered* society, in which social roles largely determine the meaning of persons' communicative actions. *Person-centered* societies, on the other hand, seem to explicitly acknowledge a fundamental psychological uniqueness and autonomy of its members. A more *elaborated* linguistic code tends to be used in person-centered societies. This code is the means for communicators to express their private views so that others will understand them.

By integrating this analysis with theories of Werner and Piaget, Bernstein's analysis of person- versus position-centered speech becomes a way to analyze individuals' messages. Werner's work on autonomous speech (Werner & Kaplan, 1963) highlighted the developmental changes toward being able to adopt views of psychologically distant persons, a point reminiscent of Piaget's account of the shift from egocentric to socialized speech as a function of perspective taking. In sum, the person centeredness of a child's language (or for that matter, an adult's) should reveal his or her relative degree of social-cognitive development.

Thus the constructivist perspective expects systematic relationships between the complexity of one's interpersonal construct system and message strategies. As one acquires a more complex representation of other persons, the increase in complexity should be associated with a gradual shift from position- to person-centered language use. These specific claims of constructivists have been supported in numerous studies, in which individuals' construct system development is assessed and related to the degree to which their message strategies reflect person-centered quality (i.e., adapt to the listener's perspective; see review by Burleson, 1987).

Parental Messages. To return to the study of the effects of parental messages on children, first recall the model in Figure 4.2. This model of parental reflection-enhancing communication tests the basic premises of constructivism as they relate to parents and children individually and the link between parents and children. The theory being tested is that parental social knowledge and how well it is developed directly influences the encoding of messages. These parental messages influence, in turn, the child's cognitive and communicative development.

Two different parental strategies have been examined in relationship to these child outcomes: regulative messages and comforting messages. Note how these particular strategies represent the two dimensions of the general parenting model (Figure 4.1). Mothers' regulative messages are based on the legitimate power of parents to control or modify children's thinking or behavior (Applegate, 1990). Such messages are maximally reflection enhancing when children are encouraged to reason through aspects of situations, to anticipate consequences, and to act appropriately. On the other hand, comforting messages belong to the domain of parental nurturing behavior. These strategies are reflection enhancing when parents acknowledge and legitimize the child's feelings while also assisting the child in understanding feelings and how they are influenced by particular circumstances.

Note that *reflection enhancing* is a quality of parental communication. Variation in the reflection-enhancing quality of a message lies in the degree to which it explicitly expresses parental understanding of other persons, brings this to children's attention, and encourages children to respond to appropriately. Parental messages that are highly reflection enhancing paint for children a social world that is full of complex relationships among people.

The empirical support for the model is preliminary, but quite compelling. The complexity of mothers' interpersonal construct systems is systematically related to the reflection-enhancing quality of their messages to children (Applegate et al., 1992). In addition, highly cognitively complex mothers tend to use a greater number of reflection-enhancing messages to influence children's thinking or behavior than less cognitively complex mothers (Applegate et al., 1985). Mothers apparently use such messages consistently; a high correlation was obtained between quality of regulative and comforting strategies across situations examined. Relative to their peers whose mothers' talk encouraged little reflection, children of reflection-enhancing mothers tend to have higher cognitive complexity. They also use message strategies that are person centered and are more likely to be socially accepted by their peers (Burleson, Delia, & Applegate, 1990).

Summary. Reflection-enhancing communication appears to influence children's interpersonal construct system development by fostering development of a logic about persons as unique, psychological beings, which then impacts the child's interpersonal communicative behavior. This model stresses examining variation in parental social knowledge and messages, relative to (1) parents' immediate and socialization goals, (2) the degree to which environmental features are highlighted for the child's attention, and (3) the degree to which the child is encouraged to reflect on his or her actions and consequences for others. Thus conceptualized, reflection-enhancing messages do a lot of work. In fact, Applegate et al. (1992) suggested that these highly complex messages may allow parents efficiently to pursue many socialization goals simultaneously, for example, for children to behave appropriately, to develop the capacity for self-regulation, to understand one's behavior and its consequences, and to reflect on the implications of actions while pursuing one's goals, all as the basis for future activities.

Note also the attention to parental beliefs of parents and how these may be made public through reflection-enhancing communication. At a fundamental level, parental messages may illustrate for children different concepts of communication: communication as a simple vehicle of expression versus communication as the practices of unique individuals in which actions are aimed at the pursuit of goals (Applegate et al., 1992; see also O'Keefe, 1988, for a discussion of broadly defined cultural logics underlying message design). However, there are only a small number of studies on parental communication using the constructivist model. Given its initial support, more attention to this perspective is warranted. Furthermore, this is only one program of study that applies the general constructivist perspective. Constructivism provides a framework for studying communication in use and in development across the life span of persons, both as a function of cognitive development and as subject to immediate environmental influences (see Burleson, 1987). Qualitative differences in messages may be readily assessed along a hierarchy from position- to person-centered language use. Differences in language use can be examined as they reflect persons' conceptions of others and relationships with others (i.e., interpersonal construct system development) and of communication in general. Finally, although not stressed in this overview, culture's influence on communication processes can be investigated via a constructivist orientation.

SUMMARY AND CONCLUSIONS

The earliest studies of parent-child interaction were strongly influenced by a conception of the child as either a blank slate or innately evil. This became the argument for strong parental intervention in children's lives. Thus the role of the environment is stressed in unidirectional perspectives. Even when the possibility of a child's inherited characteristics is acknowledged, parenting is focused on either accelerating or enhancing what is already there or on countering more negative inherited tendencies. The perspective itself accommodates both continuous and discontinuous explanations of developmental course. It also generally assumes a cumulative effect of parental actions. That is, the plastic, passive child is built up gradually over time by the parent. In short, what the parent does determines what the child becomes.

Parental behavior has been analyzed along two orthogonal dimensions (control-demandingness and warmth-responsiveness), which appear to interact to affect a variety of outcomes. From the literature, one may conclude that parents' behavioral dispositions are continuously exhibited in actions throughout the socialization process. The strength of these findings in Western white middle-class cultures is further supported by studies of parent-child interaction in other cultures that have isolated the warmth and control dimensions of parental behavior (e.g., Bronstein-Burrows, 1981). Clinical impressions of parenting behavior are consistent with the above-cited empirical studies of parenting behavior. For example, Satir's (1988) descriptions of *boss, leader and guide,* and *pal* parent types are built on the interaction of parental warmth and regard for the child with an instrumental, goal-oriented control dimension.

There is no need to belabor the observation that the warmth-control model has certain limitations for communication studies. There are other, more specific frameworks available, including the parental style taxonomy of Baumrind (1967) and the constructivist analysis of reflection-enhancing parental messages. Neither has generated a great deal of research in the communication discipline, although perhaps they should. The insightful analyses of each raise numerous possibilities for future research, and would both continue and improve research on parent-child interaction from a unidirectional perspective.

As will be highlighted in later chapters, unidirectional orientations, although capable of providing an extensive amount of information, seldom are realistic enough to capture the complexities of parent-child interaction. For example, Baumrind (1980) has acknowledged that "a unidirectional linear causal model cannot account for the intense variations in behavior that human beings are capable of" (p. 648). The next chapter summarizes research on the three exemplar variables from a unidirectional orientation.

5

The Child as Clay:
The Unidirectional Approach
to Three Variables

INTRODUCTION

From a unidirectional standpoint, socialization is seen as the goal and purpose of parenting. Thus research is generally directed at answering the question, "How do parents achieve this goal?" The purpose of this chapter is to synthesize research on the proposed role of the parents in shaping selected, traditionally studied child outcome variables: self-control, self-concept, and communication competencies.

SELF-CONTROL

Research on compliance-gaining strategies forms the core of the discussion here due to the unidirectional stance that these parental attempts are direct causal agents of child compliance, internalization, and development of a moral conscience. A substantive body of work supports the notion that parental strategies are linked to self-control (Harter, 1983). Relationships between parental strategies and aspects of self-regulation have been confirmed (see e.g., Holden & West, 1989; Moore, Mullis, & Mullis, 1986). Issues of child safety and adoption of social and cultural norms, among others, are of utmost importance to society (Harter, 1983). In infancy, parents attempt to influence children to protect children from harm and ensure survival. Later on, the emphasis is to teach society's rules and norms and, ultimately, to promote moral development.

Noncompliance of young children is reported by parents to be one of the most problematic issues they face (Forehand, 1977). Conflict between mothers and 4-year-olds has been found to occur on the average of 1.5 times in every 5 minutes (Eisenberg, 1992). Although most people think of how to survive the early age of the so-called terrible twos, issues of compliance extend to adolescents, as anyone who has encountered a teenager will attest. Compliance gaining overlaps significantly with the concept of control discussed earlier. Three constructs related to control emerge: coercion, induction, and love withdrawal (Rollins & Thomas, 1979). These basic modes also align fairly closely with Baumrind's parenting styles. *Coercion* is a clash of wills between parent and child, in which the parent exerts significant pressure on the child to behave. This is usually considered a high-power-assertive technique and may include physical force, physical punishment, and/or deprivation of privileges. Authoritarian parents seem disposed toward such power-assertive orientations (Baumrind, 1967).

Induction is aimed at avoiding a clash of wills (Hoffman, 1970). "It is an influence attempt that places rational maturity demands on children, offers, [and] explanations" (Peterson & Rollins, 1987, p. 478). Induction is reasoning with and explaining to the child. This is a low-power-assertive technique (see reviews by Marion, 1983; Putallaz & Heflin, 1990). Induction styles were observed to be commonly used by authoritative parents (Baumrind, 1967).

The third control technique, *love withdrawal,* has been studied less frequently than the other two. It is parental behavior that indicates disapproval of the child with the implication that love will not be restored until the child changes his or her behavior. Love withdrawal "may be devastating emotionally because it poses the ultimate threat of abandonment or separation" (Hoffman, 1970, p. 285). Tactics include ignoring or isolating the child as well as explicit messages of rejection, disappointment, or coldness. Love withdrawal has generally been considered a high-power-assertive technique. It is most notable in descriptions of the permissive style of parenting (Baumrind, 1967).

In addition to these three basic control types, *warmth,* or nurturance, has emerged as a overall dimension related to compliance. Although warmth overlaps some with the styles above, and what exactly constitutes a warm message is unclear, warmth (nurturance) has received enough research attention to warrant separate consideration.

Despite the resemblance, compliance-gaining and control attempts are not the same. They differ in that compliance-gaining strategies are down a level of abstraction from control styles. That is, compliance gaining is studied as concrete communication-based behaviors. Table 5.1 compiles a relatively exhaustive list of basic strategies. Due to variations in conceptualization, labeling, and operationalization, the categories are not mutually exclusive. Furthermore, researchers vary considerably in the level of specificity in which they are interested.

Not all of the strategies listed in Table 5.1 will be discussed, because some that have been detailed in descriptive investigations have not been studied in association with child outcomes. Thus generalizations about the potential links between parental communication and the child outcomes cannot be offered about all strategies. Rather conclusions concerning the four general types of control—coercion, induction, love withdrawal, and warmth—will be summarized.

Generalizations

The same communication strategies chosen by parents to elicit immediate compliance in the young child may not elicit long-term compliance in the young child or internalization or moral conscience in the adolescent (Hoffman, 1970; Peterson et al., 1985). These general findings have held in recent research (see Crockenberg & Litman, 1990).

Pragmatically, the hardiest conclusion emerging from decades of research is that the greater the parental coercion, the less the compliance and internalization (Honig, 1985; Putallaz & Heflin, 1990). Coercive power-assertive strategies such as physical punishment and bargaining with threats are presumably frustrating to the child, as they tend to negate the child's growing autonomy, sense of self, and ego development. The most predictable outcomes of parental coercion are child anger and aggression and, behaviorally, in the long run, less compliance. Even strict behaviorists do not advocate highly coercive tactics, because they reinforce aggression and avoidance.

Coercive or high-power-assertive techniques may be effective for immediate compliance (Lytton & Zwirner, 1975). However, Kuczynski (1984) found that even in immediate situations, 4-year-olds were less compliant with mothers using high-power techniques than were children whose mothers used induction. Moreover, the more often power-assertive strategies are used, the less often and fully the child complies with parental instructions over time.

Another point of agreement concerns induction. Consistent use by parents of inductive messages appears to encourage both immediate and long-term

TABLE 5.1

Compliance-Gaining Strategies, Explanations, and Examples

Strategy	Definition	Communication Example
Physical coercion		
a. Physical punishment	Physically reprimanding	Spanking, slapping the hand
b. Physical restraint	Physically moving or restraining the child	Moving the child from standing on the back of the couch; grabbing his arm before he hits his brother
Verbal coercion	Expressing displeasure, criticism, or threat	"You did a bad job"; "You can't do anything right"
Verbal prohibition	Verbally commanding child to stop or change behavior	"Don't do that"; "Stop it right now"
Love withdrawal	Temporarily removing affection or attention; includes separation	Sending child to his or her room; making child sit in the corner; ignoring child when he or she cries
Bargaining		
a. Coercive	Threatening punishment	"I'll send you to your room if you don't eat your vegetables"
b. Reward power	Offering a promise or bribe	"I will give you candy if you eat your vegetables"
Distraction, verbal or nonverbal	Offering an alternative to the child's objectionable behavior	"Look, here's a ball you can roll" (as the parent gently removes the small item the child has put in her mouth); shaking a rattle so a baby will stop crying
Appropriate physical contact (sometimes restricting)	Nonverbally acknowledging the child; nonchalantly restraining the child	Hugging or reassuring pats; matter of factly holding child on lap so she or he cannot run around during church
Nonverbal guidance	Directing the child's attention physically to the task	Holding the child's hand and walking her over to the toys and pointing to them

TABLE 5.1
Continued

Strategy	Definition	Communication Example
Appropriate timing	Awareness of the child's state of involvement; awareness of number of commands sent	"Please brush your teeth after you finish that game" versus "Brush your teeth now"; also "Please brush your teeth" versus "Brush your teeth, put your pajamas on, get your teddy bear and book"
Verbal positive reinforcement	Verbally praising or acknowledging the child	"Wow, you got your pajamas on all by yourself"; "What a good girl"
Play	Engaging in play with child	Playing tea party
Parental compliance	Allowing child's request	"Yes you can play outside"; "Yes I will read you a story"
Synchrony, reciprocal action, responsiveness	Staying in tune with the child; interacting with the child; following the child's lead	*Child:* "Squish the clay." *Mother:* "Okay, now let's make a pancake with the squish." *Child:* "Okay, Mommy." as opposed to *Child:* "Squish the clay." *Mother:* "I have a better idea. Let's roll it out like this." *Child:* "I don't want to do it that way."
Tutelage	Offering guidance or restructuring the situation	"Let's build a tower" (instead of throwing the blocks)
Induction	Offering an explanation, reason, or consequence of the deed	"If you touch the stove you will get burned"; "It's hot"; "You'll get hurt"

compliance by the child (Kuczynski, 1983). Induction also predicts internalization and moral development among adolescents (Higgins, 1991; Hoffman, 1975). This last finding has significant implications for researchers and practitioners concerned with problems of undesirable adolescent behavior. Such behavior has been attributed to conflicts between adolescents and parents rooted in the move toward stronger alliances with peers and greater independence from parents. The concern of parents appears to center on their adolescent children's emotional separation and perceived denial of parental values. However, giving up childhood dependencies on parents does not necessitate either emotional separation or denial of values. It does, however, require "the freedom to explore and experiment and protection from experiences that are clearly dangerous" (Baumrind, 1991, p. 60). Baumrind (1991) has found that adolescents who are "self-regulated, individuated, competent individuals" have authoritative parents (p. 60). Recall that such parents tend to rely on induction.

It should be noted, however, that within induction, the content of parental reasons has seldom been investigated. There is likely considerable variation in reasons. They may, for example, center on the dilemma of others or the logical consequences of a child's actions for self and others. Thus reasons may vary in efficacy as compliance-gaining tactics. Kuczynski's (1983) findings were inconclusive and thus caution against assuming that all reasons are equally effective.

There is a mixed bag of findings relative to love withdrawal, which perhaps only emphasizes the need for research in this area. First, the effects for the child are theorized to be similar to those associated with physical punishment (Maccoby & Martin, 1983). Love withdrawal, like physical punishment, induces short-term compliance. But persistent use may lead to child anxiety and a lack of cooperation over the long term. However, the hypothesized effects of love withdrawal are seldom found (Brody & Shaffer, 1982; Peterson & Rollins, 1987).

There are at least three accounts for the equivocal findings. The first is related to parental tendencies to combine strategies. Indeed, love withdrawal is often accompanied by other compliance-gaining tactics (Chapman & Zahn-Waxler, 1982). Not surprisingly then, considerable variation in outcomes has been observed. When used in conjunction with warmth and affection, love withdrawal appears to be positively associated with moral development. The association does not hold, however, when love withdrawal is administered in a "cool and aloof" manner (Brody & Shaffer, 1982).

Second, operationalizations of love withdrawal vary dramatically and in several ways. For example, in addition to verbal messages (e.g., "I won't love you until you clean up your room"), love withdrawal has been operationalized as isolation. Isolation can vary from *time-out*, in which a child faces the corner, to the extreme of locking a child in a dark closet. At this extreme, isolation is considered unethical, and its use banned in certain populations (Anderson & King, 1974). Nevertheless, milder forms of isolation have been effective in both research and home settings, especially when used in combination with other techniques, for example, when coupled with an explanation.

And finally, speculation as to the label *love withdrawal* is raised. By definition, love withdrawal implies that the child perceives removal of parental love. However, the withdrawal of love may not be inferred by the child in many techniques classified as love withdrawal. Or the reverse may be true; techniques not seen as love withdrawal by researchers may be perceived by the child as such. Also, the long-term implications of love withdrawal are not well known or understood.

A final generalization concerns warmth. Warmth, in terms of sensitivity and expression of positive affection, appears likely to prompt strong self-guides (Higgins, 1991). Some specific examples of this warmth include appropriate physical contact such as hugging, patting, and physical guidance (Marion, 1983). Hugs and pats offer warmth and support through positive nonverbal contact. Physical guidance also serves an important function in attracting and keeping the child's attention. Quinn (1987) referred to warmth in a conceptually similar manner as humanistic parenting, which he contended to be formative of moral conscience.

Warmth may also be considered positive and supportive *involvement*. Here reference is made not to a specific compliance strategy, but rather to the general pattern of interaction between mother and child. A relatively consistent finding is that the overall amount of maternal play with the child is linked to child compliance (Lytton, 1980). Mothers who invest time and energy playing with their children likely reap the benefits of compliance in both those specific play interactions and in other interactions. In addition, mothers who spend a significant amount of playtime with their children and who invoke induction have the highest likelihood of achieving compliance from their children (Putallaz & Heflin, 1990).

Many social mold orientations are grounded in learning theory. It is logical, then, that parental reinforcement after gaining compliance has been investigated as well. Although discussion has concerned strategies aimed at gaining compliance, reinforcement is in essence a compliance-gaining strategy. As any learning theorist would vow, well-timed reinforcement heightens subsequent compliance. The timing should be positive and immediate, especially for young children. Positive reinforcement fits with the warm pattern noted by Higgins (1991) and the authoritative parenting style. Yet positive reinforcement for compliance is relatively rare. When a child does comply, the most common response by the mother (more than 50% of the time) is no response (Lytton, 1979, 1980). The next most common response is a neutral comment. The third most common response to a child's compliance is another request by the parent. Positive responses, even a simple "Good girl" or "Thanks," were the fourth most likely. It is no wonder that obedience of children tends to be "erratic" (Lytton, 1979).

Conclusion

Parents face a daily, often hourly, problem: How to get the child to mind. In general, the authoritarian, authoritative, and permissive parenting styles discussed in the previous chapter are associated with certain tactics. Researchers and practitioners are interested in the long-term effects of such strategies on the child.

In sum, conditions that gain immediate compliance do not necessarily foster internalization or moral development. Rather, though coercive or controlling strategies have been associated with immediate short-term compliance, these appear to be detrimental to child socialization in the long run. Controlling strategies have been negatively associated with self-esteem, academic achievement, and creativity (Peterson & Rollins, 1987). Induction, and other low-power-assertive, high-support messages are posited to promote immediate compliance, internalization, and the development of moral conscience. Findings concerning love withdrawal are mixed. Finally, as compliance strategies are seldom used individually, more research into the combined effects of such strategies is needed.

The questions confronting scholars of communication are the following: Is there a way of talking with a child that will aid compliance and moral development? Does the content of the message matter? Or does the warmth associated with it? What about the effects of mixed strategies? And are child-parent interactions at this early age related to moral conscience in adulthood?

The compliance-gaining research brings into question the widely held assumption that early experience is formative. Because studies seldom go beyond adolescence, it may be that compliance-gaining strategies of parents lack predictive power for their children's adult morality.

Finally, even if direct links could be determined for the right way to parent to create ultimate moral socialization, the same compliance strategy may not have the same outcomes in other cultures or co-cultures. Maccoby (1984) argued, for example, that physical punishment is more frequent among American blacks than whites. She raised the possibility that the greater frequency of physical punishment among black families makes it normative so that the experience is less negative (if negative at all) for a black child than for a white child. Maccoby's (1984) study illustrated "dangers of generalizing the findings" concerning parent-child compliance strategies and the possible enhancement of internalization and moral development from one cultural group to another (p. 215). The questions of what is normal and what route is best are reflected here.

SELF-CONCEPT

Discussion of self-esteem flows nicely from a discussion of compliance, because the way a parent exerts pressure on the child influences the child's evaluation of himself or herself. For example, induction appears to be related to the development of a good self-concept (Mills & Grusec, 1988). Clearly, this represents a unidirectional orientation to the development of self-concept. Although James (1890) would not be considered a unidirectional scholar, he did foreshadow the modern-day preoccupation with the causes of self-hood. He discussed self-esteem in terms of the sources of, and the impact of society on, the person's sense of self.

From a unidirectional stance, the origin of self-esteem and locus of control is usually explained from one of two theoretical positions: (1) symbolic interactionism or (2) social-learning theory.

The symbolic interaction model contends that children's self-concept is derived from reflected appraisals of significant others (usually parents). From Cooley (1902) and Mead (1934) comes the idea that people learn to see themselves as significant others see them. This approach contains three elements: self-appraisal, actual appraisals of significant others, and reflected appraisals.

(a) Self-appraisals result from the individual's perceptions of others;
(b) the individual's perceptions are fundamentally accurate readings of others' behavior and attitudes; and
(c) the actual behavior and attitudes of others produce the individual's self-appraisal. (Margolin, Blyth, & Carbone, 1988, p. 211)

Early symbolic interactionists also credited the child with significant influence on self-development and on society. However, this insight has been almost completely neglected by unidirectional scholars. Note in the above list, the child is only implicitly acknowledged in terms of perceptions. The second theoretical stance is social-learning theory. Modeling and reinforcement have been invoked to explain the development of self. Social-learning theory holds that modeling is a primary process leading to socialization. Children who are exposed to high-self-esteem models are more likely to perceive themselves as having a high self-esteem (Bandura, 1978). Reinforcement emphasizes contingent responses. "Contingency is defined as a probabilistic relation between a person's action and an event" (Skinner, 1986, p. 361). Remember that although social-learning theorists do accept that both the child and environment are important for the child's development more emphasis is placed on environmental forces.

The interactive nature of self and environment can readily be seen in regard to locus of control. Learning theorists are increasingly interested in issues of locus of control as fundamentally related to self-esteem (e.g., Skinner, 1991). A young child's awareness of self as the agent of cause and effect (i.e., locus of control) may well form the base of self-esteem (Franks, 1985). This new interest is somewhat ironic, as Cooley (1902) proposed this relationship almost a century ago. Yet once more, within a unidirectional framework, parental input is still considered to carry more weight.

Generalizations about parental effects on children's self-concept follow. Research on locus of control is presented first, because it is frequently considered foundational to self-esteem. Findings relative to self-esteem are then summarized.

Locus of Control

From a reinforcement perspective, people achieve a greater sense of control when they perceive that outcomes are contingent on their own efforts (Lefcourt, 1976; Phares, 1976). From this stance, a parental task is to help establish this sense of cause and effect as early as possible in infancy. That is, parents should help the child see the relationships between his or her actions and the results. Through interacting with the world, the infant early on begins to grasp an understanding of causality. Causing things to happen is the medium through which the young infant begins to exercise control and to understand cause and consequence more fully (Gurin & Brim, 1984, p. 283). In a similar manner, Gordon, Nowicki, and Wichern (1981) concluded, "If the child's performance of certain behaviors is contingently rewarded by his [sic] parents, he comes to expect reinforcement for these behaviors in the future. Since such expectancies tend to generalize, this child is likely to develop a general, internal locus-of-control" (p. 50).

Self-Esteem

The legacy of the symbolic interactionist approach adapted to unidirectional research is an almost religious fervor in the belief that self-esteem develops via the child's interaction with significant others in the environment. Despite some recent doubts about the link between the appraisals of others and self-appraisals (e.g., Felson & Reed, 1986), one's self-esteem is still considered to be molded predominantly by the primary group (e.g., the family) or significant others (e.g., parents).

What is currently known about the antecedents of self-esteem comes predominantly from three classic studies: Bachman (1970), Rosenberg (1965), and Coopersmith (1967). These researchers adopted a unidirectional orientation to search for parenting behaviors impacting self-esteem. Primary attention will be accorded to Coopersmith (see also summaries and interpretations by Harter, 1983; Maccoby, 1980).

Coopersmith (1967) proposed that parental acceptance and positive regard were critical antecedents of high self-esteem. He obtained considerable support for his hypotheses. Parents of high self-esteem boys were described as follows:

(1) They were accepting, affectionate, and involved, treating the child's interests and problems as meaningful, and showing genuine concern; (2) They were strict in the sense that they enforced rules carefully and consistently, and sought to encourage children to uphold high standards of behavior. (3) They preferred noncoercive kinds of discipline, for example, denial of privileges and isolation, and typically discussed the reasons why the child's behavior was inappropriate; (4) They were democratic in the sense that the child's opinions were considered in decisions such as the hour of their bedtime, and the child participated in making family plans. (Harter, 1983, p. 338)

Rosenberg's and Bachman's conclusions are similar to those of Coopersmith. Rosenberg (1965) found high self-esteem in high-school boys and girls to be related primarily to parental interest in the child. Bachman (1970), like Coopersmith, studied boys and found self-esteem to be associated with parental affection and fairness, and inclusion in decision making.

All of these foundational studies are based on self-reports; in general, observational studies have been scarce. Coopersmith examined children's self-reports of self-esteem and maternal reports of parenting. Rosenberg and

Bachman both relied on retrospective self-reports of children and their memories of earlier parenting.

Generalizations

Given that the parental behaviors hypothesized to aid high self-esteem are virtually isomorphic with those hypothesized to aid internal locus of control, generalizations will be drawn across the two constructs. The vast majority of studies, whether based on perceptions or behaviors, confirm the same overall patterns. Because the similarity in findings is much greater than in the other two exemplar variables and given the ultimate goal of the *unidirectional* orientation to unearth the one best way to parent, this albeit unrealistic one best way can be clearly enumerated. These generalizations have been compiled from several sources. Studies and reviews on locus of control used to draw the list of enhancing parental behaviors include Chance (1972); Chandler et al. (1980); Chapman et al. (1990); Crandall and Crandall (1983); Crandall et al. (1965); Damon (1983); Findley and Cooper (1983); Gecas (1989); Gordon et al. (1981); Harter (1983); Krampen (1989); Lefcourt (1976); Loeb (1975); Rotter (1966); Scheck, Emerick, and El-Assal (1973); and Skinner (1991). Self-esteem literature drawn on is Felson and Reed (1986); Gecas (1971); Gecas and Schwalbe (1986); Grotevant and Cooper (1985, 1986); Harter (1983); Isberg et al. (1989); La Voie (1974); Leaper et al. (1989); Loeb, Horst, and Horton (1980); Maccoby (1980); and Sears (1970).

Parental behaviors consistently associated with high child self-esteem and/or internal locus of control include:

1. Warmth (also studied as nurturance, responsiveness, support, or acceptance), including statements of praise and the absence of criticism.
2. Contingent reinforcement (appropriate positive reinforcement or punishment).
3. Suggestive, as opposed to directive, statements during interaction.
4. Nonrestrictive behaviors and remarks (also studied as curiosity-promoting behaviors).
5. Encouragement of children's independent behavior.
6. Involving the child in developmentally appropriate decisions.
7. Flexible parenting (also studied under the idea of being open to the child's good reasons).
8. Avoiding high-power-assertive techniques, especially physical punishment, instead using induction.
9. Relatively high demandingness.

This list would be what pure unidirectional researchers might advocate if writing a parenting manual. As will be seen in upcoming chapters, this is an unrealistic and simplistic picture of the complex dynamics of parent-child interaction and the variables of self-esteem or locus of control. To facilitate high self-esteem, developmental and family researchers generally concur that both warmth and control dimensions should be demonstrated in parental actions. Consistent positive associations are obtained between parental warmth and support behaviors and children's self-esteem (Growe, 1980). However, there is some confusion surrounding the construct of parental control in relationship to self-esteem and locus of control. Sears (1970) found that fathers' control and punishment is associated with lower self-esteem in boys; Bachman (1970) obtained similar findings. Likewise, Buri et al. (1988) indicated that strong disciplinary practices by parents have negative effects. Though there are major differences between Coopersmith's concept of control and the behaviors studied by Sears (1970) and Buri et al. (1988), the latter researchers' findings have been interpreted by some as contradicting Coopersmith's report of firm, demanding parental discipline as positively related to self-esteem.

Findings related to the control dimension are more compatible than they first appear (see reviews by Growe, 1980; Steinmetz, 1979). Contradictory findings may be explained as a matter of how constructs like control, discipline, or punishment were operationalized. Very simply, "parental authority may have a negative or positive effect upon self-esteem depending upon the *type* of authority that is exercised" (Buri et al., 1988, p. 280, emphasis added). Consistently, high-power-assertive techniques are associated with low self-esteem.

Self-esteem research brings into focus the paradox of being firm and consistent yet also flexible with children. Control behaviors engender both positive and negative consequences. For example, restrictive parental actions impede children as they seek to develop mastery and autonomy. Directive messages, particularly when children are playing, prevent active learning through experimentation. On the other hand, the benefits include defining limits for children's acceptable behaviors. Rules, regularity, and predictability provide structure and security for children. These may also be metacommunicative messages of parental concern and respect for the child. Parental permissiveness allows children the freedom to make mistakes and learn from them, but with too much freedom children may wonder where they stand with their parents. Finally, permissiveness in the early years may backfire later, for example, when parents try to establish rules like curfew for teens.

The key appears to be in the balance of these behaviors and also in the ability to apply minimally sufficient pressure (see Lepper, 1983). Unidirectional researchers advocate that parents be consistent and firm, yet listen to, value, and take into account the child's opinions and be flexible enough to allow exceptions to rules (e.g., Gordon et al., 1981). This seems to be excellent advice. Adolescents with the highest self-esteem scores reported their parents to be accepting, to use less psychological control, and not to be overly firm. Stated simply, evidence to date indicates "optimal self-concept development takes place in an atmosphere of acceptance that allows the adolescent autonomy and the opportunity to learn competencies" (Litovsky & Dusek, 1985, p. 373).

Conclusion

The description by Coopersmith (1967) of parenting practices promoting self-esteem continues to ring true several decades later in unidirectional research. This is astonishing, because his study focused on a sample of only boys in a limited age range. Yet his findings have been supported for both sexes, across a wide range of ages, and by researchers from different disciplines. The same basic dimensions of parental behavior—support (warmth) and control—emerge as critical factors in study after study. The parent of a child with high self-esteem and an internal locus of control very closely resembles Baumrind's (1967) authoritative parenting style.

Despite the similarity and strength of the evidence, numerous issues lurk. First, no one theoretical model clearly accounts for everything. The appraisals of others (as stressed by symbolic interactionism) and modeling and reinforcement (social-learning theory) appear to impact self-concept and self-esteem.

Second, given the correlational nature of most studies, almost every writer acknowledges that cause and effect are difficult to determine. Interpretations of the link between parenting behavior and child self-concept could run the other direction (per Bell, 1968). Nearly all reports contain the "customary caveat that there may well be reciprocal effects of child on mother which in some fashion lead a child's high self-concept to produce maternal warmth" (Sears, 1970, p. 269). Social mold theorists tend to discount such interpretations, however. Next, the primary group may have different members at different points in development. Parents are generally the significant others during infancy, but do they remain significant as children's social networks expand? Some scholars contend that parents maintain a strong and influential foothold in the primary group. Studies have found that adolescent identity is more closely related to positive relationships with parents than with friends (e.g., O'Donnell, 1976). However, there are numerous other candidates for inclusion in the primary group such as peers, day-care staff, and teachers. Scholars tend to agree that as part of ego development adolescents are expected to become more autonomous from parents and more connected with peers (Leaper et al., 1989). Adopting a developmental perspective, Isberg et al. (1989) concluded that parental influence diminished with youth ego development. The composition of the primary group probably does change across the developmental span. Note, however, that this is still a unidirectional orientation. Only the source of influence has changed.

Finally, unidirectional conclusions are directly related to the issue of the formativeness of early experiences. Some believe self-evaluation, formed when young, remains relatively stable across time. Yet prospective studies are lacking. Instead, studies are based on retrospective data: young adults' recollections of their self-esteem earlier in life and/or perceptions of the parenting they experienced. Although this method invites critique on the basis of validity, it has been argued that what the parent does is not as important as what the child perceives. It can be concluded that the perception of the parent as warm and nurturing, accepting, and so forth is tied consistently to self-concept.

In general, unidirectional researchers believe they have solid evidence for at least a quasi-causal relationship between parenting styles and self-concept. There remains a question of the direction of this influence. The phenomenon may be one of mutual influence. Or parental communication might be a response to their perceptions of their child's self-esteem. Given the number of self-report studies and the relative lack of interaction studies, the questions salient to those interested in interaction are the following: Are actual communicative differences in parental talk related to the child's self-concept in a causal manner? If so, what is the nature of this talk? Is there a pattern of communication that fosters normal or optimal self-esteem and locus of control? What proportion of the child's self-concept can be accounted for by parental communication and what proportion can be accounted for by the child's perceptions or reconstructed memories or innate tendencies? Finally, if communication is indeed casually related to early self-concept, does it retain a lasting effect into adulthood?

COMMUNICATION COMPETENCIES

Trying to make generalizations concerning the function of caregiver input in the development of children's communication is like trying to recapture the contents of Pandora's box with a butterfly net. Overall, the environment appears to serve a functional role with respect to some facets of communication. There remain many questions as to which types of environmental influences may be related to which aspects of communication. The basic question has been framed as, "What forces propel the young child into language use?" (Schaffer, 1989, p. 1). Given the predominant concern of social mold research with parental input and styles, discussion will be organized around maternal input and its potential effect on child communication competencies. This logically leads to the foci of the discussion being the social interactionist position and its challengers. (Note the words *mother* and *maternal* will be used here, because these reflect the participants in the vast majority of research on caregiver speech. This is not to imply that fathers or other adults may not serve as primary caregivers.)

For the purpose of this volume, maternal input has been divided into five nonmutually exclusive categories: (1) motherese, (2) features of maternal speech, (3) overall amount of maternal verbal stimulation, (4) interaction style, and (5) conversation. As conceptualizations of conversations between child and mother generally focus on mutual interaction, the fifth category will not be covered in this chapter. Conversation is more suitably postponed until the chapters on bidirectionality.

Motherese

A major tenet of social interactionism is that caregiver input is causally related to child communicative competencies. Of historical interest, Hess and Shipman (1965) first assessed the relationship between maternal input and language acquisition. Since that time, volumes have been filled with studies seeking to ascertain if indeed there is a relationship between motherese and child language or communication skills and, if so, which maternal features impact which aspects of children's language and/or communication.

Although the characteristics of motherese have been well documented in the general American culture (see Chapter 3), the motherese hypothesis is controversial: "These SPECIAL [sic] properties of caretaker speech play a causal role in language acquisition" (Gleitman, Newport, & Gleitman, 1984, p. 45). A counterposition is that motherese may simply be a culturally determined style for speaking to infants, bearing neither a direct nor indirect function to language facilitation (Ochs & Schieffelin, 1984).

The investigation of the effect of motherese has been a scholarly conversation that has the flavor of a tennis match. Consider the exchanges between Furrow, Nelson, and Benedict (1979); Gleitman et al. (1984); and Newport, Gleitman, and Gleitman (1977). Newport et al. (1977) first reported that there was little relationship between maternal input and language acquisition. A similar study conducted by Furrow et al. (1979) obtained the opposite result. In accounting for Newport et al.'s findings, Furrow and colleagues faulted the Newport team's statistical treatment of the data. In response, Newport and colleagues reanalyzed their data and provided additional evidence in support of their initial findings (Gleitman et al., 1984). The volleying continues even today, as other researchers tally their scores. For example, Hoff-Ginsberg (1990) found that "the pattern of results obtained . . . supports the notion that maternal input does influence the development of syntax" (p. 85).

In addition to direct links to children's competencies, potential indirect effects of motherese have been posited. It may be that a child's limited attention and memory span accounts for motherese. Perhaps motherese helps maintain the child's attention (e.g., Foster, 1990). Getting and keeping a child's attention may be a necessary prerequisite for language learning, but the tactics that accomplish this may not be necessarily directly related to language learning (e.g., Nelson, Hirsh-Pasek, Jusczyk, & Cassidy, 1989). Another possibility is that motherese may make it easier for the child to engage in conversation and hence indirectly aids in the development of syntax (Hoff-Ginsberg, 1987, 1990; Snow, Perlmann, & Nathan, 1987). The child is simply allowed practice of communicative skills, which subsequently impacts communicative development.

Adding to the motherese controversy are cross-cultural and co-cultural studies of mother-child interaction (e.g., Ochs, 1988; Ochs & Schieffelin, 1984). Children from all cultures acquire language within the realm of normal variation, despite tremendous variability in the way parents talk (or do not talk) to their children. Such cross-cultural studies have been used by those forwarding innatist explanations as "proof" that motherese cannot serve a facilitative function. But such arguments have not gone unchallenged.

Motherese, also known as baby talk (BT), as a unique register of language used with young children has been evidenced in numerous cultures (see review by Andersen, 1990). For example, not only is BT well documented in Japan but it is similar to American BT in terms of a simplified register (Toda, Fogel, & Kawai, 1990). In addition to BT registers in other countries, there is evidence of caregiver language variation in nonmiddle-class white Americans (e.g., Miller & Garvey, 1984).

Cross-cultural data also have been interpreted as supporting the motherese hypothesis. "There is increasing evidence that children do not have to solve the socio-linguistic puzzle all by themselves" (Andersen, 1990, p. 73). Kaluli mothers, in line with their cultural conventions, speak for the child, instead of directly to the child (Schieffelin & Ochs, 1983). In interactions with others, the mother answers for the child. The mother uses a high-pitched tone speculated to mark the "language as appropriate for the child to utter" (Andersen, 1990, p. 73). This is frequently followed by *ellma,* which translates to "say it." This is used with infants, and older children are expected to repeat verbatim what the mother has modeled. Such prompts have been documented in South Africa as well (Demuth, 1986). Demuth (1986) proposed mothers may well be teaching social communicative competencies to help children "recognize social situations and respond appropriately" (p. 51).

The same features of middle-class American BT are not necessarily the same features of BT in other cultures. Interactionists contend that the failure to find the same *type* of BT in certain cultures does not constitute evidence of an innatist position. Rather it may simply illustrate how various cultures value the role of adults in teaching the native language to children, and the particular skills seen as conventionally appropriate to learn (Haslett, 1990). If, as Andersen (1990) maintained, the characteristics of motherese are different, researchers have been examining the wrong variables. If the skills stressed vary between cultures, researchers have been looking at the wrong communication indices. Interactionists contend that in other cultures, it is simply not yet known which aspects of motherese to investigate relative to which aspects of a child's communicative competencies.

At a different level, differences in BT between cultures may reflect cultural beliefs having little to do with language learning or teaching. Mother-child communication is the means through which children are socialized, regardless of specific qualities of maternal speech (Ochs & Schieffelin, 1986). For example, Japanese retain many of their traditional beliefs and values of child rearing despite much westernization. Toda et al. (1990) speculate motherese serves to reinforce the hierarchical structure in Japan; BT communicates to a child his or her place in the social hierarchy.

To summarize, some scholars contest a language- or communication-enhancing function, instead proposing that culturally specific modes of maternal talk serve a more general function of socialization. Proponents return the volley; just because motherese is culturally determined does not imply BT is not useful for communication development in that culture. Hence, cross-cultural researchers are not in agreement as to the functions of motherese. Nevertheless, there is at least some implicit agreement; a maternal register exists in most societies. Moreover, scholars concur characteristics of BT are culture specific. Questions that remain include the following: What are the features of BT within various cultures? Which, if any, facilitate communication competencies, attention getting, and/or socialization? In short, the function of motherese "has become a pivotal issue in the language learning literature" (Nelson et al., 1989, p. 55).

Features of Maternal Speech

Syntax has been studied primarily in relationship to child grammar (as reflected in the review of BT above). Most investigations of caregiver syntax focus on child syntactic development as the outcome variable. In contrast, discourse and illocutionary features are aspects of maternal speech often studied in regard to communication. These features are not mutually exclusive sets.

Discourse features are elements of speech that connect utterances into more or less coherent streams of discourse: imitations, expansions, extensions, and acknowledgments of the child's speech. An *expansion,* for example, is a maternal utterance that extends a child utterance, usually into a grammatically correct one. Consider the following interchange:

Child: **Green doggie.**

Caregiver: **There is a green dog.**

An extension prolongs a preceding child utterance by incorporating the child's topic. A caregiver takes the child's subject and adds new information. Consider:

Child: **A doggie.**

Caregiver: **A big green doggie.**

In addition, maternal self-repetition, unintelligible remarks, maternal self-answers, and so forth, are studied as discourse features (see Cross, 1977; Stafford, 1987).

Illocutionary features refer to the pragmatic intent, or "force," contained in an utterance, that is, whether the utterance serves to command, question, obtain another's attention, acknowledge the other, and so forth (see Dore, 1978; Searle, 1969).

The study of certain discourse and illocutionary features of caregiver speech holds the most promise for discovering relationships between maternal input and children's language and communication development. In general, these features are thought to serve a teaching mechanism via two functions. The first is to present to the child more "correct" forms of speech.

Such utterances provide the child with informative feedback and additional opportunities for learning (Ellis & Wells, 1980). Second, such speech is considered to show caregiver interest in, and support of, the child. This creates a conversational environment allowing the child opportunity to practice speech skills.

Though features such as these may be related to syntax acquisition, it is more probable that such features are related to global child communication competencies. Wells and colleagues (e.g., Ellis & Wells, 1980; Wells, 1985a, 1985b, 1986; Wells & Gutfreund, 1987) have found significant effects of differential maternal use of discourse and illocutionary features on various areas of child communicative progress. Specifically, child competencies such as comprehension, vocabulary, semantic range, functional or pragmatic use, rate of development, and general conversational competence appeared to be influenced by maternal input. Longitudinal studies have found maternal discourse and illocutionary force features to be positively correlated with the child's mean length of utterance, semantic range, vocabulary, and rate of language development (see Wells, 1985a, 1985b).

The interpretation of such findings opens the possibility that such features reflect a generally warm or responsive maternal environment, and it is this responsiveness to the child that serves to facilitate communication competencies. For example, questions or suggestions, rather than commands, have been associated repeatedly with general language competencies. It is thought that commands are representative of a more controlling environment that, in turn, negatively impacts the development of communication (McDonald & Pien, 1982).

Overall Amount

Numerous studies have shown that the sheer quantity of talk directed toward a child may be related to communicative development. Clarke-Stewart (1973) found that caregiver verbal stimulation (basically the amount of talk to a child) was the variable most highly related to the global index of child communication abilities. Recent studies continue to find effects for the amount of verbal stimulation a child receives. Overall amount of direct verbal stimulation has been significantly related to many facets of verbal progress (e.g., vocabulary). Researchers staunchly maintain that the results of such studies reflect the direct influence of the mothers' input and are not dependent on child characteristics (e.g., Olson, Bates, & Bayles, 1984; Olson, Bayles, & Bates, 1986).

Interaction Style

Interaction style refers generally to patterns of maternal communication that are relatively stable across time and situations. Two approaches to style are described. The first set of studies originates from sociolinguistic research, and examines speech characteristics of mothers of very young children. The second group summarizes recent constructivist research on reflection-enhancing communication of mothers of school-age children.

As studied from sociolinguistic orientations, style concerns the potential effects of combinations of various maternal discourse features, illocutionary force features, and amount of stimulation. The premise is that such features combine to form an overall style of interaction (e.g., McDonald & Pien, 1982). The critical overarching construct is responsiveness, credited as the key to verbal progress (Maccoby, 1980; Schaffer & Collis, 1986).

Despite some day-to-day variations, the interaction styles of mother-child dyads are quite stable (e.g., McDonald & Pien, 1982; Olson et al., 1986). McDonald and Pien (1982) found that mothers could be classified into two groups, those with a desire to converse with their children and those with a desire to control their children. Conversing mothers engaged in frequent questions and positive acknowledgments. They infrequently used directions, repairs, and spontaneous declaratives (defined as maternal utterances unrelated to the child's talk or activity). Controlling mothers used frequent directives, negative acknowledgments, spontaneous declaratives, but infrequently asked children questions. Inequality of participation was notable. Controlling mothers tended to "monologue," allowing the child little opportunity to participate in conversation. The implications of these findings are interesting. As noted several times earlier in this volume, mothers who elicit conversation and respond to their children may aid their children's communicative development. Controlling mothers may impede communication competencies. Recent research has provided further support for McDonald and Pien's (1982) work (e.g., Pratt, Kerig, Cowan, & Cowan, 1992).

In a similar vein, Nelson (1977) found that children of mothers with a directive or intrusive style had a relatively slow rate of communication progress compared with the children of mothers with a more suggestive and responsive style. Likewise, Akhtar, Dunham, and Dunham (1991) found such features to relate to relatively slow rates of vocabulary production. These researchers proposed that whether directiveness is measured syntactically or pragmatically, "directiveness has been negatively correlated with measures of the child's subsequent language development" (Akhtar et al., 1991, p. 42).

Others have investigated sensitive responses. Optimally, the sensitive adult is responding promptly and appropriately. Such an adult reinforces the child's basic sense of self-worth and allows opportunity for participation and interaction so the child may develop linguistic competencies (Harris, Jones, Brookes, & Grant, 1986; Tomasello & Farrar, 1986).

From a different perspective, constructivist researchers in communication (see Chapter 4) have obtained similar findings in regard to maternal influence on children's communication development. Constructivists have analyzed the reflection-enhancing quality of mothers' regulative (i.e., controlling) and comforting (i.e., nurturing) messages. Differences in message quality were studied in relationship to children's social-cognitive and communication development in a short-term longitudinal study. Children's overall level of social-cognitive development, their relative mastery of persuasive and comforting skills, and overall use of receiver-focused communication in the first year was predicted by mothers' use of reflection-enhancing message strategies (Applegate et al., 1992). Quality of maternal communication in the second year predicted those same child outcome variables, plus children's affective perspective-taking and listener-adapted skills.

Reflection-enhancing maternal communication appears to have significant consequences for children's communicative development. When mothers use a communication style that encourages children to reason through situations, anticipate consequences of their actions, and act accordingly, children develop characteristics apparently critical for competent communication. They exhibit higher cognitive complexity, which is in turn related to greater use of person centered message strategies. Not surprisingly, these children are more socially accepted by their peers (Burleson et al., 1990).

Generalizations

Contrast the following summary statements. "The findings of several studies in recent years support the conclusion that properties of the speech children hear influence their rates of syntax development" (Hoff-Ginsberg, 1990, p. 85). Versus, "In general, input seems to have a fairly limited usefulness in the acquisition of grammar" (Foster, 1990, p. 140).

Despite these and other conflicting summaries, most scholars downplay the role of input in the development of *grammar*. The quote offered by Foster (1990) was truncated. Complete, it reads: "In general, input seems to have a fairly limited usefulness in the acquisition of grammar. It may, however, have more of a role to play in the development of pragmatic skills." The potential for environmental forces playing a role on numerous aspects of communication seems probable (see e.g., Schaffer, 1989).

Scholars of child language and communication virtually agree that, at some level, the environment "is all important: if children are not exposed to languages, they will not learn them" (Foster, 1990, p. 138). However, it is equally clear that "beyond the simple exposure, the precise effects of the input are little understood" (p. 138).

To close, as Rutter (1974) concluded two decades ago, "Putting the evidence together, probably the single most crucial factor for the development of verbal intelligence is the quality of the child's language environment; how much he [*sic*] is talked to [and] more than that, the richness of the conversational interchange he experiences" (p. 92). As evidenced by recent studies and reviews, a responsive, conversation-eliciting speech environment appears to aid children's development of communication competencies. In essence, it is conversational involvement that appears to matter the most.

Conclusion

The reader may recall the question asked in the opening of this section concerning the forces that propel a learner into language. Schaffer (1989) answered his own question: "After an unprecedented surge in research over the last two decades or so we are still no nearer to providing anything even approaching a definitive answer to this question" (p. 1).

Conclusions are difficult to draw given the vast array of maternal input variables and child outcome variables studied. Schaffer (1989) argued that the debate concerning the relative weight of maternal speech in influencing child language and communication has been somewhat off target. This is because very different research agendas have been set forth. Those in favor of endogenous factors typically study syntax. Those focusing on exogenous factors have studied more global domains of communication.

Clearly, the jury is still out on whether or not nature or nurture is more prominent in language and communication development. Likewise, debates concerning the extent to which the child is active in the environment, whether the child has innate language-learning structures, whether caregiver speech facilitates the acquisition of grammar and, if so, in what arenas and to what extent, represent just a few of the continuing controversies. If one were to randomly peruse research pieces in the 1980s and early 1990s, one is likely to encounter "proof" of the role of maternal speech in facilitating grammar; one is also likely to encounter "proof" against much of a maternal role. At times, the same data and findings have been interpreted as support for both basic positions. Nowhere else in the social sciences do we see positions held to and debated with such vigor, tenacity, and frequent myopia.

There is a majority view on the acquisition of language and communication development. When sifting through the numerous reviews, meta-analyses, and empirical studies, maternal input loses where *grammar* is concerned.

The evidence in support of maternal input as facilitative of *numerous facets of communication competence* (other than grammar) is much more consistent. Yet there remain more unanswered questions than answered ones. From a unidirectional framework, the most striking issue of contention remains the nature-nurture controversy.

Even if the relationship between caregiver speech and child language and communication were to be entirely disproven, unidirectional researchers would still consider caregiver speech to be an important communication variable in other realms of child development. Several areas have been studied as outcome variables of maternal input. For example, the overall amount of maternal input has been related to cognitive and social competencies (Clarke-Stewart, 1973; Olson et al., 1984; Putallaz & Heflin, 1990). One program of study has found that maternal input influences the language learning style adopted by the child (McCabe, 1989). Similarly, the constructivist orientation proposes that the effect of maternal input is on the child's social knowledge, via greater differentiation and organization of the interpersonal construct system (see Applegate, 1990). In addition, maternal input has been related to child aggression, conformity, creativity, and dependency. The list of outcome variables could continue, because there are many areas of potential influence of parent-child interaction (for reviews see Clarke-Stewart, 1988; Rollins & Thomas, 1979; Steinmetz, 1979).

SUMMARY AND CONCLUSIONS

Upon reviewing compliance gaining, self-concept, and communication competencies, one proposition is unambiguous. The primary inquiry of social mold researchers seeks a prescription for how parents should interact with children to bring about optimal development. The question posed is, "What is the best way for the parent to enhance socialization?" It cannot be doubted that parents mold their children's behaviors, personality, and development to some degree. Yet, the formativeness of this molding in the long run is clearly in need of investigation. Much of the discussion has centered on the mother as the significant other, that is, the primary socializing agent. An important question is raised by Rosenberg (1979), however, when he asks who these significant others are. He points out that all "others" are not equally significant to children. Significant others change across time with maturation and expanding social contacts (Harter, 1983).

Despite trends toward more elaborate mutual influence and systemic models, unidirectional models are not to be dismissed lightly or entirely. Schaffer and Crook (1979) argued for the importance of continuing to explore questions from this orientation. Although mutuality between parents and their child is clear, bidirectional perspectives ignore the "obvious fact" that parents do have to take the initiative most of the time. Parents do have purposes and goals that they need to convey to their children and with which they expect children to comply. Although "children may be able to influence their parents, the far greater power of the parents cannot be ignored" (Schaffer & Crook, 1979, p. 989).

In conclusion, one prevailing theme concerns parent-child interaction in which a parent is firm or demanding as well as warm or responsive. Questions must be raised, however, as to the optimal level associated with each dimension, and how they are to be balanced. How firm is firm? How warm is warm? And how consistent is being consistent? Moreover, the way in which warmth and control are expressed by parents most likely should change in response to the child's maturation.

Though a unidirectional framework has served as the cornerstone of child development research for decades, Clarke-Stewart (1988) noted that the approach is not complex enough to account for adult-child interaction. Generalizations from unidirectional perspectives about the parents' effects on the children are dwindling (Clarke-Stewart, 1988). A unidirectional model is simply not a realistic representation of adult-child interaction (Rollins & Thomas, 1979). If it were, then scholars could simply focus on parental input, child outcomes, and a parenting manual developed on the basis of such information (which has been done frequently in popular literature on the basis of such unidirectional cause-and-effect research).

As has been repeatedly noted, the ever-present question left unexplored from a unidirectional orientation is whether parental communication could be primarily a response to the child's characteristics rather than the cause of them. "The problem of determining cause-effect sequences . . . bedevils socialization research generally" (Schaffer, 1989, p. 19). Yet, correlational data are generally interpreted as support for such causal linear effects by unidirectional researchers, despite the usual caveat of "correlation does not have to imply causality." The recognition that the study of interaction must be more than one sided prompted the development of bidirectional models.

6

Through the Looking Glass: An Overview of Bidirectional Approaches

INTRODUCTION

This chapter outlines the bidirectional perspective relative to research on parent-child communication. Two general classes of theory and research subsumed by this rubric are identified and discussed. These views may be conveniently labeled (1) mirror-reverse orientations, as identified by Peterson and Rollins (1987), and (2) mutual influence orientations. A reversal in the idea that certain communication patterns are a causal factor in the emergence of schizophrenia is discussed to offer an example of mirror-reverse orientations. To illustrate mutual influence approaches, social referencing is briefly discussed.

Recall that from a unidirectional approach a researcher explores the relationship between types of parental communication and successful child development. From the two bidirectional perspectives, in contrast, researchers address a two-part question. First, to what extent do children affect parents? Causality is assumed to run in the opposite direction from the unidirectional approach. Second, in regard to mutual influence, the question moves away from unidirectional views to ones more aligned with the definition of interpersonal communication offered in the Overview. The driving question is thus, "How do child and parent mutually communicate, influence, and respond to each other?"

TYPES OF BIDIRECTIONAL ORIENTATIONS

The assumption of the unidirectional perspective is that parental interaction serves the goal of successfully integrating children into adult society.

Bidirectional approaches also generally posit socialization as the ultimate goal of parent-child interaction. However, bidirectional approaches do not presume parents to be all powerful; that it is they—and only they—who determine what a child becomes. Bidirectional research has not grown out of any one theoretical perspective. This is not to imply bidirectional research is devoid of theory. As will be seen, trait theories, innatist theories, and especially symbolic interactionism have all informed bidirectional research. Regardless of theoretical heritage, however, bidirectional researchers highlight the major question, "Who is influencing whom?"

Children are seen as influencing parental behavior, just as parents influence children's. This shift may be attributed to the particular conception of "the child" as fundamentally active, rather than passive, in nature. The blank slate has been broken; the child studied from bidirectional perspectives is not something to be "written on" at will by others. In its place is a unique individual who, from birth, changes the lives of other people. Thus researchers emphasize the stance that infants are predisposed to be social and are born with rudimentary skills that immediately immerse them into "conversation" with parents (see comprehensive review of literature on infants' capabilities by Field, 1990). This has had a profound effect on the features incorporated into bidirectional models. First, the inherited nature of the child, and its effects on the child's own behavior, must be taken into account. Second, thinking shifts to considering the child as a partner with the parent in interaction and socialization.

Bidirectional advocates conceptualize interaction and socialization as reciprocal processes. Not only are children being socialized but so too are parents regarded as developing members of society (albeit in different ways). Thus parent and child occupy two roles simultaneously, that of socializer and socializee.

> The parent-child relationship initiates a child into the social world and reshapes components of the adult self-concept into identification with parental roles. Much of what occurs between parents and children transforms a biological organism into a human being and confronts adults with a new set of experiences and responsibilities. Through this facet of the socialization process, parents and children acquire the knowledge, attitudes, skills, values, and expectations that allow them to become increasingly integrated into new social relationships. (Peterson & Rollins, 1987, p. 471)

Through their actions, children are seen as having a significant influence on the socialization of parents (Goodman, 1985b) and, in turn, their own development.

As noted above, theories and research adopting these assumptions can be divided into two contrasting categories. The first, which has been labeled mirror reverse, is simply the flip side of the unidirectional perspective. Ways in which children affect parents are explored. More truly bidirectional in scope are mutual influence theories. The parent-child dyad is prominent in such models, and research tracks how parent and child synchronize and regulate their interactions and generally influence each other.

Mirror-Reverse:
Children Influencing Parents

Unidirectional orientations implicitly assume some mutual influence between parents and children, even if that influence is primarily a function of children's maturation (Bartle, Anderson, & Sabatelli, 1989). Bidirectional approaches make the assumption of mutual influence explicit and focus specifically on it. Taking the reverse tack and attending to children's influences on parents is like looking in the mirror of unidirectional research and seeing its reflection. The child occupies the role of socializer in the bidirectional perspective. Children's behavior may shape or change parents. Thus the label *mirror reverse* is proposed.

In the 1950s, Sears (1951) observed that the study of children's socialization and the parental role in it would benefit from adoption of bidirectional models. Yet it was almost 20 years before the commonsense idea that children influence parents was considered as a theoretical tenet. Bell's (1968) seminal paper explicitly challenged the idea that children were the only individuals being socialized within the family. Reinterpreting findings of socialization studies, Bell demonstrated that the child may be quite significant in parental socialization. It should be noted that Bell did not argue that parents were without influence on children. Instead, he articulated the position that children affect parents. Convincing empirical evidence for this claim soon followed (e.g., Bell & Chapman, 1986; Bell & Harper, 1977; Belsky, 1981) Common sense suggests that the birth of a child changes the marital partners (and older siblings, if any). Generally, families find that they must adjust to the infant, particularly in terms of its gender, innate temperament, and developmental level (Belsky & Vondra, 1985). First-time parents are unquestionably taken into uncharted territory. This in turn brings stress to both individuals and relationships (Entwisle, 1985). The transition to parenthood changes the relational patterns and life-styles of the married couple (Crnic & Booth, 1991). New mothers and fathers both report the addition of new daily hassles and sometimes the aggravation of old ones.

Where unidirectional theories end and bidirectional ones begin is not always clear. At the core of the controversy over the usefulness of unidirectional socialization models and mirror-reverse models is the issue of cause and effect. Parenting has traditionally been studied as it represents an individual parent's relatively stable characteristics (i.e., personality). However, parenting behaviors can be interpreted readily as *responses by parents* to children (Lewis, 1981). Rather than certain patterns of parental actions causing high self-esteem, for example, children with high self-esteem may elicit a particular set of parental behaviors. Likewise, a child's compliance makes it easier for a parent to be nondirective and nonjudgmental. And an outgoing toddler is probably going to be more engaging in conversation than a toddler who tends to observe. But is the child that much more influential than the parents? It depends.

Such contingencies can be illustrated by thinking about "types" of children (i.e., in terms of temperament or traits). Parents may be more likely to influence infants in the middle ranges of temperament (Buss & Plomin, 1984). Children at the extremes (in one way or another) appear to have relatively more influence on parents. For example, a persistently fussy baby influences the parents to respond differently from the way they would to an easy baby (Clarke-Stewart, 1988). Children with developmental delays are more stressful to their parents than are "normal" children (e.g., Crowell & Feldman, 1988). And what might seem to be the blessing of an extremely bright child may actually be a stressor for parents (Frey & Wendorf, 1985).

Turning the Tables on Schizophrenia Research. An exemplar of the mirror-reverse orientation, and its implications for clinical practice, is found in the history of research on communication patterns and schizophrenia. In the late 1950s, the Palo Alto group proposed that specific characteristics and patterns of parental messages created schizophrenia in children (Bateson, Jackson, Haley, & Weakland, 1956). Much of the research focused on a paradoxical message form labeled the *double-bind.* Double-binds are messages that are contradictory in some way (Jackson, 1959; Sluzki & Ransom, 1976). For example, a mother might say to her child, "Go ahead, play with your friends," while at the same time sniffling and dabbing her eyes with a tissue. In this case, the verbal message (i.e., giving permission to play) is contradicted by the nonverbal actions (i.e., perhaps a display of the mother's feelings of abandonment). Numerous early investigations supported this theory. In one study, for example, individuals suffering from schizophrenia reported greater maternal use of double-bind messages than individuals without that psychological disorder (Berger, 1973).

The possibility of reverse effects—from the child to the parent—was not considered a viable hypothesis until much later. When this perspective was taken, studies such as that published by Liem (1980) suggested that the behaviors of schizophrenic children set in motion the abnormal patterns noted in their interactions with each parent. Such work provided evidence that the mirror-reverse explanation could not be dismissed. It was clearly possible that the child suffering schizophrenia might initiate dysfunctional patterns of communication with parents. To pause for a moment, some clarification is necessary. As will be demonstrated later, the model of family interaction explicated by the Palo Alto group has implications far beyond the disorder of schizophrenia. Also, although this group of scholars takes a systems approach, it is still quite useful to illustrate bidirectional principles, given that systems approaches both include and extend bidirectional views.

To sum, parents are influenced by children. The mirror-reverse paradigm allows for numerous outcome variables of *parents* to be studied as caused by children's behavior. A key difference between the unidirectional and mirror-reverse approaches has to do with intentionality. Although influencing parents, children are not credited with adultlike motivation for their actions. Infants and young children do not have the goal to socialize their parents in the same way parents generally pursue the goal of raising children. Lack of intentionality does not negate a child's actual influence, however. Through their characteristics, developmental progress, and behavior, children exert effects on parental behavior, on parent-child interactions, and hence on their own development (McKinney & Peterson, 1987; Smolak, 1987).

Although there is agreement among bidirectional researchers that the child is an active agent, some scholars imply that the child is in some way a "negotiator with the social surround" (Connell & Wellborn, 1991, p. 47). Many such social approaches are unclear as to what the child brings to the bargaining table, beyond minimal concurrence that the child is somehow developing. Temperament was mentioned above. Connell and Wellborn (1991) reviewed other possibilities including emotions and psychological needs, biological drives, self-esteem, and needs for power achievement and affiliation. Consideration of needs and drives exemplifies how both psychoanalytic and humanistic doctrines are germane to questions of bidirectionality as well.

It should be obvious that mirror-reverse approaches are concerned simply with the influence of one individual (the child) on another (the parent). The dyad, however, becomes central when one moves to mutual influence models.

Mutual Influence:
The Child's and Parent's
Influence on Each Other

Studies of adult-adult communication accept as a given that conversational partners coordinate and regulate interaction via their individual behaviors

(Cappella, 1981, 1991). However, this bidirectional concept has been applied only recently to the study of parents and children. Once unorthodox, this stance on parent-child interaction has become widely accepted in many disciplines, among them developmental psychology (e.g., Clarke-Stewart, 1978; Grusec & Lytton, 1988), family sociology (e.g., Huber & Spitze, 1988), communication (e.g., Fitzpatrick & Badzinski, 1985), language studies (e.g., Snow, 1984), family relations (e.g., Engfer, 1988), and human development (e.g., Worobey, 1989). All generally agree that "parent-child relations are a joint enterprise involving tightly woven sequences of interaction" (Peterson & Rollins, 1987, p. 487). Both within and across disciplines, there is a trend toward research that examines parents and children as simultaneously and mutually regulating, and achieving various levels of synchronization with, each others' behaviors.

One potent factor arguing for adoption of mutual influence models is the unequivocal fact that children change as they mature. Adults basically have no choice but to respond to this development. Oftentimes, this premise is not acknowledged explicitly. But even in hard-core unidirectional theories, where parental actions cause child outcomes, scholars assume parental behavior adapts to children's developmental achievements. If they did not, researchers would be trying to find examples of mothers using motherese with teenagers. In short, parents and children adapt to the child's changing social, cognitive, emotional, physical, and communicative abilities.

Mutual influence theories are not solely concerned with adaptation, however. Interactional synchrony is a major research topic. It may be described quite simply as the *goodness of fit* between the child and parents (Belsky & Vondra, 1985). When certain characteristics of the child mesh with those of the parents, more fluid message exchange is experienced by both parties. Cappella (1991) has recently urged communication researchers to consider possible biological origins of interactional synchrony. This is likely only part of the explanation. Parents' psychological characteristics may also be important factors mediating synchronous interaction with children (Sameroff, 1975). Considered together, an encompassing framework for theoretical development is obtained. Moreover, compared with mirror-reverse theories, such a framework is truly bidirectional.

There is much evidence that parents and children reciprocate behaviors and that, over time, interaction patterns may develop. For example, mothers and infants are each more likely to engage in vocal activity when the other is vocalizing (Anderson, Vietze, & Dokecki, 1977). Along the same line, infant vocal responses to maternal speech seem to act as reinforcement for the mother to keep talking (Anderson et al., 1977; Smolak, 1987). In addition, the more negatively a parent feels and reacts to a baby's crying, the more likely the baby is to cry (Wilkie & Ames, 1986).

Substantial data on synchronized reciprocal interaction in parent-child dyads have been collected (see review by Cappella, 1991). Adults and 3- to 6-year-old children accommodate their rate of speech to the other's conversational tempo (Street & Cappella, 1989). Such synchrony has been observed at a very early age in several areas. Cappella (1991) reports several studies by others that document synchronized interactions between child and mother in terms of vocal rhythms and/or movement anywhere from the child's age of 30 hours to 11 months (e.g., Berghout-Austin & Peery, 1983; Stern, Hofer, Haft, & Dore, 1985). In short, studies demonstrate the early onset and pervasiveness of synchrony in parent-child interaction, suggesting that a full account of synchrony may require a conceptual role for biological origins.

Social Referencing. Considerable research suggests that infants are aware of the goings-on about them and that they act on the environment with increasing competence as their motor and sensory capabilities develop. Their actions in interaction with others also suggest increasing abilities to interpret the social meaning of what they perceive. These two ideas are brought together in the research on social referencing.

Social referencing focuses on infants' and toddlers' communicative activities to acquire information from caregivers. The definition of social referencing most commonly used is "the use of one's perception of other persons' interpretations of the situation to form one's own understanding of that situation" (Feinman, 1982, p. 445). Such information appears to be used by children to guide their immediate actions and interactions with caregivers and other persons. Thus social referencing illustrates key principles of mutual influence models of parent-child communication. This research also illustrates how what is known about biological and social origins and the development of human behavior may be integrated to provide a relatively complete account of parent-child communicative processes.

Two theories of social referencing have been proposed to explain a pattern of infant information-seeking behavior that typically emerges at around 9 months of age (Campos, 1983; Campos & Stenberg, 1981; cf. Feinman, 1982, 1983, 1985). The specific behavioral pattern was first documented in an extensive series of studies testing Piaget's theories on perceptual development. The Campos research group was particularly interested in the relationship between depth perception and fear in infants. These studies used the visual cliff, an apparatus consisting of a sheet of clear acrylic plastic suspended over a marked dropoff. Although the dropoff clearly looked dangerous from the perspective of anyone looking down on it, it was of no consequence for the child's safety because the acrylic plastic surface was suspended like a bridge over the cliff.

Crawling toward the simulated dropoff, 9-month-old infants typically hesitated when they perceived the edge of the cliff. Crossing over, however, tended to be variable. Some children, who could obviously perceive the dropoff, would ignore it and make a beeline across it. Others would also cross, but take an indirect route; yet other children did not cross over at all.

In seeking to explain the apparent lack of fear in some infants, Campos and colleagues began to note the facial expressions of the infants' mothers standing on the other side of the cliff. Some mothers would smile to their infants, while others might look down at the dropoff as their children did and show concern. It seemed that the infants understood that the emotional expressions of their mothers provided information about this ambiguous situation, and the infants used it to govern their own behavior. Subsequent investigations confirmed that mothers' expressions predicted whether or not the child crossed the visual cavern (e.g., Sorce, Emde, Campos, & Klinnert, 1985). Infants who accessed an expression of happiness from their mothers, encouraging them on, crossed over the visual cliff, whereas infants who saw an expression of concern or fear on their mothers' faces refused to cross.

The account of social referencing developed by Campos and Stenberg (1981) stressed, in addition to perceptual developments, the evidence for early communication based on emotional displays among humans, the role of cognitive appraisal, and the availability of trusted persons as sources of information for infants.

Campos and colleagues argued that infants are prewired to use and act on the information provided by emotional displays of others. *Emotional communication* can occur because of humans' innate abilities to produce and interpret facial displays of emotion, which further appear to have universally understood meanings (Ekman, 1972). Social referencing grows out of this early communication of infants and caregivers based on affective displays. Having learned that others can provide useful information, infants actively seek it in new, or ambiguous, situations. When the child's current knowledge is insufficient to base his or her action on, Campos and Stenberg asserted, the child looks to, or references, another person for the needed information. Once obtained, the information then may (or may not) be used by the child to guide behavior and/or emotional responses.

It is at about 9 months of age when certain visual and motor skills are sufficiently developed to enable the behavioral pattern described above. Given the infant's still-limited verbal comprehension, other persons' facial displays appear to be the primary source of social information for the infant. Information is sought from available and "reliable" sources, for example, from mothers (Zarbatany & Lamb, 1985) or fathers (Dickstein & Parke, 1988). The unavailability of a trusted referent in an ambiguous situation, owing to either his or her absence or the fact that the trusted individual's face is hidden from the child's vantage point, may produce frustration or anxiety.

A complementary conceptualization of social referencing to that outlined by Campos and co-workers is that proposed by Feinman (1982, 1983, 1985). Feinman contends that social referencing is a basic process of communication. From its onset in infancy, the process of social referencing continues to be significant for shaping social interaction across the life span of individuals.

Feinman's theoretical framework is grounded in central tenets of sociological theory and symbolic interactionism. The concept of the reference group as the primary source of social information is extended to consider how an individual (e.g., a parent) serves as a referee for the child. The paradigm case of social referencing in this view is when an individual changes his or her apparent interpretation of an object or situation on the basis of the information provided by the referenced target. In essence, Feinman proposes a theory of the social construction of reality originating in infancy.

An expanded range of information sources and processes are outlined. For example, Feinman maintained that researchers should explore verbal cues in the environment as well as emotional cues (à la Campos and colleagues). Feinman suggests that not only does the child actively seek information from others but information may also be imposed by others on the child. This process of imposition is demonstrated by a simple, well-known situation. Consider the toddler eagerly groping for a vase, paying no attention to others. The mother may call out, "Rebecca!" and then display a stern expression while shaking her head from side to side. Both the child's active information seeking and the mother's imposition of information are described by Feinman as processes of direct social referencing. In contrast, indirect social referencing is the process of the child's vicarious access of cues not necessarily intended as information but available within the social context and used by the child to guide his or her actions.

There is considerable empirical support for central claims made by Campos and Feinman; however, the research has been quite narrow in its scope thus far. Research has been laboratory based; researchers have manipulated various unusual toys (e.g., robots or spiders operated by remote control) to create ambiguous situations for children to react to (e.g., Gunnar & Stone, 1984). Only a few studies have considered children's referencing mothers for information concerning other individuals who are present but unfamiliar to the child (e.g., Feinman & Lewis, 1983). Furthermore, studies of social referencing in naturalistic settings are virtually unheard of to date.

Regardless of whether one examines Feinman's or Campos's account, social referencing is depicted as a process of mutual influence between parents and children. Children, as much as parents, share knowledge about their interpretation of the situation and thus influence each others' behavior. If one were to synthesize the Campos and Feinman accounts, the result would be a conceptual framework that would allow a researcher to consider genetic and environmental influences at the individual level, development over time, and interactional processes. In sum, this theoretic provides an integrated image of the influence of nature and nurture in the study of parent-child communication.

Bretherton (1984) proposed that researchers should explore infants' and toddlers' social referencing as a significant communication process in its own right and because of its implications for social-cognitive development and social construction of reality. In addition, social referencing models also suggest somewhat continuous development of children's communication competence. By focusing on the process of social referencing in a longitudinal design, researchers may better understand how children apply the lessons learned from early interactions based on emotional communication to their development of strategic behavior in social interaction.

SUMMARY AND CONCLUSIONS

This chapter sketched basic premises of the bidirectional perspective and further identified two general classes. First, the child influences the parent. The reversal of effects was discussed, and studies on the etiology of schizophrenia were cited to illustrate the implications of this view for research and practice. The second view encompasses a fuller (and one might argue the "true") definition of bidirectional as mutual influence between parents and children. Models highlight the interrelationship of genetic inheritance, development, and interactional dynamics (e.g., synchrony and reciprocation) to demonstrate the theoretical usefulness of this approach. Social referencing was included as a current research example of mutual influence models. Social referencing considers potential interactions of inherited characteristics of the child and their influence on early behavior and the experiences gained and interpretations made from social interaction with parents. More important, as an example of a mutual influence model of parent-child communication, social referencing highlights an interactive communication process between children and parents that may be of significance across the life course.

To summarize, a core idea of bidirectional perspectives is that interactions are expected to change over time. However, research has been historically preoccupied with infants and preschoolers (Collins & Gunnar, 1990). Research on parent interactions with middle-school-aged children and adolescents is increasing (see Collins & Russell, 1991, for a comprehensive review). The need for continued investigations across time and age groups is obvious.

The stage is now set to illustrate more specifically the similarities and differences between the unidirectional and the bidirectional orientations. Research evidence from this perspective on self-regulation, self-concept, and communication competencies will be discussed in the next chapter.

7

Through the Looking Glass: Bidirectional Approaches to Three Variables

INTRODUCTION

In this chapter, research findings from bidirectional orientations relative to the three child variables are discussed. Specifically, mirror-reverse and reciprocal views on mutual influence processes in self-control, self-concept, and communication competencies will be examined. Generalizations and conclusions concerning each of the three exemplar variables will be forwarded.

SELF-CONTROL

Self-control has been approached from almost every theoretical orientation imaginable. The theme underlying these diverse studies is centrality of parental responsiveness and/or sensitivity to the child. Furthermore, within a bidirectional framework, the child as active participant in determining self-control is paramount. As indicated in Chapter 3, discussion will continue to center on compliance.

Children's activities and characteristics are related to parental attempts to gain compliance. To illustrate the basic idea of bidirectionality, consider child ego development. Parental compliance attempts vary in response to a child's level of ego development. Recursively, ego development plays a role in determining parental choice of strategy (Isberg et al., 1989). Moreover, adolescents, due to their growing independence, sometimes do not comply regardless of parental strategy. When a bidirectional orientation is adopted, some level of noncompliance is considered completely normal. By comparison, unidirectional researchers consider compliance a mark of successful parenting; noncompliance is considered failure. Clearly from a unidirectional stance, a child's failure to mind is a result of parental incompetence (Patterson, 1982).

Unidirectional and bidirectional orientations in general posit considerable adult communication skill, but in different ways. From the first view, parental skill is in directing and influencing the child. From the second, skills involve listening to, adapting to, and being open to the child's influence. More important, however, within a bidirectional perspective parenting skills may be entirely irrelevant.

Three broad categories, all congruent with bidirectional claims, will be covered. The first concerns compliance as driven by the child. Next, bidirectional research findings relative to maternal choice of strategy as mediated by the child's developmental level are considered. Finally, true bidirectional interaction and compliance is reviewed.

Child-Determined Compliance

Noncompliance or compliance is often unrelated to parental communication skill. Children may simply choose not to comply, regardless of parental skill. Noncompliance is frequently studied in dysfunctional families or is taken as a sign of a dysfunctional family. Yet Kuczynski and Kochanska (1990) astutely observed that noncompliance is quite normal.

How does one explain the commonplace noncompliance that occurs regardless of parental communication strategy? Possibilities are numerous. Some simply claim that toddler negativism is a normal developmental stage (Gesell, 1928; Wernar, 1982).

From a social interactional viewpoint, compliance is seen as determined by the child, not the parent (Anderson, Lytton, & Romney, 1986). Compliance, or lack thereof, is explained by the child's need to say no. The occasional *no* to a parent may help the child achieve a sense of independence and autonomy. Eisenberg (1992) concurred that noncompliance is not only normal but is necessary. There may be hidden costs of parental demands for complete obedience. Children may "pay a price for their obedience in the form of lower levels of spontaneity, creativity, and self-esteem" (Eisenberg, 1992, p. 23).

Noncompliance may be a context in which children develop their own interpersonal influence strategies as they try to forestall parental compliance attempts (Kuczynski & Kochanska, 1990; Kuczynski, Kochanska, Radke-Yarrow, & Girnius-Brown, 1987). Noncompliance can serve to give children practice in their own compliance-gaining skills. The key term is *practice.* Messages that respond to characteristics of another person are more likely to persuade that person. Often children can identify such pertinent characteristics of the target of persuasion but cannot use that knowledge in creating persuasive messages (Clark & Delia, 1977). Developing a repertoire of persuasive behaviors appears to be crucial for engaging in person-centered (or perspective-taking) communication. Children may be developing and practicing this repertoire in their refusals to comply.

Nevertheless, research on discipline and compliance has largely neglected children's endeavors to persuade parents. Despite the usual spotlight on child noncompliance, mothers are far less compliant to children's requests than children are to mothers'. Eisenberg (1992) demonstrated that conflict episodes between child and parent are useful for the development of oppositional and negotiation strategies: "Arguments over child noncompliance may be especially important for the development of reasoned arguments as children justify more often when they behave noncompliantly" (p. 35).

Children's obedience may be contingent on their interpretation of the parent's request or "why they perceive their parents or others as attempting to control and modify their behavior" (Lepper, 1983, p. 313). Lepper extends the same line of reasoning to internalization.

Trait theorists contend toddler temperament predicts noncompliance. Rowe (1990) reinterpreted Lytton and colleagues' (1980; Anderson et al., 1986) findings on compliance and argued that noncompliance is a case of "reverse causality." From Rowe's standpoint, some children are predisposed genetically to conduct disorder, and it is this predisposition that drives parental strategy choice.

Maternal Choice of Strategy

Somewhat like their social mold counterparts, bidirectional researchers do suggest some strategies are more likely to result in compliance than others. Bidirectional strategies that yield a higher probability of compliance appear to be grounded in parental sensitivity to the child's maturation and current activities. The mother chooses the strategy, but the choice is based on the child. Regardless of the strategies chosen, it is the child who ultimately accepts or refuses the attempt.

As just noted, the child's general development is a mediator of maternal choice of strategy (Eisenberg, Cialdini, McCreath, & Shell, 1987; Lytton et al., 1988). Also, a child's level of comprehension mediates compliance (Kaler & Kopp, 1990). Thus it may be that lack of compliance has been confused with a lack of comprehension. To illustrate, noncompliance can often result because the child simply did not understand, hear, or remember the request.

Emotional level and ego development also mediate compliance (Labouvie-Vief et al., 1989). As children's egos mature, parents emphasize patterns of separation (for individual identity development) as well as closeness (Leaper et al., 1989). Such patterns also help further children's ego development. Thus the interaction between child characteristics and parental communication appears to be of some significance.

Other investigations corroborate the claim that responsiveness and sensitivity predict compliance (Honig, 1985; Parpal & Maccoby, 1985). To illustrate: Proactive means of seeking compliance, such as providing alternative distractions or anticipating situations likely to induce noncompliance, have been found to be related to both compliance and self-control (Holden & West, 1989). At times compliance can be achieved most efficiently by allowing the child to complete his or her current activity before requesting compliance. When the play activity is a forbidden one requiring immediate cease and desist (such as coloring on the wall), a parent can be sensitive to a toddler's pleasure in coloring. Rather than simply demanding that the child stop, giving the child paper to use is a response more sensitive to the child's current activity. As the child matures, explanations can be offered as to why coloring the walls is not an acceptable pastime. Indeed explanations have been found to be offered more and to increase the probability of compliance as the child matures (Kuczynski et al., 1987). Note that, in general, these parental tactics are low in assertion of parental power.

Research is sparse on adolescent compliance (however, see Baumrind, 1991). Obviously as the child matures, the substantive issues that parents face change. In earlier adolescence, compliance may be sought in routine matters such as household duties and dressing habits. In older adolescence, the number of daily (or hourly as compared with toddlers) hassles decline, but concerns and conflicts about topics such as dating and alcohol use increase (Carlton-Ford & Collins, 1988). Peterson and co-workers (1985) reported that adolescent self-regulation may be (1) obedience due to surveillance, (2) compliance due to internalization, and (3) guidance by internal moral principles. Like younger children, teenagers are also struggling with issues of independence and autonomy. Interest is in how parent and child *mutually* enhance the transition from obedience as the result of parental surveillance to engaging in correct behaviors because of the evolution of moral conscience. This cognizance of mutuality leads directly to reciprocal orientations to compliance.

Reciprocal Orientations

Compliance is a joint undertaking (Schaffer, 1984) as is morality (Smetana, 1983). The central proposition is that initial compliance breeds further compliance (Honig, 1985; Lepper, 1973, 1983). Effective adult-infant and adult-child interactions in activities such as feeding, soothing, play, and talk build reciprocal, mutually satisfying patterns of cooperation. The greater the parental involvement with the child, the more likely greater child compliance will emerge. In a similar vein, it has been argued that parents should accept some noncompliance. Parents who interact with children as if their demands are legitimate tend to have children who regard parental requests as legitimate as well (e.g., Parpal & Maccoby, 1985).

Likewise, synchronized interactions in general seem to foster compliance. In a unique study, Rocissano, Slade, and Lynch (1987) found that mother's synchrony with the child in a tea party task resulted in the greater likelihood of the child carrying out the tea party instructions. They found that if the mother positively responded to the child's play requests, the child would respond to the mother's play requests as well. The tea party was a smashing success. But when mothers were out of synch, perhaps having their own agenda for a tea party, the party was more likely to end in frustration or tears. The child would not follow the mother's request, nor would the mother follow the child's. In other words, parents who frequently comply with their children's requests more consistently elicit compliance from their children than parents who do not.

As just observed, resistance may beget resistance. Moreover, parental perceptions or attributions about the child's noncompliance may contribute to the parents' lack of cooperation. Some parents attribute child noncompliance to undesirable traits or dispositions. Mills and Grusec (1988) speculated that such parental biases could underlie responses to the child. Hence, parents negatively overreact to the child's noncompliance. Such negative reactions further escalate conflict and child resistance. The child in turn responds with more power-assertive techniques. The "child's resistance and hostility deepen further until eventually the parent loses power altogether" (Mills & Grusec, 1988, p. 191). Given this interplay, they concluded that power dynamics of parent-child relationships are intimately and mutually associated with one another.

Generalizations

In addition to findings from research studies mentioned above and below, several excellent reviews are used to draw conclusions (e.g., Marion, 1983;

Maccoby & Martin, 1983; Parpal & Maccoby, 1985; Putallaz & Heflin, 1990). The chief generalization captures the essence of bidirectional positions. Compliance is no longer seen as a result of choosing the correct magic formula. The child plays a significant role in whether or not compliance occurs, regardless of the incantation invoked. Compliance may be contingent on the child's attributions concerning the parental request. In addition, noncompliance may be based on children's needs to challenge authority. These are normal processes. The studies cited above concerning the child's role are unique. In general, there is a dearth of research on the effects of children's commands or requests on parental responses. Kochanska and Kuczynski (1991) contended that the consequence of this lack of research is the continued, potentially inaccurate, portrayal of the adult as most likely to be more powerful and to be the driving force in compliance.

Second, the developmental status of the child may drive the interaction, thus arguing well for parental sensitivity. Clearly, compliance will be more likely when compliance requests are phrased in words understood by the child. Futhermore, the quantity of instructions should not overload the child's cognitive ability to process them. For example, adults frequently issue a series of commands or requests. Although more time-consuming for parents, compliance is more probable if the parent gives one request, lets the child respond to it, gives another instruction, and so on. As the child gets older, he or she can remember and carry out more requests in a series. An 8-year-old *may* remember to put away his shoes, hang up his coat, and wash his hands all in one request. A 3-year-old is likely to be in the closet playing with her shoes. It is doubtful that this behavior is conscious disobedience. Rather, it may be due to a simple inability to remember the next step because she is distracted by how interesting all the shoes in the bottom of the closet are.

In addition, continued compliance is more apt to occur if each act of compliance is positively acknowledged before another request is given. Similarly, obedience is also more probable if the request is accompanied by parental displays of support. To illustrate, a parent could give a hug at the time of the request or after compliance. In short, strategies may precede the request or, alternatively, may follow the compliance.

Holden and West (1989) remind us that the development of child self-regulation requires parental self-discipline. The level of involvement, responsiveness, and sensitivity to developmental demands requires quite a lot of energy. For example, creativity in the form of providing preemptive distraction, as opposed to postnoncompliance discipline, comes "at a cost of physical and mental effort" for the parent, especially with young children.

Finally, responsiveness and compliance by the parent to the child's requests seem to foster responsiveness and compliance. Clearly, there is evidence that mutuality occurs (Crockenberg, 1987).

Conclusion

The consistent conclusion, based on a wide range of theoretical orientations and diverse methodologies, is that sensitive, developmentally appropriate care fosters long-term harmony. However, it is equally true that in many instances compliance is simply beyond the parents' control due to the active nature of the child. Compliance is not merely facilitated by reciprocity, nor is noncompliance always a need to say no. Rather, Lepper (1983) contended, compliance is truly a reciprocal interaction process. The dichotomy between compliance and noncompliance is too simplistic. He asked:

> What constitutes "substantial compliance?" Does pushing everything under the bed or into the closet constitute cleaning up one's room? Can a board game in progress be left on the floor? And so forth. The answer to questions of this sort may depend not only on the parents' initial intentions and goals but also on a complex and interactive process of negotiation and compromise between parent and child. (Lepper, 1983, p. 319)

In a similar vein, Higgins (1991) inquired, does the parental and child view of compliance match? When matches occur, caretakers respond in positive manners, via reassurance. With a mismatch, negative sanctions are more likely to be used such as punishing, criticizing, and the like. Furthermore, Landauer, Carlsmith, and Lepper (1970) urged "rather than trying to discover what makes certain children obedient, or certain mothers obedience-compelling, one should try to discover what makes a particular adult-child pair likely to have a relationship conducive to compliance" (p. 610).

The reader is encouraged to read the work of Patterson (e.g., 1986), which explores the interactive process of compliance and differences in several perspectives on compliance research.

SELF-CONCEPT

Recall from earlier sections on self-concept that unidirectional models conceptualize self-esteem as a mechanical transmission process from parent to child. Self-concept is seen as a photocopy of another's evaluation. A bidirectional perspective to self-concept extends beyond social mold views. The child's *interpretation* of experience and related actions are included as influencing self-concept. However, evidence relative to this claim is only now emerging.

Human action and the construction of knowledge and meaning in interaction with significant others are highlighted, following the original views of Mead (1934). His greatest contribution was a move away from the photocopy metaphor and the belief that a child's mind is a blank slate (Franks, 1985). Symbolic interactionism unquestionably considered the child as mutually shaping his or her own self-concept and the concept of others.

Four broad types of studies are considered here. Some have emanated from symbolic interactionism; others are eclectic, not driven by theory, but rather targeted toward Bell's proposal that the child affects parents. Studies that have explored how a child's level of self-esteem affects the communication of parents with the child are discussed first. In addition, arguments for the lack of effects of parental communication on the child's self-concept (due to child characteristics) are considered. A direct mirror-reversal orientation is then noted. Finally, mention is made of more truly reciprocal findings.

The well-documented association between parental support and child self-esteem has come under scrutiny. The prevalent assumption is that parental support causes a child's level of self-esteem. A mirror-reverse proposal is that the child's sense of self and accompanying behaviors influence the parental communication. For example, low-self-esteem children tend to be defensive, depressed, and/or engage in defiant behaviors (Felson & Zielinski, 1989). Such behaviors tend to evoke negative responses from parents instead of supportive ones (e.g., Rosenberg, 1965). Thus the child's competencies may produce the supportive environment, or lack thereof, not vice versa (Margolin et al., 1988).

Such studies lead to the possibility that children with various positive characteristics and communication patterns may inspire positive and supportive communication from their significant others. The child's already established self-esteem and associated behaviors earn the rewards (i.e., the type of parental communication) they receive. This in turn reinforces the child's initial level of self-esteem.

Various investigations have examined potential child-driven characteristics and behaviors in the formation of self-esteem. From a symbolic interactionist perspective, children seek and interpret appraisals of others. Perhaps children look to different significant others in different domains. To illustrate, children may look to parents for feedback in regard to academics and athletics. For feelings of self-worth concerning their physical appearance, however, children may seek evaluations from their peers (Felson & Reed, 1986).

Yet, parental communication with a child has been considered relatively unimportant by some due to characteristics of the child such as an already established level of self-esteem. One proposal is that self-esteem serves as a select memory filter or schema (Markus, 1977). Children of high and low self-esteem may receive similar supportive or nonsupportive behaviors from parents. Children with high self-esteem focus on and remember the positive and supportive actions; children with low self-esteem focus on and remember nonsupportive and negative parental communication (Eder, 1988; Margolin et al., 1988). Hence children's perceptions of parental communication may bear little or no resemblance to the actual communication of the parents.

In a similar manner, children's individual differences in sensitivity to feedback from others may influence their self-concept. Lack of awareness to feedback results in the inability to incorporate feedback into self-concepts (R. Edwards, 1990). If indeed some individuals are insensitive to feedback and hence do not utilize that feedback to form their self-concept, this would render communication from others unimportant for such individuals. This proposal obviously merits further consideration by those interested in communication.

Research also indicates that children shape their parents' sense of self to a surprising degree (Stryker & Statham, 1985). Mothers' self-esteem may be damaged by stressful relationships and responsibilities of parenting teenagers, whereas fathers' self-esteem appears to be enhanced by high levels of positive communication with teenagers (Demo, Small, & Savin-Williams, 1987). Thus looking at the mirror-reverse, children affect parents' self-concept.

A more reciprocal, as opposed to mirror-reverse, orientation has sometimes driven research. One study found that parental behavior affects child self-esteem and child self-esteem affects parental behavior in equal magnitudes (Felson & Zielinski, 1989). Furthermore, children have some veto power over their parents' communication. This forms a role-bargaining relationship between parent and child, which ultimately affects the self-concepts of both individuals (Stryker & Statham, 1985).

Skinner (1986) found that the relationship between mother sensitivity and child activity and subsequent perceptions of control is reciprocal. Moreover, children's perceived control of their environment was the best predictor of maternal sensitive initiation.

Generalizations

Despite the small base of research, several generalizations may be offered. Children influence their parents' self-concept, at least to some degree. Also, high- versus low-self-esteem children elicit different messages from their parents. Children's perceptions of self-esteem are undoubtedly highly correlated with perceptions of parental attitudes and memories of parental communication toward them (Harter, 1983). Perceived and recalled parental respect, liking, appreciation, affection, and unconditional regard are positively correlated with self-esteem (Margolin et al., 1988). This frequently replicated result should come as no surprise given that the majority of studies on self-esteem continue to be questionnaire based. It has been argued that this is appropriate given that it is the child's perception of parenting that is the important filtering variable. This is represented in the proposals concerning memory filters and the ability to incorporate feedback.

The suggestion has also been put forth that parents are not the only primary group. In some cases, the primary group may differ in regard to topic area. Nevertheless, it can be concluded that the child's self-concept and parental communication (or at least the child's perception of parental communication) operate to influence each other reflexively.

Conclusion

From a bidirectional orientation the child is viewed as playing a formative role in the emergence of self-concept, locus of control, and ego development. Child behavior influences parental behavior and parental self-esteem. In turn, parental behavior feeds back into the child's sense of self. Child self-esteem may also serve as a perceptual filter that biases the child's memories and perceptions of parental behavior. At this point, determination of whether the child's self-esteem or the parental supportive behavior came first is an open question.

In sum, the theory is relatively old. The child has long been presumed to play a more or less active role in socialization of self. Yet this idea is relatively new in research. At this point there is little direct research on the reciprocal nature of the development of self-esteem or on the children's role in their own development.

The only truly unequivocal conclusion is that children's perceptions of parental warmth are highly correlated with their own self-esteem. Some argue that such perceptual variables, albeit intriguing, offer little guidance for practitioners.

It should be clear by now that bidirectional researchers have taken a rather dim outlook to claims of the exclusivity of others in shaping self-esteem. Pushing the point, some have argued that there is little evidence of parental influence on children's self-concept. Schrauger and Schoeneman (1979), for example, found no clear indication that children's self-perceptions are influenced by parental feedback. The majority of studies they reviewed involved late adolescents and adult populations, though. These researchers cautiously concluded that children are potentially susceptible to the molding of self-concept by parents. Still, the question of the formativeness of such influence past adolescence remains salient. Given the presumed importance of communication in the formation of self-esteem and the pragmatic implications for personal competence associated with possessing high self-esteem, this question of which comes first, parental communication or child self-esteem, warrants the attention of communication scholars. The most plausible answer may not be found in a unidirectional model but in a reciprocal conceptualization, in which both parents and children participate in shaping their own and the others' self-concept.

COMMUNICATION COMPETENCIES

As with the other variables discussed, language and communication research also reflects a shift from unidirectional to bidirectional approaches. If there is general awareness that children affect mothers and mothers affect children, it seems only reasonable that they do also in language and communication processes (Lamb & Easterbrooks, 1981). Few would argue against the claim that communication is a two-way street, but one cannot tell that from a unidirectional perspective. The essence of bidirectional research is, "What are the contributions of child and mother to early interaction and hence to language and communication development?" However, there remains a preoccupation with the primary caregiver, still generally considered to be the mother. Hence, we will continue to use the word *mother.*

Conversation research may play a key role in bridging traditional linguistic and diverse aspects of communication (Jacobs, 1986). The bulk of the following discussion surrounds *conversation* in some way, shape, or form. Language and communication will be interwoven among the topics to reflect the concept of communication competencies. For organizational purposes, child-parent conversation is divided into four admittedly overlapping categories. First, fine-tuning is discussed. Next is the argument for adult-child conversation-like routines as the basis for the emergence of communication. Third comes the early turn-taking nature of conversation-like interaction. Finally, synchrony will be discussed. Generalizations and conclusions will be offered across the four categories.

Fine-Tuning

The fine-tuning hypothesis, in its simplest form, states that the caretaker adjusts speech to the level, or just above the level, of the child's cognitive and communicative abilities. When the adult fine tunes, the child is provided with input data that are highly appropriate to linguistic needs (Cross, 1977). The fine-tuning hypothesis, in its broadest version, does not specify which features of speech are adjusted. Yet, the only aspect of fine-tuning that has received much research attention is the syntactic fine-tuning hypothesis. The proposal is that simplified language input helps language learning by providing a good data base from which grammar can be constructed.

Because fine-tuning is often thought to facilitate children's language acquisition, fine-tuning is in many ways reminiscent of a social mold approach. Again, it is clear that separations between unidirectional and bidirectional are not clear. Yet, adult fine-tuning is a mirror-reverse phenomenon; the mother is the one assumed to adapt her language to the child's communication development (see Cross, 1978).

Fine-tuning receives mixed support in the literature (Foster, 1990). Several studies have found adult input being adjusted to, or slightly above, the current abilities of the child (e.g., Furrow et al., 1979; Murray, Johnson, & Peters, 1990). Yet, other studies fail to show such relationships (e.g., Gleitman et al., 1984; Newport et al., 1977). A third opinion is that fine-tuning takes place in early prelinguistic stages but is discontinued once the child has some initial words (e.g., Barrett, Harris, & Chasin, 1991). Thus pervasiveness of fine-tuning is not well documented. Unlike motherese, there are many cultures in which no evidence of fine-tuning has been found.

Assume for a moment that fine-tuning does occur. The question of a facilitative function still remains. Do fine-tuned messages really aid children in acquiring language? Or is fine-tuning simply a response? Researchers finding evidence for fine-tuning can seldom make strong claims as to its tutorial role. Cross's (1978) work indicated that fine-tuning played little role in aiding the child's syntactic development. She concluded that the caregiver adjusts speech up as the child matures, simply to keep pace with the child. Weber-Olsen's (1984) synthesis indicated that maternal grammatical adjustments do not account for language acquisition. Rather the child's listening and processing strategies do. Others maintain a facilitative function for fine-tuning. Yet it is language comprehension, not production, that is enhanced (Murray et al., 1990; Van Kleeck & Carpenter, 1980). There are several explanations for the inconclusive results. One is researchers' inability to determine the latency between exposure and acquisition, and thus researchers may not look for correlations at the right time (Foster, 1990; Hoff-Ginsberg, 1985). Mixed results also occur because different scholars examine different aspects of maternal speech and different aspects of child speech.

Bruner (1983) proposed that maternal fine-tuning helps the child master language in a general sense. Maternal fine-tuning lets the child understand the mother, and hence, converse with her. "The important thing is to keep communicating with [children], for by doing so allows them to learn" (Bruner, 1983, pp. 38-39).

In addition, some have explicitly stated that the child may drive the fine-tuning. For example, children with long mean length of utterances may stimulate maternal talk. Or a child with high levels of curiosity may influence maternal discourse (Yoder & Kaiser, 1989). In essence, Yoder and Kaiser (1989) "argue that child-driven and mother-driven" models of fine-tuning are equally feasible. "In actuality, bidirectional influences" on fine-tuning are probable (p. 146).

In sum, fine-tuning is bidirectional by definition in that maternal speech is affected by the child. However, for most advocates of fine-tuning, unidirectional assumptions are operating. The position held is that fine-tuning is a causal molding of child characteristics. Yoder and Kaiser (1989) have called for a more explicit recognition of the bidirectional nature of fine-tuning. Finally, most salient here is Bruner's observation that fine-tuning enhances conversation between mother and child. Obviously, the unanswered questions are, "Does fine-tuning exist?" "And if so, to what extent is it driven by the child versus the caregiver?" "What functions are served by it?"

Routines as Linguistic Foundations

Joint interaction episodes (JIEs) are interactions in which individuals jointly focus and act on the same object or topic, usually in a playlike routine (Schaffer, 1989). At issue is the extent to which such interactions are facilitative of language development. Many social interactionists claim that mother-child participation in JIEs is essential for the child's language development. The primary function of such games is providing a "shared routine and interaction opportunity that is sufficiently predictable and practiced so that both can take their turns successfully" (Snow, Dubber, & De Blauw, 1982, p. 57).

The proposals of Bruner illustrate this position quite clearly. According to Bruner (1983), the emergence of grammar is contingent on prior learning of prelinguistic routines between child and caregiver. He argued that all natural languages exhibit a form of topic-comment structure. JIEs are organized by shared attention (topic) and mutual action (comment). Through play routines, the child's attention is drawn to communication and its structure. The child develops hypotheses as to workings of language and communication. The mother provides feedback confirming or disconfirming the child's hypotheses.

Bruner demonstrated joint enterprises and the formation of routines in feeding, bathing, and playing in prelinguistic encounters. In these encounters mothers standardize the interaction. "At the outset, in this process, the mother is almost always the agent of the action, the child the recipient or 'experiencer' " (Bruner, 1983, p. 13). Yet language learning is viewed by Bruner as bidirectional because it involves negotiation between two people. "A format [routine] is quintessentially transactional: What one party does is contingent on what the other has done and what each anticipates the other to do" (Bruner, 1981, p. 44). When parent and child are jointly engaged in a routine, the parent initially plays both roles. However, as the child becomes more experienced through the mother's guidance, the child takes over a role. "As the child mastered components of the task, he [*sic*] was free to consider the wider context of what he could do, to take over more of the complementary activity" (Wood, 1980, p. 282). The mother no longer plays both roles, having handed over a role to the child. As a concrete example of a verbal game, initially the parent says both "Knock, knock!" and "Who's there?" As the child grows in competence the mother gradually hands over more of the routine to the child. The child begins to take his or her part in the game and eventually becomes an initiator of the game, not just the "experiencer." That is, the child learns to answer "Who's there?" and learns to initiate the "Knock, knock!" This process is referred to as *scaffolding* (e.g., Wood, Bruner, & Ross, 1976). A critical point is that learning language is not only learning grammar but also learning how to use language. Scaffolding aids mastery of both.

There are numerous social interactionist positions; Bruner's theory serves as an example. The global proposition is that children who experience JIEs are provided with an opportunity, if not a prerequisite, to learn the basics of language and conversational skill (see Foster, 1990). Like many social interactionists, Bruner apparently regarded the transition from prelinguistic to linguistic communication as continuous. Language is mapped onto the existing prelinguistic structure. The adult is the crucial guide, and adult-child routine conversations are prerequisites to language. However, the child is endowed with a language acquisition support system (LASS) to aid in abstracting the rules for the linguistic system. Like most other interactionist positions, though the environment is given priority, some innate mechanisms may operate as well. Positions such as these have come under attack. They are often critiqued as insightful metaphors, but no more than that. They lack any real power to explain the emergence of grammar or communication (Shatz, 1982).

Turn Taking

The position taken by many social interactionists is that the fundamental feature of social interaction in infancy, turn taking, provides a discourse structure without which the rules of language could not be learned (Kaye & Charney, 1980). The foundation of language and communication lies in the routines that are predicated on a turn-taking structure.

The phenomenon of turn taking has been intensively studied in adult-adult interaction under such labels as bidirectionality, synchrony, and reciprocity (Cappella, 1981). (Synchrony as a separate, yet related, topic is discussed momentarily.) The salience of turn taking is underscored by recalling the definition of interpersonal communication articulated by Cappella (1987; see also Overview). By this definition, both individuals exchange messages. Both partners actively participate. Both influence and are influenced by the behaviors of the other. Turn taking is inherent to interpersonal communication.

Such conversational models have also been applied to adult-child interaction research. Mutual influence in turn taking constitutes the "basic building blocks in establishing parent-child bonding and in influencing cognitive and language behavior" (Welkowitz, Bond, Feldman, & Tota, 1990, p. 221). Turn taking is pervasive in most of the activities involving infants and mothers: feeding, bathing, dressing, and prelinguistic conversations in which infants' facial expressions count as turns (Brazelton, Koslowski, & Main, 1974; Kaye, 1977; Nelson, 1977; Snow, 1977a; Stern, 1974; Trevarthen, 1977).

A debate arises surrounding the relative contribution of the two parties. Given the conversational skills of the mother and the lack thereof in the child, "obviously" the mother leads the conversation. Prelinguistic conversations are notably asymmetric. Mothers initiate and maintain continuity in the discourse by imputing meanings to the infant's movements or expressions. The key point is that the mother credits the child with intentionality and interprets behaviors as if they were intentional conversational interchanges (Kaye & Charney, 1980). From this position, "Any apparent two-way interaction is just that—apparent and not real" (Murray & Trevarthen, 1986, p. 16). The mother is filling in the gaps and making noninterchanges into interchanges via her own responsive interpretations.

Above it was noted that "obviously" the mother leads the conversation. The *obvious* has come under close scrutiny. Turning the coin, many contend the child is significantly more active from birth than the above would lead one to believe. Indeed, the child's contribution is now receiving increased attention. "The infant's responsiveness to what the mother does is communicative, in the sense that it is effective in influencing the course of the interaction and is contributing" to the interaction (Murray & Trevarthen, 1986, p. 27). Kaye and Snow have been faulted for ignoring the participation of the infant. This leads us to a mutually responsive view, as opposed to a simple mirror-reverse one. Indeed, in and beyond infancy, rather than the mother leading the conversation, child and mother are both influenced by and influence each other; either may take the lead (see Welkowitz et al., 1990).

This meets the definition of interpersonal communication forwarded in the Overview: An exchange of mutually influencing behavior. From this view, conversation does not rely on the *as if* infants were conversing, rather infants are indeed conversing. In other words, this position sets aside the explanation of early dialogue as parental interpretation of the child's actions in favor of seeing caregiver-child interaction as reciprocal and mutually influencing. A mutual influence orientation posits true interpersonal communication between parent and child from birth. Thus it is maintained that infants are communicative beings (e.g., Murray & Trevarthen, 1986).

Synchrony and Sociability

Questions raised time and again with respect to early parent-child interaction are the following: "To what extent is the child 'social' at birth?" and "To what extent does the ability to engage in social interaction emerge as a result of adult guidance?" Research on synchronization tackles these questions of nature versus nurture (see Harris et al., 1986). Synchrony in turn taking has also been called conversational congruence, symmetry, pattern matching, and coordinated interpersonal timing. Scholars do not agree that turns are necessarily synchronous, or that conversational rhythms are biologically influenced. But scholars do agree early communication, although not intentional, is synchronized and mutually influencing.

Compared with other research areas discussed in this volume, studies of interactional synchrony best demonstrate the impact of nature on parent-child communication. It appears that infants are biologically predisposed to be social and that communication ability is innate, expressed quite early, and impacts the mother (Dimitracopoulou, 1990).

> From the time of birth the infant is an active, not a passive, participant in his or her social environment. It is now accepted that the newborn infant is biologically designed for survival in a social context. Therefore, the infant is of necessity, a "born communicator." (Thoman, 1981, p. 186)

Studies have consistently documented the synchronous nature of neonate and infant actions (see review by Cappella, 1991). In sum, the infant may be biologically predisposed to turn-taking activities.

Communication is based in the behavioral rhythms of the two partners and mutual adaptation (Thoman, 1981). Thus a strong case for the importance of synchrony, or more precisely the lack of synchrony, is made by Cappella (1991). Cappella proposed that parents and children who are biologically predisposed to different physiological rhythms will be out of synch in their interaction patterns. This is speculated to lead to difficulty in laying building blocks of communication. Asynchronous interactions may also influence cognitive development. Moreover, attachment formation between parent and child has been proposed to be susceptible to biologically mismatched rhythms (Welkowitz et al., 1990).

Generalizations

Adult-child conversation is often accorded an assisting role in the emergence of the child's language and communication skills. Conversation is clearly interactive in nature. Frequently, the adult is seen as the critical guide in this process and is credited the lead role.

Let us tentatively conclude that in recent research on Western cultures the bulk of the evidence comes down in favor of the existence of fine-tuning. Those who agree fine-tuning exists are divided on its function. Some maintain fine-tuning helps the child engage in conversation, hence fine-tuning indirectly facilitates communicative competencies. Yet, Wells's work not only is supportive of the existence of fine-tuning but credits it with a strong role in assisting language acquisition and communication development (see Wells, 1985a, 1985b). It is most likely that some aspects of parental communication are fine-tuned and others are not. Thus the conclusion offered in Chapter 5 is reiterated. Although grammar may not be particularly susceptible to environmental influences, more general communication competencies may be.

Turning to the second category discussed, parent-child routines do indeed have characteristics of conversations. No controversy exists. The most striking similarity between the routines and conversations is turn taking. Turn taking underlies many mother-child games and routines. The controversy is whether such routines are necessary or even helpful in the development of communication competencies. Agreement is far from being reached.

That mothers and children take turns is readily observable. Yet, scholars' positions concerning the relative contributions of mother and child and the extent to which the child is actively social come under heated debate. At least from the bidirectional orientation, the majority argue that the child is an active social being.

Early interactions are generally synchronous in nature. But what are the relative contributions of mother and child? Overall, contributions from both biological and social origins are being recognized. The infant may be biologically predisposed to reciprocal, synchronized social interchanges. Parents participate in these interchanges, extending them to build what may be the foundation for the child's development of language and communication.

Conclusion

In sum, this section has focused on fine-tuning, routines, turn taking, and synchronization. The major issue under debate is whether or not such features actually lay a foundation for communication or are simply metaphorical. Other issues include the relative contribution of mother and child: How much of the conversation is imposed by mothers and how much may be attributed to innate properties of the children? Questions centering on the intentionality of the child versus imposed intentionality (as seen by the mother) are raised. In addition, the innate sociability of the child is brought to attention.

Perhaps the dilemma here revolves around the issue of control in the mother-child interaction. It obviously can be argued, as unidirectional scholars have, that the overwhelming discrepancies between maternal and infant abilities are sufficient to say that the mother is in control. The infant is without a linguistic system and is physically dependent. The mother is skilled in language and, as noted above, it is her responsive adjustments and attributions that keep dialogues dialogues. Contrariwise, others see the infant, even the neonate, as an innately skilled communicator. Some researchers adopt the position that "one cannot not communicate" (Watzlawick et al., 1967, p. 49). Taking this stance, it becomes "easier and easier to attribute a near-equal role to the infant, regarding his or her contribution to the encounter" (Worobey, 1989, p. 9). Yet, both sides agree on two fundamentals. There is mutuality in mother-infant interaction, and on some level the interactions are social. That is, whether viewed as symmetrical or asymmetrical, innate or learned, routines are mutual. Without question, the infant is less skilled than the mother initially. The child grows in skill, perhaps as a result of scaffolding. Routines are conversation-like in regard to turn taking. This is true regardless of who imposes these turns. Most important is the contention that early conversation is, in one way or another, linked to later emergence of language or communication. The linking mechanism is often considered to be routine, conversation-like interaction.

SUMMARY AND CONCLUSIONS

Although the concern is obviously still with variables of the child as related to parent-child interaction, research discussed in this chapter is quite different from that using a unidirectional model. The notable change is a movement from the stance that only the child changes in response to parental communication to one in which both the parent and child change in response to each other's behaviors; children shape parents; parents shape children. Rather than focusing on child effects on parents and vice versa, the primary focus is on mutual interchanges.

The reader has likely noted the skewed nature of the information presented relative to the age of the child. It is rare to find studies of children's effects on their parents beyond infancy. And the studies of infants' effects on parents are concerned almost entirely with synchrony before emergence of verbal speech (but see Yoder & Kaiser, 1989). Older children are beginning to receive more research attention.

> Children who are older than infants have substantial influence on their parents. That is, the young acquire power in the parent-child dyad, and their role performance elicits behavior responses from their parents. Youth also identify keynote issues and challenge the attitudes, expectations, and role behavior of adults. (Peterson & Rollins, 1987, p. 489)

It is generally acknowledged that parents do have more influence on a child than vice versa, at least initially. Even in hard-core bidirectional models, the distribution of the influence is not assumed to be equal. The distribution of power begins to shift with the child's development. Yet some challenge this position. Several allusions to the infant's and child's power have been made throughout. And, as will be demonstrated in later chapters, infants have a great deal of power in disrupting entire households.

Many child effects on parents remain to be discussed. For example, research has begun to explore the consequences of the child on the marital pair; that is, a child may *create* marital discord. When one moves beyond the parent-child dyad into the parents-child triad, one approaches a systems perspective. Thus issues involving effects beyond the dyad will be discussed in the next two chapters. A caution is offered; simply because disciplines are incorporating systems perspectives does not mean that bidirectional research has been abandoned. Systems models may best be thought of as inclusions and extensions of bidirectional models. This subtle shift from bidirectional to systemic will be evident in the next chapters.

8

The Family as a Spiral of Recursive Feedback Loops: An Overview of the Systems Approach

INTRODUCTION

This chapter and the next are concerned with systems frameworks on parent-child interaction. First, basic premises of systems theories are outlined. Next, the following seminal systems orientations directly related to parent-child interaction are described: the pragmatic perspective of the Palo Alto group, the ecological perspectives of Bronfenbrenner and Belsky, and the interpersonal relationships perspective of Hinde.

Although systems models examine patterns of all elements in the systems and are concerned with how all of these elements effect all others, those interested in child development and parent-child relationships put the most emphasis on how "the family system serve(s) the young child" (Honig, 1991, p. 519). Primarily, this chapter is devoted to tracing the emergence of research foci in systemic orientations: mother-child versus father-child interaction, a comparison of differential mother-child/father-child interaction, the marital relationship, and finally, sibling interaction.

THE SYSTEMS APPROACH

Expanded theoretical conceptualizations are required to examine relational communication patterns beyond the dyad. Triadic interactions (such as both parents and the child) as well as the influence of larger sociocultural patterns must be taken into account. A general system theory was briefly described in Chapter 2. The basic "model of interaction within a systems point of view involves a spiral of recursive feedback loops" (Minuchin, 1985, p. 290) or "What circles are happening in this family?" (Bavelas & Segal, 1982, p. 103).

Examining interactive effects of relationships on the family as a whole is quite different from a unidirectional approach, which largely ignores the parent-child relationship and focuses instead on the parental evocation of child effects. The focus of systems frameworks on mutual influence reflects an extension of bidirectional perspectives. Indeed, systems frameworks are perhaps most easily understood as inclusions and extensions of bidirectional views.

Comparatively little research from a systems standpoint has been conducted on parent-child interaction. Systems approaches to family therapy were originally used to treat young children (Combrinck-Graham, 1990). Yet, attention shifted to marital couples, adolescents and young-adult children within the family, and aging parents (Zilbach, 1986). Only quite recently have family therapists and clinical researchers rediscovered children as family influences. Many family therapists believe that difficulties children experience may not lie within themselves but rather are manifestations of family difficulties. Similarly, they recognize that children can initiate change in a troubled family (Combrinck-Graham, 1990).

Social science researchers are just beginning to explore the phenomena therapists and clinical researchers have been investigating for some time; all individuals and relationships within the family interactively and reflexively shape all other family members and relationships. Moreover, all local interaction is framed within, and influenced by, sociocultural patterns (Minuchin, 1985). The sheer complexity of accounting for so many factors may be one reason so few scholars have attempted such a comprehensive research undertaking. Considering the dyad as the unit of analysis is not simple. When a second child is born, complexity increases exponentially. The triad is extended to a tetrad. Two siblings in a family creates a sum of six dyads. It becomes overwhelming when all relationships between extended family members come into consideration as well. Although improvements in research methods and statistical techniques have allowed systems research to be slightly more feasible, the changing American social scene has most likely provided the impetus for Western researchers' adoption of this perspective. For example, the entry of women into the American work force has promoted long-overdue consideration of the father's role in socialization (e.g., Lamb, 1981; Parke, 1981). In addition, consideration of the effects of divorce has led to the identification of a critical relationship between persistent marital discord/conflict and child socioemotional development. Intriguingly, the relationship between the parents' general happiness with each other and child socioemotional development appears to hold whether the marriage is intact or dissolved (e.g., Emery, 1982).

Theoretically, systems views move beyond cause-and-effect relationships. Instead, the concentration is on sequenced patterns of interactions and mutual influence as defining relationships. However, acknowledgment of cause and effect within the family system is made by most systems theorists (but not all, see Chapter 9). Hence, on the surface, seemingly contradictory assumptions persist.

However, these apparent contradictions are actually integral parts of most systemic positions, which usually include and extend unidirectional and bidirectional views. In regard to unidirectional views, Hinde (1989) adamantly insisted, "All 'child outcome' measures are not to be dismissed" (p. 160). Likewise, much of Belsky's work explicitly includes ramifications for system members, as does the work of the Palo Alto group. Furthermore, investigating interactions in terms of mutual cause and effect (i.e., a bidirectional framework) is not inconsistent with a focus on sequenced patterns of interdependence.

Just as effects can be multidirectional, they can also be either direct or indirect. Direct effects are "those interactions that represent the influence of one person on the behavior of another when both are engaged in mutual interaction" (Lewis, 1987, p. 458). Indirect effects, according to Lewis (1987), may be of two types. The first is "sets of interaction that affect the target person, but that occur in the absence of that person" compared with the second type, which includes interactions "that occur in the presence of the target person even though the interaction is not directed toward or does not involve that person" (p. 458).

In short, when viewing a family as a system, "parenting affects and is affected by the infant, who both influences and is influenced by the marital relationship, which in turn both affects and is affected by parenting" (Belsky, 1981, p. 3).

THREE SYSTEMS PERSPECTIVES

These commonalities among systems views aside, there is no one systems perspective:

The varieties of family therapy practice and family systems theory range from those derived directly from psycho-analysis (psychodynamic family therapy of Ackerman and followers, Bowen systems therapy, contextual therapy of Boszornmenyi-Nagy, and objects relations therapy); to those primarily centered around expressiveness and communications (Satir's conjoint therapy, symbolic-experiential theory of Whitaker); to those focused on organization (structural family therapy of Minuchin); and to those derived from the ecosystems models of Bates and the hypnotic practices of Milton Erickson (strategic family therapy of Haley and the Palo Alto Group and systemic family therapies of the Milan group). Each of these "schools" of family therapy has been a nucleus for elaboration, revision, and change. (Combrinck-Graham, 1990, p. 501)

Three systems approaches most germane to parent-child communication are outlined below. See Bochner and Eisenberg (1987) for a catalog of systems theories used within social scientific research.

The Pragmatic Perspective

Students of communication are probably most familiar with the pragmatic perspective. In fact, this approach has become nearly synonymous with *systems* in the communication discipline. The research team associated with the pragmatic perspective is known as the Palo Alto group, originating from the Bateson project on schizophrenia mentioned in Chapter 7. The assumptions of this team have been articulated best by Watzlawick and co-workers (1967).

Of particular concern here are four concepts associated with this approach. First, the definitive characteristic of the pragmatic perspective is its regard for only *observable* patterns of communication. Psychological processes are generally not considered. Second, a fundamental concept is that of *homeostasis,* which was first applied to human systems by Haley (1959). Homeostasis functions to maintain equilibrium within the family system; it is not necessarily a healthy property. The family often seeks to keep the status quo, even at the expense of dysfunctional behavior. Many families actually seem to need their dysfunctional behaviors to maintain the family system (Jackson, 1957). Third, although Watzlawick et al. (1967) presented many insights, axioms, and proposals concerning *communication* patterns, they are probably best known for their axiom, "you cannot not communicate" (p. 51). This axiom implies that every behavior is communicative. Recall this particular axiom was used to buttress the position that the infant is an innate communicator as discussed in Chapter 7. Finally, the Palo Alto group claimed *control* is at the heart of all relationships. Accordingly, the pragmatic perspective has served as the impetus for many relational control studies and development of schemes for coding adult couple interaction (e.g., Rogers & Farace, 1975). Such schemes are being extended to family interaction (e.g., Gaul, Simon, Friedlander, Cutler, & Heatherington, 1991).

Ecological Systemic Approaches

A primary concern of systemic ecological perspectives is to describe both the immediate and more remote social settings (Peterson & Rollins, 1987). The primary factors taken into account are (1) chronological systems (i.e., changes in the family and child across time) and (2) social systems. Thus ecological theorists see the family as part of a much larger social system.

Bronfenbrenner (1979, 1986, 1989) has done the most to advance an ecological systemic perspective of parent-child interaction. The purpose of his model is to delineate "external influences that affect the capacity of families to foster the healthy development of their children" (Bronfenbrenner, 1986, p. 723). To understand childhood development and the microsystem of parent and child, a seemingly infinite number of environmental variables impinging on the parent and child must be considered. Of utmost importance are life course events and the transitions across them made individually by all family members. In addition, "the interaction of genetics and environment in families; transitions and linkages between the family and other major settings influencing development" are all part and parcel of the environment that influences parent-child interaction (Bronfenbrenner, 1986, p. 723). Such settings include day care, peer groups, the school, parental job environments, public policies, and the like. Note that although there is a great deal of interest in the mutual interaction between the child, the parent-child dyad, and extrafamilial environmental factors, the ultimate goal is still the investigation of the consequences for the child.

Belsky (1981, 1984) derived an ecological system perspective directly from Bronfenbrenner's. Belsky agreed that one must take into account the aforementioned variables to understand parent-child interaction. Yet Belsky's model centers on relationships and roles as opposed to individuals. Specifically, he noted three major influences on parenting. These are the background and resources of the parents, the individual characteristics of the child, and the stress and support the parents experience from the extended system (Belsky, 1984).

Interpersonal Relationships Perspective

The final systemic approach discussed here is the most compatible with a communication-based view of parent-child interaction: the interpersonal relationships perspective of Hinde (1979, 1989; Hinde & Stevenson-Hinde, 1987, 1988b). The dynamics of interpersonal relationships are the driving forces in parent-child interaction. The child must be studied as "a social being, formed by and forming part of a network of relationships" (Hinde & Stevenson-Hinde, 1987, p. 2).

The concentration is on "relationships, and on how relationships affect relationships" (Hinde & Stevenson-Hinde, 1987, p. 16). Relationships endure over time, through separations, and may be carried out in the forms of memories of and expectations for interactions (Hinde, 1988). In essence, this draws a distinction between interpersonal relationships and interpersonal communication, which are often perceived as synonymous.

Hinde concisely tied together the unifying theme of relational perspectives: Given that relationships affect relationships, what are the consequences for children? This outlook places significance on the formativeness of early experience into adulthood. Thus the traditionally studied mother-child interaction is highly salient. Yet it is only one of many relationships. Relationships with fathers, grandparents, siblings, and other family members are also paramount.

Researchers using this framework are not ignoring the larger environmental context. Rather "we must come to terms with two dialectics—between the characteristics of individuals and interactions on the one hand, and between interactions and relationships on the other, with two-way cause-effect influences in each case" (Hinde & Stevenson-Hinde, 1987, p. 3). These relationships and interactions are impinged on by social norms, the sociocultural structure, and other aspects of society. In addition, individuals and the relationships between individuals also influence society (Hinde, 1984).

Thus Hinde (1989) also concurred with Bronfenbrenner's general view of numerous levels of systems of varying complexity. Nevertheless, the stance taken is that "the most important aspect of the context is the interactional and relational one" within the networks of the immediate and extended family (Hinde & Stevenson-Hinde, 1987, p. 4).

In sum, Hinde has not claimed to offer a theory. He cautioned that the interpersonal relationships perspective should be wedded to other approaches. In fact, Hinde (1989) acknowledged the similarity between more traditional family systems approaches and relationship approaches. Child consequences have been stressed more by Hinde than by most other systems theorists. He advocated the merging of perspectives to further the understanding of child development processes. His work has served as a bridge between systemic researchers and child development researchers. Simple, obvious, yet often overlooked advice has been offered by Hinde and Stevenson-Hinde (1987): "It is essential at this stage to remain eclectic" (p. 17).

All three systems perspectives reviewed contain marked similarities. All consider nested levels and systemic relationships within and between these levels. Moreover, they all concede that the general sociocultural structure and norms are substantial factors to be considered. Most important, all emphasize the patterns and processes of interactions.

MOVEMENTS TOWARD FAMILY SYSTEMS RESEARCH

The recognition that men are part of families has promoted systems research. Initially men were studied only in terms of the impact of their absence (Belsky, 1981). When considering men as part of a family, interest has generally only focused on their role in the marital dyad. This led to research on the "family" as composed of two dyads: the wife-husband and mother-child. More recently, men have been investigated as potential parenting figures.

But are fathers more involved with their children today than they were 10, 20, or 30 years ago? Based on their interpretation of the findings of numerous studies conducted in the late 1980s, Harris and Morgan (1991) concluded, "despite considerable research interest, social scientists have found little evidence of a shift toward a more active father role" (p. 531).

Moreover, when men are examined as parents, it is not usually in conjunction with mothers as parenting partners, but rather apart from mothers (e.g., Cath, Gurwitt, & Gunsberg, 1989). "This exclusive concentration on the father is as short-sighted as the previously popular exclusive research focus on mothers. To fully understand parental correlates of children's development, it is necessary to examine relations with both mother and father simultaneously" (Clarke-Stewart, 1978, p. 467). Nonetheless, the inclusion of the father-child dyad serves to expand examinations of parent-child interactions beyond the mother-child dyad.

Family Systems Research

Attention is now turned to research advancing a systemic understanding of parent-child interactions within the family. Although much of the research discussed below is not truly systemic, it reflects the historical movement toward and contributions to systemic orientations.

The first item on the agenda is mothers and fathers in interaction with their children. The second major category considered is the nature of the marital relationship. Third, the presence of more than one child in the same family and sibling relationships are examined. Finally, research reflective of a more truly systemic nature is noted. Recently a few attempts have been made to study complex interactions of multiple family members within a systems paradigm.

MOTHERS AND FATHERS
IN INTERACTION WITH CHILDREN

Research has most often compared the tenor of mother-child interactions to that of father-child interactions and explored different outcomes for the child. A few studies have looked at triadic interactions.

Mother-Child Versus Father-Child Interaction. Regardless of the limited number of comparative studies, some conclusions are consistent across disciplines and methodologies. The generalizations offered below come predominantly from reviews by Belsky (1981), Grusec and Lytton (1988), Harris and Morgan (1991), Maccoby and Martin (1983), Parke (1978), and especially Parke and Tinsley (1987), as well as the work of Lamb (e.g., 1977a, 1977b; Lamb & Easterbrooks, 1981).

Unequivocally, mothers still spend more time with infants than do fathers. Even in dual-earner marriages, mothers retain the primary caregiver role (Darling-Fisher & Tiedje, 1990). However, it appears fathers play as much or more with their children than do mothers (e.g., Clarke-Stewart, 1978; Pleck, 1985). When fathers play with children, they engage in a qualitatively different type of play than mothers do. Mothers engage in nurturing play, for example, close face-to-face games, peek-a-boo, and pat-a-cake. When fathers play with children, it is generally roughhousing, such as bouncing and lifting. Intriguingly, fathers are preferred playmates, but when young children are afraid or upset, they prefer their mothers (Lamb, 1977a, 1977b). Clarke-Stewart (1978) speculated that fathers themselves are not preferred as playmates, but rather the type of play in which they engage is simply more fun for the young child. She concluded that, at least for children under 2, children are more secure with their mother in times of distress.

Across middle childhood through adolescence, children and parents spend a decreasing amount of time together (Montemayor & Brownlee, 1987). Mothers spend more time with their older children than do fathers—up to twice as much, even through the age of 16 (A. Russell & Russell, 1988, G. Russell & Russell, 1987). In fact, some studies have revealed that in dual-earner families a sizable percentage of fathers engage in no one-to-one time with their offspring (Crouter & Crowley, 1990).

In regard to conversation, adolescent talk with fathers narrows to a small number of topics, predominantly instrumental goals and activities. Talk with fathers is also characterized by a control function concerning issues of discipline and setting boundaries, for example, "Curfew is 10 p.m." (e.g., Papini & Sebby, 1987). Mothers talk with their children more and over a greater range of topics than fathers. Along the same lines, adolescents report more self-disclosure to their mothers than fathers (Wilks, 1986). Mother-adolescent interactions are more likely to involve personal and social issues as well as instrumental ones.

Differences in the interaction patterns of children with their mothers versus fathers have been highlighted here. Despite this, there may be at least as many, if not more, basic similarities than differences (Clarke-Stewart, 1978; Parke & Tinsley, 1987). A growing number of descriptive and comparative studies provide evidence that both mothers and fathers are psychologically involved and serve as attachment figures for their children (Belsky, 1981; Maccoby & Martin, 1983).

Child Outcomes Associated With Mother's Versus Father's Interactions. Numerous studies have supported the claim that sensitive, responsive caregiving (whether by mother or father) is associated with optimal development in nearly every domain of child competence (Lamb & Easterbrooks, 1981). In contrast, Belsky (1981) claimed that the only uncontested generalization about paternal involvement is that it is likely related to some overall emotional and/or cognitive development. Grusec and Lytton (1988) raised the question as to whether or not fathers are as effective primary caregivers as mothers. Their answer: "Men can be as responsive to babies as women are, but in practice are not" (Grusec & Lytton, 1988, p. 202). Thus they claimed that even when the father is the primary caregiver, the mother is more nurturing and serves as a "better" primary caregiver.

Presence of Both Mother and Father. Adding the father to explorations of parent-child interactions creates not only another relationship (the father-child) but also changes "the mother-infant dyad into a family system comprised of marital and parent-infant relationships" (Belsky, 1981, p. 5). Hence considering the mother and the father jointly as parenting figures represents a marked advance in systemic models.

Numerous studies indicate that a parent behaves differently with a child when alone than when the other parent is present. Most studies focus on how the mother changes her interaction with the child given the father's presence. Overall, parent-infant and parent-toddler interaction decreases whether assessed at home or in a laboratory (Belsky, 1979; Clarke-Stewart, 1978; Lamb, 1977a, 1977b). Parents interact with each other more and direct interaction with the infant is reduced. Reduction of interaction with the child is more striking for fathers than mothers (Crouter & Crowley, 1990).

In contrast, others report that basic interaction patterns of mothers and children do not change in the presence of the fathers (see review by Parke & Tinsley, 1987). Some patterns of interaction do seem to be subject to influences from the presence of the father, while certain other aspects of mother-child interaction are less susceptible. Parents smile more toward children and engage in more exploratory play with the child when the spouse is present. Moreover, there are also areas of increased interaction as the parents play off of and support each other. Also, some activities are not necessary affected. There is no indication that feeding and rocking increase or decrease when both parents are present (Grusec & Lytton, 1988; also see Clarke-Stewart, 1978). Conflicting findings aside, the critical point is stated by Parke and Tinsley (1987): "Overall these studies indicate that parent-child interaction cannot be understood by a sole focus on the parent-infant dyad" (p. 596).

THE MARITAL RELATIONSHIP

Belsky (1981) theorized that the relationship that begins the family —the marital relationship—influences children, and children in turn influence not only individual parents but also the marital relationship. The claim that relationships affect relationships is repeatedly supported by research.

The literature concerning the marital relationship is organized around three general themes. First, the quality of the marital relationship is seen as causally related to children's development. Second, the influence of the quality of the marriage on parenting and/or parent-child relationships is of interest. Competing compensatory and spillover hypotheses have been proposed. Third, the child may also be an intrusion on the marriage. This creates discomfort in the marital relationship (Easterbrooks & Emde, 1988).

Marital Quality. Before proceeding, attention is drawn to the fact that research under the rubric of marital quality has involved concepts that are differently labeled marital satisfaction, happiness, harmony, adjustment, quality, and so forth. There are crucial distinctions among these conceptualizations (see Fitzpatrick, 1987). However, Norton (1983) has demonstrated the extremely strong correlations among the various measures and claimed that these constructs are essentially indexes of global subjective experiences of the participants.

Conflict and discord are also considered part of the marital experience. However, to quote Margolin (1988), "marital conflict is not marital conflict is not marital conflict" (p. 193). In fact, conflict may be defined on at least three dimensions: process, content, and/or duration (Emery, 1982). Variations in marital conflict on any, or all, of these dimensions may have uniquely different implications for child outcomes. At present, these potential relationships remain largely unexplored. This is surprising considering the widespread consensus that it is the experience of interparental conflict that may be negatively linked to children's social development. When investigators have differentiated between intensity, duration, manner, and the like, this will be brought to the reader's attention.

The goal in this section is to draw unity among the findings of these concepts, referring to the overall nature of the marital experience. Hence terms such as *unhappy, dissatisfied, conflicted, discordant,* and the like are used interchangeably. This is not meant to dismiss the often meaningful differences in these terms, but, as noted previously, all are viewed as general indices of the quality of the marriage. In short, both concepts, satisfaction and discord (conflict), yield indices to the adjustment of marital partners. From this literature, several generalizations can be drawn.

Consensus emerges concerning the relationship of marital quality and child consequences. The experience of interparental conflict is negatively associated with children's socioemotional development and general social conduct (see reviews by Emery, 1982; Grych & Fincham, 1990; Margolin, 1981; Rutter, 1981). The case that marital discord is related to a host of less than desirable child consequences is built from evidence from a variety of research studies (see summary by Emery, 1982). From these studies continuing conflict between parents, and not divorce, eventually emerged as the critical factor negatively impacting children's adjustment. Subsequent research has both supported and expanded on this basic claim.

At an early age, children appear to be sensitive to the experience of marital discord. Toddlers as young as 10 months of age respond to others' negative affect (Cummings, Zahn-Waxler, & Radke-Yarrow, 1981). And the children's *affective* responses to the experience of marital conflict extend well into adolescence (see e.g., Peterson & Zill, 1986).

The form of the child's behavioral response changes over time. A marked increase in prosocial responses and a noticeable decline in displays of anger occurs from infancy to toddlerhood (Cummings, Zahn-Waxler & Radke-Yarrow, 1984). Furthermore, as preschool children mature, their tendency to respond prosocially to adults' negative emotional displays increases (Denham & Couchard, 1991).

As marital conflict increases, the behavior of children becomes more problematic (e.g., Emery & O'Leary, 1984; Jouriles, Bourg, & Farris, 1991; Peterson & Zill, 1986). As the number of conflictual interactions increased, toddlers were less likely to ignore these episodes and instead became angry or distressed, or attempted to mediate the conflict (Crockenberg, 1985; Cummings et al., 1981). Cummings et al. (1984) reported that children who experience more frequent conflicts between their parents continued to produce more distressed reactions through the early school years. Furthermore, the relationship between increased marital conflict and child problems appears to hold into the adolescent years. The National Surveys of Children found that adolescents' depression-withdrawal, antisocial, and impulsive-hyperactive behavior increased linearly with marital conflict (Peterson & Zill, 1986).

Not all children respond to parental discordant marriages in the same manner (Cummings, Pellegrini, Notarius, & Cummings, 1989; also see Cummings, 1987). Individual children's responses across time evidence considerable consistency (Cummings et al., 1981, 1984).

Several factors are thought to mediate the general negative impact on the child (Emery, 1982). These are the age and possibly the gender of the child, the support system of other adults available to the child, the cognitive maturity of the child, the length of time the child lives in the discordant environment, the parents' ability to mask and protect the child from the discord, and certain temperamental characteristics of the child.

Marital Quality and Parent-Child Relationships. Some studies have provided evidence of the effects of marital discord on parent-child relationships. Here interest is in how the relationship between the parents may influence— directly or indirectly—parenting, parent-child interaction, and/or parent-child relationships.

In general, marital disruption is related to poor parent-child relationships as reported by children. Peterson and Zill (1986) found a linear trend between conflict and youths' evaluation of their relationship with their parents. This seems to hold in general, although some studies have found sex differences in the effect of marital distress on parents' relationships with girls or boys (e.g., Amato, 1986).

In 1981, Belsky hypothesized that the support a parent receives from the spouse may facilitate positive parenting. Today, there is good evidence for this claim. Husband's support is generally related positively to maternal parenting competence. A father appears to influence a mother's positive affect toward their child by being supportive of her emotional caregiving (Parke & Tinsley, 1987). Turning the tables, competent parenting by males seems to be even more contingent on a supportive marital climate than is maternal caregiving. The marital satisfaction of the mother is associated with increased *paternal* involvement (e.g., Harris & Morgan, 1991; Volling & Belsky, 1991).

Two competing hypotheses have been proposed concerning parental involvement with the child as a function of marital quality. One is the *compensation* hypothesis. That is, a spouse may compensate for the lack of love or affection in the marriage by investing that emotional energy in the parent-child relationship. Studies by Goldberg and Easterbrooks (1984); Brody, Stoneman, and Burke (1987); and Engfer (1988) all provided some evidence of this phenomenon. Nonetheless, compensation, or the situation in which the child is substituting for spousal affection, may be a catalyst for negative family dynamics. By strengthening the bond between one parent and child, the bond between husband and wife may be weakened (Minuchin, 1974). Bonds such as these may reflect a lack of differentiated roles within the family (Combrinck-Graham, 1990). Thus compensation appears to represent inappropriate role management and differentiation; such overlapping of roles may operate to maintain a negative cycle within the entire system. Moreover, this condition of enmeshment of the parent-child dyad is seen as an index of an unhealthy family system (Combrinck-Graham, 1990). What is critical here is that enmeshment is presumed to be detrimental for the child's development (Olson et al., 1983).

The other hypothesis is the *spillover* hypothesis. This suggests that harmony, or lack thereof, in the marriage is somewhat contagious; that is, it spills over into parent-child relationships. In other words, happy marriages would create positive parent-child relationships whereas the opposite would be true of less happy marriages (Engfer, 1988).

Another alternative concerns the father's acceptance of the fathering role. Admittedly, the proposition is highly speculative. Nevertheless, Margolin (1981) proposed the following:

> Regardless of the amount of active paternal involvement, the father's level of comfort or discomfort with his child is likely to influence the quality of the father-child relationship, as well as to affect the father's self-image as a parent, and the mother's perception of her husband in this role. Additionally, it may be that the very lack of paternal involvement intensifies the mother-child relationship with collateral repercussions for the marital relationship. (p. 174)

Interestingly, this speculation has not been forwarded concerning maternal involvement, perhaps reflecting a Western cultural bias that maternal involvement is a given.

Child Influences on the Marital Relationship. Recall from the overviews of bidirectional and systemic views that children socialize parents and parents socialize children. Children introduce a couple to parenthood. Investigations into the transition to parenthood were conducted in response to Hill's (1949) claim that changes accompanying parenthood are so sudden and stark they constitute a crisis for the marital pair.

Undoubtedly, the child modifies husband-wife interaction patterns and the marital relationship (Parke & Tinsley, 1987). Accommodating a child into the family system changes the status quo, upsetting the system's prior equilibrium (Kreppner, 1988). All current relationships within the family are rearranged; the infant "reinvents the family" (Combrinck-Graham, 1990, p. 503). This point is perhaps best made by the research on the transition to parenthood. Following the birth of the first child, the prognosis for the course of the marital relationship is somewhat grim (Engfer, 1988). The birth of a child has detrimental repercussions for marital satisfaction, which typically does not increase again until children leave home. Such findings stand in stark contrast to conventional wisdom that the birth of the child can change bad marriages into good ones. It is possible that a child can serve as the glue holding a marriage together (Huber & Spitze, 1988). The child may provide a couple with something in common to talk about, which might in turn draw them together. But in general, negative alterations in the marital relationship are much more probable (Belsky & Vondra, 1985).

Communication between the spouses changes with the birth of a child. The fundamental premise of much research on the connection between children and marital satisfaction is that the child disrupts communication in the marriage, which in turn results in a decline in marital quality (Belsky & Rovine, 1990). Sillars and Wilmot (1989) speculated that "communication in companionate areas suffers the most, as a greater percentage of communication is devoted to decision making and conflict resolution" (p. 235).

The addition of a child has an indirect effect on marital relationships as well. Role strain and physical exhaustion are reported by the wife. Often the infant's sleep cycles affect the mother's exhaustion level, which affects, in turn, the marital relationship. The wife may become disinterested in sexual relations, which may exacerbate marital discord (Belsky, 1981, 1984).

The preceding discussion sounds as if all children had the same effects on all marriages. However, the extent to which the marital relationship changes in reaction to the birth of a child is contingent on numerous variables. Child temperament is one factor influencing parents and hence their parenting and the marital relationship. For example, exhaustion impacting parenting abilities and marital role strain may be aggravated in the case of a child with a difficult temperament (Easterbrooks & Emde, cited in Engfer, 1988). Additional factors include the initial marital satisfaction level, the timing of the birth of the child in each parent's and in the marriage's life cycle, and whether or not the pregnancy was planned (Lewis, 1988a, 1988b). In addition, it has been proposed that marriages with strong friendship foundations are likely to suffer less damage than those based largely on romance (Belsky, Rovine, & Fish, 1989).

To oversimplify, although the direction of cause and effect is obviously unclear and many factors mediate the situation, happy babies and happy marriages tend to co-occur.

MORE THAN ONE CHILD: THE SIBLING SUBSYSTEM

Seldom do researchers consider interactional patterns between parents and more than one child. This section presents research on siblings as related to parent-child interaction and as related to sibling relationships. Numerous reviews and studies are drawn on, including Cicirelli (1985), Cicirelli and Nussbaum (1989), Huber and Spitze (1988), and Schvaneveldt and Ihinger (1979) as well as research by Dunn (e.g., 1988a; Dunn & Kendrick, 1982a; Dunn & Stocker, 1989) and others.

Despite documentation that as the number of children increases so does the probability of overall family conflict and parental role strain, nearly all the studies summarized previously have employed just one child. This is done by limiting samples to families with only one child or (the more usual strategy) artificially limiting the focus by selecting one child as the target. When the presence of more than one child is considered, researchers customarily limit samples to two-child families. However, contemporary research is turning toward the relationships between siblings as influencing other family members and relationships among other family members (Cicirelli, 1985). It is not questioned that the arrival of a sibling prompts changes in the interaction between the mother and the firstborn child (Dunn, 1988b).

Traditional research on families with more than one child has focused on structural variables such as the effects of family size or birth order. Although reviews indicate that birth order effects are largely unsupported, family size appears to be a predictive factor in parent-child interaction. Less interaction between a parent and any one child in a larger family is explained via a *dilution* model. That is, children must share limited family resources (e.g., parental attention). Nonetheless, Harris and Morgan (1991) found that the number of children in a family increased the father's participation in the family, yet the father's involvement with any one individual child was not any greater. Some suggest that the marital couple can impact the development of each child by limiting the number of children born and considering the spacing of siblings (e.g., Dunn, 1983).

Parental treatment of the siblings may play a crucial role in whether or not feelings of rivalry and hostility versus affection develop between the siblings. Schvaneveldt and Ihinger (1979) speculated that parent-child communication about the impending arrival will soften the impact on the parent-first child relationship after the second child is born. Indeed, when mothers discuss the younger sibling with the older child, sibling rivalry and feelings of displacement are less likely to occur or at least are less intense (Cicirelli, 1985; also see Dunn & Kendrick, 1982a).

Closely related phenomena are how the children perceive the parents' behaviors and how parents actually do act. Siblings' perceptions of differential treatment accorded them in terms of time and attention from the mother matter to children (Dunn, 1988b). Children are aware of and monitor differential treatment toward their siblings and respond to it. The child's perception of impartiality and shared time and attention has been proposed as a crucial mediating variable. Sibling conflict and parent-child conflict tend to be higher when siblings perceive partiality (Adler & Furman, 1988).

Along the same lines, Parke and Asher (1983) suggested that the quality of sibling relationships is linked to the overall quality of individual mother-child interaction. Close relationships between mother and child do not ensure peaceful sibling relationships. However, harmonious sibling relationships may promote harmonious mother-child relationships. Finally, a variation of the compensation hypothesis may occur. Dunn (1988a) has proposed that if the mother and firstborn have a poor, detached relationship, the second child provides a playmate to offer the sibling warmth and affection lacking from the mother. Dunn also noted that when the marital subsystem is dysfunctional, atypically strong bonds may develop among siblings.

Recently, adolescents' perceptions of their sibling relationships have been examined in association with their perceived relationships with both mother and father. In brief, adolescents with warm relationships with mothers and fathers reported less sibling hostility and rivalry. Moreover, children who spent time in one-to-one activities with their fathers felt more warmth toward their fathers and also had the least negative and most positive feelings about their siblings (Stocker & McHale, 1992).

Finally, it has been argued that understanding sibling relationships has been held back by Western cultural biases that overestimate the salience of parents in influencing individual children and sibling relationships. Some have claimed that parents in Western societies are preoccupied with sibling rivalry and jealousy (e.g., Zukow, 1989). However, some cross-cultural evidence indicates that siblings are effective (indeed sometimes primary) agents for the cognitive, social, and language development of each other (Zukow, 1989).

Systems

Very few studies actually examine many of the systemic assumptions discussed earlier in this chapter. One study that comes very close to a systems view is reported by Belsky, Youngblade, Rovine, and Volling (1991). They mapped changes in the relationships between the mother-child relationship and mother-child and father-child interaction patterns over a 3-year period. This study is notable in that it is observation based and longitudinal.

These researchers found that as men's marital satisfaction declined in terms of love for their spouses and increased doubts about their marriage, men became more negative in interaction with their children. Husbands in love with their wives and secure with their marriages expressed more positive affect in interaction with their children. Children of the fathers with a negative marital experience also interacted more negatively with their fathers. Child negativity may further contribute to the father's unhappiness in the marriage. Contrawise, women who became unhappy in their marriages did not manifest this change in interaction style with children. Actually, such wives became more positive and supportive of the child.

Note the systemic issues raised by this study. Do and to what extent do positive (and perhaps overstrong) bonds between mothers and children lead to fathers feeling loss of love, thus reducing involvement with children? Or does the mother-child bond develop in response to fathers' negative behavior? Does the mother strive to buffer the child from the father's negativity? Would this type of subsystem coalition be unhealthy for the child in the long run, as most family therapists would argue?

SUMMARY AND CONCLUSIONS

An overview of systems theory has been presented. Concepts especially relevant to the study of parent-child interaction were highlighted and three widely known systems approaches were reviewed. Finally, general findings emanating from systemic type studies were identified and discussed.

Systems theories have had an enormous impact on the field of family therapy, especially in clinical psychology. Ideally, therapy, theory, and research should work reflexively. Unfortunately, this has seldom happened. Although numerous schools of thought and applications exist in clinical practice and many theories have been generated, social scientific research from systems perspectives has been quite sparse. Systems research is indeed expanding. Examples include studies based on Olson's circumplex model of family functioning (e.g., Olson, 1991; Olson et al., 1983). And as noted previously, a coding scheme for the analysis of triadic interactions is being developed (see Gaul et al., 1991; Heatherington & Freidlander, 1990).

Still, a page-by-page search of the descriptor *family interaction* in *Psychological Abstracts* for the years 1988-1992 revealed only three investigations that truly examined the family as a system. Myriad pieces include the word *systems* in the title or claim to be a systems approach. In reality, many so-called systems investigations examine the cause and effect of one component of the system unilaterally on another. Such explorations are not necessarily inconsistent with systems approaches, but certainly do not adequately test systems theorists' claims.

Furthermore, studies seldom address how the personalities individuals bring into a system become part of a system. From a systemic standpoint, personality traits are part of a system, but many personality traits are thought to be more accurately discussed as *relationship* traits. The recognition of individuals' personalities as affecting a family is long-standing. As a matter of fact, before family systems thinking was even conceived, researchers such as Burgess (1926) referred to the family as a "set of interacting personalities" (see also Park & Waters, 1988; Stevenson-Hinde, 1988).

Systems perspectives have advanced *conceptually* beyond cause and effect. Most scholars of systems orientations are not preoccupied with cause and effect, as scholars from unidirectional views appear to be. "When we examine the family from a systems point of view, no one person or thing . . . can realistically be identified as the 'cause' of a problem" (Yerby, Buerkel-Rothfuss, & Bochner, 1990, p. 63). Instead, the goal of research on parent-child interaction is the "description of recurrent patterns within which the child functions" (Minuchin, 1985, p. 291). However, before examining system research, we remind and caution the reader that it is difficult to avoid the trap of direct cause-and-effect thinking. But "one must never forget that the links in a supposed causal chain are in reality spider's webs" (Hanson, 1955, paraphrased in Hinde & Stevenson-Hinde, 1987, p. 10). Hence, terms such as *associated* must not be read to imply causal relationships. Alternatively, one could think of all effects as causal (Bavelas & Segal, 1982).

In the following chapter, the three exemplar variables of compliance, self-esteem, and language/communication are discussed. We will review research that moves the field toward systemic orientations and systems research that provides insight into the child variables.

9

The Family as a Spiral of Recursive Feedback Loops: A Systemic View of Three Variables

INTRODUCTION

Little truly systemic research has been conducted on the three exemplar variables of self-control, self-concept, and communication competencies. Several reasons seem apparent. First is the long-standing assumption that such variables are unidirectional outcomes of parental actions. Second, systems models are exceedingly complex: "A complete system would theoretically encompass the universe" (Minuchin, 1985, p. 290). Such all-encompassing complexity doubtless deters all but the most dauntless researchers. Related to this, although many accept systems models, these models are comparatively difficult to translate into manageable research. Much of systems research stems from clinical and therapeutic insights. It has only recently been possible to investigate such insights quantitatively. However, advanced statistical procedures capture some, not all, systemic dynamics.

Systems theorists are interested in the patterned nature of interaction within the family. Child consequences are of interest, as are the consequences for all family members. However, the processes of patterned relational interdependence are considered more important issues than questions of etiology, direction of cause and effect, and relative contribution to consequences of various influences.

But even systems theorists disagree somewhat on whether they should *solely* focus on process or a combination of process and consequences. For example, Minuchin (1985) argued that the foundational elements of developmental research (e.g., etiology, direction of effects, and quantification of influence) "do not make sense in a systems framework" (p. 300). The Palo Alto group sees no point in looking to the past for explanations of current behavior (Bavelas & Segal, 1982). Present behavior is contingent on the dynamics of the current system. Other theorists striving to integrate developmental psychology and systems theories focus on child consequences and processes (e.g., Bronfenbrenner, Belsky, Hinde). Morcover, the argument is advanced that various aspects of the system are not necessarily equal in influence (Belsky & Vondra, 1985). In other words, despite the stance taken by Minuchin and others, some researchers are concerned with the relative weight of various systemic elements.

The camps are not really as opposed as it may seem; rather priorities differ. There is agreement that all factors are influential on all family members to some extent and examination of all factors is warranted. Developmental psychologists invoking systems theories simply concentrate effort on the consequences for the child. Little regard is given to the etiology of the consequences within the system. This is consistent with the pragmatic perspective, because it is considered impossible to punctuate the beginning of the causal links within a circle (see Watzlawick et al., 1967).

The conclusions that follow should be viewed critically in light of at least two limitations of the literature. First, fathers have not been studied as members of the family until recently, thus inhibiting a holistic portrayal of the family. Second, little evidence comes from research directly implementing systemic models. Instead, insights have been obtained from unidirectional and bidirectional research that explores the effects of relationships on an individual in linear or reciprocal fashion. Then there are the quasi-systemic studies. In such studies, a systems theory drives the research and multiple family members are included in the data-collection phase. Yet, the data analyses and/or interpretations fail to carry the systemic orientation to completion. However, there is sufficient traditional research of the type noted above, supplemented by clinical research and therapeutic application, to piece together a picture of how family systems work and, in turn, to allow generalizations.

The conclusions that follow represent the progress being made toward systems views. Research will be organized into four sections: mothers and fathers in interaction with their children, the marital relationship, the presence of more than one child (the sibling subsystem), and the family as a system. As in previous chapters concerning outcomes, generalizations will be offered relative to each exemplar variable. As the same principles emerge across the three variables, a unified summary will close the chapter.

SELF-CONTROL

Family systems practitioners have had much experience with compliance and the lack thereof. Problematic disobedience is a primary reason children are referred for counseling. Concern for noncompliance is amplified when one recalls compliance has been proposed to be rudimentary to internalization and moral development. Child disturbances, such as extreme chronic noncompliance, are a result of disturbances in the system, not merely disturbances of the child (Sameroff & Emde, 1989).

Mothers and Fathers in Interaction With Their Children and Self-Control

Differences between paternal and maternal compliance-gaining attempts reflect first the mother's role as primary caregiver (Lytton, 1980). Even after adjusting for the greater amount of time mothers spend with children, mothers engage in more attempts to gain compliance when interacting alone with children than do fathers. Thus some have been surprised to discover that there are apparently more similarities than differences in mothers' and fathers' compliance techniques.

Yet the differences that do exist are dramatic. Parents' most common response to compliance is no response, but fathers tend to be even less responsive to child compliance than mothers (Lytton, 1979). Furthermore, when children disobey, fathers tend to be demanding and severe. They react with more overt physical behavior, such as slapping or restraining the child. Mothers, on the other hand, use more verbal responses such as admonishments, criticisms, or verbal threats or tend to favor inductive strategies (Hetherington, Cox, & Cox, 1978; Lytton, 1980). An extensive meta-analysis by Brody and Shaffer (1982) revealed induction by mothers to be associated with advanced moral reasoning. Maternal use of high-power-assertive techniques was negatively associated with moral development. Associations with moral functions and maternal love withdrawal were mixed. Interestingly, few links between paternal control style and children's moral development were found consistently across investigations.

Children may respond differently to the same strategies, depending on which parent invokes them. For example, fathers' use of rewards gained compliance but mothers' use of the same tactic did not (Lytton & Zwirner, 1975; McLaughlin, 1983). Children are also more apt to obey fathers' compliance attempts, regardless of the nature of the attempt. Grusec and Lytton (1988) speculated that because fathers engage in fewer compliance attempts overall, children may pay more attention to them.

The father's presence unequivocally changes the character of the mother-child compliance interactions (see Lytton, 1980). Mothers tend to provide more positive acknowledgments to children when fathers are present. Even though mothers make more compliance requests than fathers, when both are present the rate of maternal requests drops. Regardless of the strategy mothers adopt, the sheer presence of the father increases the likelihood that mothers will gain children's compliance. When a mother's request is followed by a father's request, child compliance increases. Fathers' compliance-gaining success rate is unaffected by mothers' presence, however.

The Marital Relationship and Child Self-Regulation

Many different studies provide evidence of interrelationships between child compliance and marital quality.

MARITAL DISCORD

Children are less compliant to requests made by parents experiencing significant marital conflict (e.g., Jouriles, Pfiffner, & O'Leary, 1988; Webster-Stratton, 1989). Other studies found that children subjected to persistent marital conflict in the home exhibit problematic behaviors often associated with noncompliance (e.g., Emery & O'Leary, 1984; Jouriles et al., 1980).

Parental disagreement as to how to obtain child compliance and/or administer discipline has been related to noncompliance. For example, parental disagreement on child-rearing practices at child age 3 predicted boys exhibiting undercontrolled behaviors (e.g., acting-out and aggression) at age 7 (Block, Block, & Gjerde, 1986). It is reasonable to suppose that parental disagreement may be related to inconsistent discipline, particularly as inconsistency is frequently a correlate of child behavior problems. Inconsistency seems to provoke anxiety and confusion for the child and, in turn, is related to compliance, although the mediating variables are not known (Markus & Nurius, 1984). Moreover, inconsistency is related to the development of poor self guides (Higgins, 1991) and a lack of internalization (Markus & Nurius, 1984). In sum, lack of consensus on child-rearing practices and communication of that fact to children are associated with misbehavior, noncompliance, and possibly other aspects of the child's self-regulation.

This is not to say that conflict over how to rear children causes child misbehavior, although it very well may. Rather children's noncompliance appears to be more generally embedded in negative cycles of family interaction. For example, high spousal conflict was interrelated with increased maternal negativity toward, and reciprocation of negativity from, the child

(Christensen, Phillips, Glasgow, & Johnson, 1983). There is also evidence that inconsistent discipline is related to the way in which couples conduct their conflicts (e.g., Easterbrooks & Emde, 1988). A lack of consensus on child rearing seems to relate to poor management of martial conflict, perpetuating the system of marital inconsistencies, leading to greater child noncompliance, and in turn, escalating the conflict between the parents as to how best to handle the noncompliant child.

In addition, martial discord is linked to dysfunctional parent-child alliances (Christensen & Margolin, 1988). Unhappy parents have been observed to be more controlling and less supportive of their children. Stoneman, Brody, and Burke (1989a) reported that parental induction was notably absent in the interactions they observed. Spousal conflict also related to greater use of commands and disapproval statements (Jouriles et al., 1988; Webster-Stratton, 1989).

Studies have focused more on wives' marital adjustment or stress and their compliance attempts than husbands'. A typical finding is that dissatisfied mothers find it difficult to obtain compliance from children (Webster-Stratton, 1989). Women without spousal support tend to have more problems gaining child compliance than those who do have spousal support. Hoffman (1960) reported that wives subjected to high-power assertiveness by their husbands were more likely to use high-power compliance strategies with their children compared with wives whose interactions with their husbands were more supportive. Although limited in number, the findings related to fathers, their experience of marriage, and their interaction with children generally parallel the picture for mothers. For example, children tend to be more disobedient and less mindful of fathers who report a decline in love for the mothers over the course of the marriage (Belsky et al., 1991). Similarly, fathers involved in dissatisfying marriages were more aggravated by children's noncompliance than fathers in satisfying marriages (Easterbrooks & Emde, 1988).

Inappropriate involvement of children in enduring marital disputes is also associated with children's problematic behavior. When school-age children were entangled in marital conflicts, children were subsequently observed to exhibit more aggressive and problematic behavior in general (Johnston, Gonzalez, & Campbell, 1987). When a child and one parent repeatedly side together during conflict in opposition to the other parent, *parentification* is likely (Minuchin & Fishman, 1981). The child becomes a pseudo-parent in the sense of providing more support for the adult than does his or her marital partner (Adler & Furman, 1988). In short, inappropriate coalitions are formed. Being in the position of a pseudo-parent may give the child a certain sense of power, due to the child's inappropriate connection with the one parent. Family therapists suggest the parentified child may become a disobedient tyrant. Furthermore, it has been speculated that spouses who cannot handle their own conflicts with each other create a problematic child. This allows the couple to invest effort into the "sick" child and thus avoid their marital problems (Adler & Furman, 1988).

In regard to parental perceptions, children labeled difficult by maritally stressed parents frequently are not in fact different from other children (e.g., Christensen et al., 1983; Deal, Halverson, & Wampler, 1989; Emery & O'Leary, 1984; Webster-Stratton, 1989). This suggests that poor marital relationships color parental perceptions of their children's behavior.

The notion that child problems may initiate marital discord must also be considered. For example, a temperamentally difficult child may produce marital discord (Easterbrooks & Emde, 1988; Engfer, 1988).

Several studies suggest that child misbehavior, or even the perception of a child being difficult, may negatively influence the marital relationship. For example, Block et al. (1986) reported that son disobedience preceded both marital distress and subsequent divorce.

MARITAL HARMONY

Studies of children's compliance to happily married parents provide corroborating evidence. Jouriles et al. (1988) reported that toddlers were more likely to obey mothers reporting high marital satisfaction. When children did disobey, however, well adjusted mothers tended to treat children more easily than did less well adjusted mothers. Notably, satisfied mothers verbalized fewer disapprovals of the child's behavior. Block et al. (1986) reported that parental agreement at child age 3 predicted positive outcomes for both adolescent boys and girls. Easterbrooks and Emde (1988) found that

the sharing of positive affect between parents and child was very strongly related to the extent of parental agreement about child discipline and control, and to marital harmony in couple discussion. In addition, marital harmony was related to the expression of approval and physical affection from parents to children. (p. 97)

Positive marital relations also color perceptions of child behavior. But these satisfied spouses may be wearing rose-colored glasses. They see their children as less difficult in general. For example, mothers and fathers exhibiting low conflict perceived the same level of noncompliance in their children less severely than parents in high-conflict marital relationships (Collins,

1990). Specifically, "maritally satisfied parents hold a 'positive screen' about their interpersonal relationships, which can lead them to interpret child behaviors as more positive than do objective observers" (Easterbrooks & Emde, 1988, p. 99).

In sum, spousal discord is related to parent-child interactions that reciprocate negativity and engender various problems in children. The behavior problems of the child are apt to be disruptive to the marriage and engender discord in the marriage as well. The converse appears to occur in high-quality marriages. Finally, perceptions may play a strong role in these processes.

The Sibling Subsystem and Self-Regulation

Maternal compliance techniques and/or siblings' perceptions of such techniques are associated with child aggression, the relationship between the siblings, and the relationships between the mother and each child. Research indicates that mothers use different compliance-gaining strategies with different children (Dunn & Stocker, 1989). When two children are involved in a transgression, punishment is more likely to be directed to the child perceived as the stronger of the pair. This holds regardless of which child initiates the misdeed (Dunn & Munn, 1986). In other words, parents are more likely to punish the older sibling. Dunn and Munn (1985) found that 2-year-olds and their 5-year-old siblings were equally likely to be the instigators of misdeeds. Yet, mothers were more than twice as prone to discipline the older child and to distract the younger child with an alternative activity. Recently, fathers as well as mothers have been found to exhibit more favorable treatment toward the younger child when sibling difficulties occur (e.g., Brody, Stoneman, & McCoy, 1992). These attempts by parents to maintain the peace can backfire. The younger child expects support from the mother in sibling controversy; this expectation is generally reinforced (Minuchin, 1988). The lack of punishment for misbehavior in turn allows the younger child to go awry (Dunn, 1988b).

Siblings monitor and respond to perceived preferential treatment of a sibling. Dunn, Stocker, and Plomin (1990) found that children's realization that they are being treated in a different manner from siblings has negative consequences for that child's overall well-being. In addition, punishing the stronger and sparing the weaker may strain the relationships between the siblings and the parent's relationships with both children. A child's perception of favorable treatment of another child is associated with aggressive behavior and negative affect toward the preferred sibling (Dunn et al., 1990; McHale & Pawletko, 1992). The increase in aggression and noncompliance in the weaker child appears to increase maternal stress. This stress fuels further aggression and noncompliant behaviors of both children (Dunn & Stocker, 1989). The powerful sibling likely interprets such maternal inventions as unfair, further feeding conflict between the siblings. This perception appears as part of a chain of mutual negative interactions between this parent-child pair (Cicirelli, 1985).

Children operate on principles of justice and fairness with respect to their sibling(s) (Cicirelli, 1985; Dunn, 1988b). Thus when justice is perceived as blind, child aggression decreases and parent-child(ren) relationships are more agreeable (Dunn, 1988b). On the other hand, parental perceptions of the relative difficulty of each sibling may be the factor driving parental favoritism. When the siblings are perceived to be similar in their unfavorable emotions (e.g., anger and frustration), siblings are more likely to receive equal treatment from both mother and father (Stoneman, Brody, & Burke, 1989b).

It is of little concern to most system theorists as to whether or not it is the children's perception of favoritism, parents' perceptions of the child's difficulty, or differing parental behaviors that are at root of the troubled relationships. Etiology is irrelevant; a system of negativity between all interactants is perpetuated.

The Family as a System and Self-Regulation

Myriad factors previously discussed are interwoven as systems theorists develop models of family interaction in relation to children's compliance. Child noncompliance frequently may be seen as a consequence of a disturbed family, and regardless of origin, child noncompliance helps to maintain the coercive family system (Sanders, Dadds, & Bor, 1989). For example, the noncompliant child may serve as the scapegoat for problems permeating the entire family system (Minuchin, Rosman, & Baker, 1978).

Stoneman and co-workers (1989b) have found support for their systems explanation of children's noncompliance. For illustrative purposes, they take as their starting point children with active-emotional temperaments:

Temperamentally difficult children are believed to place added stress on their parents, above and beyond the normative stress accompanying the presence of a child in the family. This added stress results in heightened parental depression and marital dissatisfaction. In turn, these negative mood states combine with decreased spousal support, which often accompanies marital dissatisfaction, to compromise competent parenting and to increase conflict between husbands and wives. The resulting use of ineffective parenting strategies leads to a lack

of parental success in modifying children's irritating behavior, thus further ac-
centuating parental perceptions of the children as difficult to manage, intensi-
fying feelings of depression and marital unhappiness, and precipitating martial
conflict. (Stoneman et al., 1989b, p. 100)

There remains a general lack of systemic life-cycle studies on self-control.
Yet one variable in a single period of the developmental span has received
much quasi-systemic research attention. This is ego development and individuation during adolescence.

The most programmatic series of studies is by Cooper, Grotevant, and
colleagues (e.g., Cooper et al., 1983; Grotevant & Cooper, 1985, 1986).
These studies are systemic in at least two ways. First, they involved family
interactions: Moms, dads, and siblings were present. Second, a developmental orientation was taken. This research pursued questions relative to father
versus mother interaction characteristics with son versus daughter. The communication of mother versus father were then associated with the sons' versus the daughters' ego development (e.g., Cooper et al., 1983). The goal was
to determine which communication features within which dyads enhance
ego development. They provided some evidence of the processes of individuation and ego development.

Although these researchers have claimed to take a systems approach to the
study of ego development, they have been criticized for this claim due to
their unidirectional data analyses and interpretation of results (see Hauser et
al., 1991; Minuchin, 1988). Although the interactions involved all family
members, the analysis was limited to dyadic comparisons.

More recently, researchers have used a systems perspective in examining
families in more complex ways. Hauser et al.'s (1991) work is systemic in
two ways. First, they employed sequential analysis to reveal dynamic aspects
of parent-child interaction. Second, they examined both parents' and
children's ego development. They found that both adolescent ego development and parent ego development predicted parents' enabling communication with the child. That is, adolescent level of ego development influences
enabling, versus constraining, patterns of interaction between parent and
child. However, like Grotevant and Cooper, Hauser et al. (1991) still sepa-
rated father and mother effects and failed to assess an overall family style.
They, too, only examined the effects of one dyad at a time.

However, the entire family system (not simply the parents' level of individuation or individuated communication with the child) serves to constrain
or enhance individuation and autonomy (Sameroff & Emde, 1989). Examining numerous factors, Sanders et al. (1989) concluded that the most impor-

tant element in the system is the reciprocal relationship of child and mother coercive and noncompliant patterns. The integral nature of family relationships is further revealed in recent work relating sibling relationships and marital discord. Dunn and Stocker (1989) observed that children exposed to marital discord often immediately react by aggressive and noncompliant play with siblings. As noted earlier, conflict among siblings can create conflict in the marriage, especially if the parents take different approaches to handling sibling conflicts (Cicirelli & Nussbaum, 1989).

Generalizations

Several conclusions can be drawn. First, mothers, and not fathers, are the persons who most often seek compliance from children. Second, there are some notable differences in strategies. Mothers appear to use induction more, whereas fathers rely on high-power-assertive strategies. Next, children apparently respond to mothers' and fathers' compliance attempts differently. Finally, the presence of fathers changes mother-child interaction, with the effect of increasing child compliance to maternal requests. Globally, the character of the parent-child relationship is related to compliance; compliance is related to the character of parent-child relationships.

The most consistent finding is that marital discord is linked to child noncompliance and problematic behavior. Conversely, marital harmony is linked to child compliance. Marital discord also relates to compliance strategies addressed toward children. A supportive spousal relationship may indirectly influence parental compliance attempts. Disagreement in the marital dyad in regard to disciplinary practices is related to problematic child behavior. Children's involvement in marital problems appears to promote problematic behavior. All of these factors theoretically interact.

Certain interaction styles between spouses, between parents and children, and between children characterize individuated relationships. Individuated relationships tend to co-occur with ego development. Similarly, the family system promotes or hinders individuation and autonomy (Honig, 1991).

Concerning siblings, parents tend to intervene in favor of the sibling they perceive to be the weakest. A corollary is that such biased interventions may increase noncompliance of both children and strain both sibling and parent-child relationships.

Finally, for those system researchers concerned with the relative weight of various systemic elements, it seems that the element most salient to child noncompliance is the mutually reflexive pattern of mother-child negative interactions. Several authors concur with a strong focus on dyadic interaction but call for more genuine systems research incorporating all family members to understand self-regulation in children and adolescents (Sameroff & Emde, 1989).

The conclusion offered from the limited number of systems studies is naturally tautological. Haley's (1959) first law of human nature postulates that families operate to maintain the system's status quo, whether this status quo is healthy or not. Accordingly, child compliance or noncompliance serves a function in maintaining the current family system. Child noncompliance is a consequence of a disturbed family and a disturbed family is a consequence of child noncompliance.

SELF-CONCEPT

Therapists employing family systems theory have focused attention on the relationship between family communication patterns and the formation of the child's self-esteem (e.g., Satir, 1983, 1988). Hence, interactional data on all husband-wife, parent-child, and child-child subsystems are relevant to understanding self-concept.

Mothers and Fathers in Interaction With Children and Self-Concept

Given the differences in mothers' and fathers' communication with their children noted earlier, a logical inference would be that mothers have more influence on children's self-concept than fathers. However, when both parents are studied, there is no consistent empirical support for either parent playing a more important role in the facilitation of high self-esteem or internal locus of control. Numerous studies find both parents play a significant role in the formation of self-concept. "It makes little or no difference for either boys or girls whether this parental quality [warmth] is exhibited by the mother or father or both" (Sears, 1970, p. 282). Adolescent self-esteem has been related equally to both maternal and paternal nurturance (e.g., Buri, Kirchener, & Walsh, 1987). Similarly, adolescents' perceptions of both parents' style were related to adolescents' self-esteem (Bartle, Anderson, & Sabatelli, 1989).

To understand such findings, consider the following. First, researchers' biases about the greater significance of mothering may be reflected in some studies. In other words, that mothers play a more formative role in the development of high self-esteem than fathers was the only conclusion possible until fathers were studied. Second, when mother and father interaction styles were compared, it was discovered that these styles are more similar than not in most aspects. Fathers and mothers express warmth to children, albeit in different ways (see Chapter 8). If warmth and sensitivity are the critical factors in the development of positive self-esteem, one should expect that the caregiver exhibiting these qualities with the child should be the most influential person, regardless of the caregiver's gender.

It has been hypothesized that a child constructs a "self" in conjunction with the roles of other family members (Satir, 1988). The notion is quite simple. From among the roles defined by family members' interactions, the child will adopt a role held by no other to differentiate self from others, even if it is negative (e.g., the problem child). Thus a child's self-concept may not be shaped by modeling significant others, rather it can be seen to develop as a complement to those persons.

Based on the general findings reported in this chapter and in Chapter 8, hypotheses could be generated as to how changes in parent-child interaction patterns due to the presence of the other parent might be related to self-concept. However, no studies that made such links were located in the literature.

The Marital Relationship and Self-Concept

Studies of marital quality demonstrate a consistent association; as interspousal conflict increases, children's self-esteem declines (Amato, 1986). Positive child self-esteem has been associated with both spouses' marital satisfaction (often indexed by low conflict) and with spousal perceptions of positive marital communication (Matteson, 1974).

Researchers adopting a systemic view report that high self-esteem in adolescents is related to a strong bond between the marital couple. Conversely, involving the child in marital problems often results in a stronger bond between a parent and child than between the spouses. Such inappropriate boundary spanning has been associated with lower child self-esteem (Bartle et al., 1989; Satir, 1983, 1988).

Recall that locus of control has been considered fundamental to self-esteem development. Children's internal locus of control is linked with parents' use of similar compliance strategies (Scheck et al., 1973). External locus of control is associated with dissimilar parental compliance-gaining styles. Children's external locus of control is even more likely to develop when one parent is inconsistent in his or her compliance strategies (Scheck et al., 1973).

Studies have related adult family members' conflict management to self-esteem in children. Mothers' communication style in marital conflicts has been related to daughters' self-esteem (Burman, John, & Margolin, 1987). Wives who consistently withdrew from conflicts with their spouses were more likely to have daughters with lower self-esteem.

As noted previously, many systems perspectives include individuals' beliefs and perceptions as important elements of the family system. There is good reason for this. Intriguingly, spouses' perceptions of marital quality appear to bias their parental perceptions of their children. For example, Margolin and co-workers (1988) found that parental beliefs about child competencies were related to child self-esteem; the specific parenting styles or observed parent-child interactions were not.

The perceptual frames of children may also play a role in the development of self-concept (Matteson, 1974). Adolescents with low self-esteem tend to perceive their parents' interactions as dysfunctional. In addition, low self-esteem children apparently interpret messages directed to them by parents as unsupportive and disconfirming. High self-esteem children reported the opposite. Matteson (1974) also reported that high self-esteem children's perceptions were more congruent with their parents' reports of their own marital communication. On the other hand, the perceptions of marital communication reported by low self-esteem children were incongruent with those of their parents.

Until this point, discussion has proceeded as if marital quality and related patterns of parenting communication cause the child's level of self-esteem. There is obviously a link of some sort. But O'Leary (1984) posed the following query: Might not such normal child problems such as low self-esteem negatively impact the parents' relationship with each other?

Limited evidence confirms such a possibility. Certain children are easier to parent, and easier parenting tends to be linked to a less stressful marriage. Children with low self-esteem and/or external locus of control may elicit a different style of parenting than their counterparts (see Chapter 7). Bartle et al. (1989) tentatively proposed that a high self-esteem child may also be easier to parent. This is related to a low stress marriage. In sum, differing levels of child self-esteem might prompt differing parental communication styles with the child, which may interact with the marital relationship. More globally, the innate temperaments of a child may impact parental interaction with the child.

The Sibling Subsystem and Self-Concept

It appears that children capitalize on their differences from siblings to individualize their personal sense of self (Bank & Kahn, 1982; Dunn & Stocker, 1989). That is, children strive to develop identities that differentiate them from their siblings. Supposedly, this helps children to avoid competing with their siblings in similar domains, especially for parental affection and attention. The proposal that differentiation from others is a primary means of forming self-concept is not new (see e.g., Erikson, 1959) and has received empirical support (see review by Schachter, 1982).

Tesser (1980) found empirical support for a model of sibling dynamics and self-esteem. Three points seem to be critical: (1) performance in a given area, (2) the importance of that area to the self-concepts of the siblings, and (3) the closeness of the relationship between the siblings. When there is a close relationship between two siblings and the domain is relevant to the self-worth of the lower-achieving sibling, that sibling is apt to engage in a comparison process, resulting in lowered self-esteem. Yet when the area of achievement of one sibling is not particularly relevant to the other sibling's self-definition, the less capable sibling actually experiences a rise in self-esteem. This effect is more likely to happen between siblings who feel close. A sibling may bask in the reflected glory of the more successful sibling, readjusting his or her self-esteem upward. Alternatively, when the domain is important a sibling can attempt to maintain or increase self-esteem by increasing his or her own performance level or by decreasing closeness with the "better" sibling. This, however, often creates friction between the sibling pair. Friction is most likely when a younger sibling outperforms an older one. Clearly, this illustrates an interesting interactive dynamic between sibling relationships and self-esteem.

Finally, consider the special case of twin siblings. Twins may have more difficulty developing individual self-concepts than do different-aged singletons. Twins are hypothesized to have quite diffuse individual boundaries, resulting in enmeshed relationships (Bank & Kahn, 1982). A relevant point here is that a lack of maternal involvement with twins has been speculated to be a factor related to this difficulty to form individualized identities (see "The Sibling Subsystem and Communicative Competencies" for an elaboration). For example, mothers report that they do not feel needed by their twin children as much as by their singletons because twins have each other (Betton & Koester, 1983). However, evidence relating mothers' perceptions to twin identity differentiation or even the notion that twins are enmeshed to damaging extremes remains anecdotal. Yet Stafford (1987) found twins were often addressed as a unit by their mothers, whereas two singleton siblings were addressed individually. Speculatively, twins' experiences of being talked to as one child, rather than as two children, could inhibit differentiation processes.

The Family as a System and Self-Concept

The dynamics of family systems with respect to child self-concept remain largely a mystery. It does appear that warm family systems are important for self-concept. Children with high self-esteem promote warmth from parents, and parental warmth promotes high self-esteem progressively and reflexively (Russell & Russell, 1989). Similarly, children's perceptions of family cohesion have been strongly associated with self-esteem (e.g., Kawash & Kozeluk, 1990).

Studies approximating a systems orientation are few and far between. Given the strong foothold of unidirectional beliefs regarding parental communication as formative of self-concept and the misapplications of symbolic interactionism that have often overlooked the child's role in the formation of self-concept, it is not surprising that few truly systemic studies on self-concept exist. However, studies reviewed from bidirectional orientations do reflect a shift away from a pure unidirectional stance (e.g., Demo et al., 1987). Furthermore, studies like those reviewed here reflect the fact that progress is being made.

Generalizations

Parental communication is seen as critical in the development of self-concept. This seems to hold both in regard to the communication between the spouses, and in the communication between the child and the parent. Also, self-esteem appears linked to the child's perceptions of parental communication.

Harmonious marriages and high self-esteem seem to correspond; unharmonious marriages and low self-esteem coincide. Strong marital coalitions also may foster high self-esteem. Alternatively, parentification may lower self-esteem. The use of inconsistent compliance strategies and/or inconsistent punishment are related to child external locus of control.

Beliefs and perceptions of both the marital dyad and the child in regard to the child's level of self-esteem may operate as worldviews. Such worldviews indirectly reinforce the child's low self-esteem and increase parenting stress and marital discord. The same pattern in reverse is speculated to hold for children with high self-esteem. In other words, although the inference might be drawn that marital discord and marital communication affect child self-esteem, this is not the implication intended. The opposite direction of influence is as easily extrapolated. It may be that children with low self-esteem influence parenting and the marriage. Children's self-concept and sibling relationships are intertwined. Finally, overall warm family environments may be the most important element in relationship to child self-concept. From a systems schema, children with positive images of themselves contribute to overall family warmth as well.

COMMUNICATION COMPETENCIES

There has been little systems research on language and communication, despite calls to the contrary (e.g., Schaffer, 1989). Biases in Western culture toward the primacy of the adult caregiver (i.e., mother) and the emphasis placed on parental input have maintained strong footholds on language and communication research. The effect has been to constrain systemic investigations into these phenomena.

The exclusion of the father is strikingly apparent in this area of study. Until very recently, research concerned with parental input into child language could virtually say, "Read *parental* as *maternal*." For example, Snow and Ferguson's (1977) classic book, *Talking With Children,* is about mothers talking with children; 15 years later, it appears that the scene has changed very little. What will be discussed is not the result of inquiries guided by systems theory; rather, it is an effort to fit available research into a systems-like frame.

Mothers and Fathers in Interaction
With Their Children and
Communicative Competencies

The overall styles of motherese as used by mothers and fathers are not drastically different, although some differences do occur in mother- versus father-to-child speech. Noting these differences between mothers' and fathers' speech styles, researchers like Lewis and Gregory (1987) have been interested in clarifying the relationship of sex of the parent and the type of speech used with the child. It appears that it is not the parent's gender, but the activities in which the parent and child are engaged that relate to differences in speech. "Different activities, by their very nature, call forth different modes of talking" (Lewis & Gregory, 1987, p. 215). Sex role expectations may be of some value in explaining differences in both mothers' and fathers' engagement in activities and hence differences in mothers' and fathers' speech. In general, mothers spend more time interacting with their children than fathers. In fact, "so great are the differences between the amounts of father-child and mother-child language that the vast bulk of motherese research simply assumed that fathers must have negligible impact upon the child's early language development" (Lewis & Gregory, 1987, p. 202). Fathers' minimal involvement with children has prompted interest in what fathers do, or don't do, when they are alone with children. Fathers apparently spend less of this time in focused interaction with the child than do mothers. For example, fathers watch more television and engage in more silent reading than do mothers when alone with their very young children (Belsky, Gilstrap, & Rovine, 1984).

Fathers seem to have more difficulty interacting with their children. Motherese and fatherese are thought to be similar (Lewis & Gregory, 1987), yet fathers do not adjust their language as dramatically in response to the child's cognitive level as mothers do (Kavanaugh & Jen, 1981). Fathers are also reported to be less responsive and to express less positive affect toward children (Tomasello, Conti-Ramsden, & Ewert, 1990). Breakdowns in father-child interactions occur more often than in mother-child interactions. Fathers appear to experience more difficulty understanding children's baby talk than do mothers. Fathers request clarification from children much more often than mothers do (Tomasello et al., 1990).

But perhaps fathers serve a special role for children's development of communication competencies. Fathers' failure to fine-tune their speech may force children to work harder to understand fathers' messages. Children's critical listening and comprehension skills may thus be encouraged (Lewis & Gregory, 1987). Also, children's experience in striving to make themselves understood by their fathers may be necessary practice for developing the skills required to make themselves understood in the outside world (Mannle & Tomasello, 1987). This claim is known as the *bridge* hypothesis (Gleason, 1975; see also Shatz & O'Reilly, 1990). Somewhat counterintuitively then, children's general communicative competencies may be aided by difficulties encountered in verbal exchanges with their fathers.

Father-child play may contribute to general communicative competencies. Fathers' games may serve a function similar to maternal preverbal routines in developing turn-taking skills and other regulatory functions. For example, fathers' games, although quite physical, are rhythmical and repetitive (Stern, 1974). Stern noted the regulative property of these games may encourage children's mutual coordination skills. Furthermore, such play interactions are characterized as joint involvement episodes (MacDonald & Parke, 1984). Hence father's play may serve similar functions as JIEs with mothers (see Chapter 7).

Beyond comparing mother-child and father-child communication, some researchers have explored parent-child dyadic interaction in the presence of both parents. Most research has focused on how the father influences mother-child interaction. Clarke-Stewart (1978), for example, found that mother-child interaction changed not only when the father was in the same room as the mother and child but also when the father was even at home. Her study has been consistently replicated; mothers talk less, respond less, and play less with the child when "Daddy makes three."

It is also interesting to note that when both parents are present, the child receives less direct stimulation from either parent compared with what the child receives when alone with a parent (see reviews by Belsky, 1984; Maccoby & Martin, 1983; Parke & Tinsley, 1987). The critical point of such findings is drawn with respect to the emphasis scholars have placed on focused one-to-one interaction in the development of language and communication skills. The decrease in direct parental involvement with the child due to the presence of another parent has generally been considered a less than optimal situation for learning language.

Some theorists, however, challenge this assumption. Simultaneous parental presence creates a situation in which there is likely to be as much, or even more talk in the environment compared with when one parent is alone with the child. Belsky (1984) proposed the addition of the second parent provides the child an opportunity to listen to marital (i.e., adult) interaction. Schaffer (1989) expanded this notion. The *overhearing* hypothesis predicts that "certain rules of language use can be learned most effectively through the child listening to conversations of others rather than through direct participation in such exchanges" (Schaffer, 1989, p. 15). Overhearing parent-parent conversations appears to help the child learn to listen and monitor conversations of others. In consequence, overhearing may be facilitative for skills children require for competent communication in contexts beyond the family.

The Marital Relationship and Communicative Competencies

Of interest here is couples' satisfaction and its relationship to mothers' and fathers' speech to children. Indeed, Pratt et al. (1992) found that marital satisfaction was correlated with elements of parental speech with children. Consistent relationships were found in studies of both conflictual and harmonious marital relationships between the quality of the marriage and the interaction with the child.

Marital discord is associated with negative message use by mothers (Stoneman et al., 1989a). For example, mothers experiencing high spousal conflict used more statements of disapproval and issued more commands (e.g., Jouriles et al., 1988). Dissatisfied fathers monologued and engaged in less equal turn taking with the child (Pratt et al., 1992). Both partners in dissatisfied marriages talked to their children with more complex speech than happily married parents (Brody, Pellegrini, & Sigel, 1986).

In contrast, a positive marital climate is related to maternal sensitivity (Lytton, 1980). Furthermore, Belsky and Volling (1987) found that good communication between the spouses, especially about the baby, positively related to fathers' increased stimulation of and responsiveness to the infant. Recall both stimulation and responsiveness have been found to be associated with language development.

The question is, "Do the different types of speech found in differing adult messages caused by the quality of the marriage correspond to children's communication competencies?" Perhaps. All of the speech features that have been evidenced in marriages less satisfying for the partners have been previously related to less communication competence in children (see Chapter 5). Harmonious marriages appear to co-occur with general communicative competencies in children (Santrock, Warshak, Lindbergh, & Meadows, 1982).

Moreover, systemic properties are evidenced. Children tend to respond in kind to negative messages used by mothers who are experiencing marital discord (e.g., Christensen et al., 1983). Also, when children are involved in marital disputes, children subsequently tend to be more withdrawn and uncommunicative both immediately and in the long-term, at least in the home environment (Johnston et al., 1987). The evidence combined suggests that interactions of maritally stressed parents and children become long-term cycles of negative communication. Regardless of the yet unclear impact of marital quality and related parental speech features on the communication competencies of the child, the level of "marital satisfaction seems to be expressed conversationally with children" (Pratt et al., 1992, p. 261). Clearly, even if speech characteristics are found to be unrelated to child communicative competence, this leaking of marital dissatisfaction via interaction with the child warrants further exploration by those interested in the dynamics of family talk.

Turning the tables, does child talk influence the marital relationship? There is little in the literature that directly addresses this question. Quite recently however, Belsky et al. (1991) reported that the amount of child talk directed toward the mother and the father seemed to play an influential role on martial satisfaction. The effect is particularly noticeable when parents are dissatisfied with the level of a child's participation in the family.

Research on adolescent self-disclosure to parents is also related to the question of how children's messages may affect marital relations. Parents frequently report that their adolescent children do not disclose to them as much as the parents would like (Olson et al., 1983). Topics taboo for parental ears include alcohol; boyfriends or girlfriends; feelings in general; and especially, self-esteem and insecurities, sex, and secrets of their friends (Zamanou, 1985). Invariably parents seem to be unable to comprehend why "We just can't communicate anymore." Teenagers generally report, "They just don't understand me" (Goswick & Jones, 1982).

These realities and perceptions seem to place strain on parent-child communication and, perhaps in turn, on the marital relationship (Williamson & Campbell, 1985). It should be pointed out, however, that such developmental stress is considered natural.

The Sibling Subsystem and Communicative Competencies

Firstborns have greater opportunity for exclusive interaction with parents than do second borns by the sheer fact that they are for a time only children (McCabe, 1989). After the birth of the second child, "the need for an adult to divide her [*sic*] attention brings about both quantitative and qualitative changes in the nature of interaction" (Schaffer, 1989, p. 12). Presumably, a base has been set for the firstborn child that he or she may draw on to further develop language and communicative skills. In important ways, communication changes for the firstborn after the birth of a second child. There are significant differences in the quality and quantity of interaction the second born experiences relative to the firstborn as well. The exact nature of the change in parent-child interaction is not clear, nor are the effects of such change. Yet it is indisputable that triadic interactions are quite different from dyadic ones.

Many studies have focused on the lack of maternal interaction with the younger child when both children are present. When both children are present, mothers talk less and respond less to the younger child than when alone. Moreover, the younger child initiates less talk with mother when the older sibling is present (e.g., Jones & Adamson, 1987). Given that mothers interact less with later-borns and that later-borns acquire language more slowly, some theorists conclude that direct one-to-one maternal speech must be salient for communication development (see Hoff-Ginsberg & Krueger, 1991; Tomasello & Mannle, 1985).

Still, some have found it is the older sibling who is left out. Dunn and Stocker (1989) summarized numerous studies to conclude firstborn children are relatively neglected when the second child is present. Mothers direct more verbalization and are more responsive to the younger child (see also Cicirelli, 1985). It should be noted, however, that researchers like Dunn are more concerned with sibling relationships in general than language and communication. Hence the conflict in findings is likely due to varied operationalizations (Dunn, 1985).

Most scholars of language and communication agree that it is the second child who lags behind communicatively, relative to the first child. Thus "there is some support for the position that later-borns suffer from inferior linguistic experiences compared to firstborns" (Dunn & Shatz, 1989, p. 400). The "reduction in access to semantically contingent speech associated with being a second born has been related to language delays in later-borns' language acquisition" (Snow et al., 1987, p. 77).

Another explanation for the slower rate of language development in second born children is that older siblings often serve as conversational partners for the child in place of the mother. Hoff-Ginsberg and Krueger (1991) found that although siblings somewhat adjusted language to younger siblings, siblings did not provide as many of the features thought to enhance language acquisition as did mothers. Hence it is maintained that "language development may proceed more slowly to the extent that the young child depends upon older children as conversational partners" (Hoff-Ginsberg & Krueger, 1991, p. 477; see also McCabe, 1989).

Children affect the caregivers' speech as well. The effects on caregivers of the simultaneous presence of multiple children is especially noticeable with twins. There is less interaction with twins than with two different age siblings. Interaction is also qualitatively different.

Singletons receive less direct maternal verbal interaction than twins (e.g., Stafford, 1987; Tomasello, Maulle, & Kruger, 1986). Furthermore, twins' mothers are less responsive to their children's verbalizations than mothers interacting with two singleton siblings (Stafford, 1987). Tomasello et al. (1986) found that joint interaction episodes were significantly shorter for twins than singletons. These studies are consistent in finding that the discourse of mothers with their twins was composed of more controlling (as opposed to conversational) discourse features than mother-singleton discourse. In sum, parents of twins have been found to give them less attention and to engage in less talk with them. In addition, when parents do interact with twins, the interaction is qualitatively different.

The importance of these observations relates to the fact that twins are consistently reported to be delayed in language acquisition (Day, 1932; Tomasello et al., 1986). Thus triadic contexts are speculated to be an impoverished language learning environment often brought about by the twin situation, which, in turn, changes the maternal mode of talk.

The belief that the presence of multiple children (whether twins, siblings, or peers) is a nonfaciliative language-learning environment has been challenged. Schaffer (1989) argued that diffusion of caregiver resources for children is not necessarily negative. Other children may contribute varied input models, numerous interaction opportunities, and therefore stimulating environments for children. These have been speculated to promote children's language and communication abilities.

Multiple children may foster social communication skills out of necessity. For example, Stafford (1986) found 2-year-old twins to be significantly more adept at sharing, turn taking, and negotiating play with each other compared with dyads of 2-year-old and 5-year-old siblings. Similar findings concerning social skills have been put forth by Dunn and Kendrick (1982b) in regard to siblings versus only children.

There is good evidence that siblings provide stimulating and varied interaction partners (Dunn & Shatz, 1989). For children beyond the very first stage of language acquisition, the fascination of older siblings is usually such that the likelihood of imitation is considerable. Such exposure and imitation likely enhances linguistic competencies (Dunn & Stocker, 1989). A facilitative effect for learning turn-taking skills and other social uses of communication have been posited (Dunn & Shatz, 1989). Finally, younger siblings' social communicative skills may be enhanced by striving to interact with older siblings. This may aid the younger child in learning to communicate with peers outside the family (Jones & Adamson, 1987). This position is similar to the bridge hypothesis concerning fathers.

The point is that the environment for simultaneous multiple children is different from an exclusive one. But is such an environment detrimental or enabling? Of course there is a third stance; it is neither. The presence of multiple children may induce a different order or sequence of learning language and communication. Thus it is neither enhancing nor hindering, it is simply different (see e.g., Jones & Adamson, 1987; Savic, 1980). Obviously, such a position has implications for the stages of language acquisition. The issue of siblings playing direct roles in enhancing sibling language acquisition and communication development, as opposed to simply being a deterrent, is in need of exploration. In any case, indisputably, children's language environments are composed in part by their siblings.

Family Systems and Child
Communication Competencies

The family system provides a vast array of opportunities for language and communication development. Even so, no studies examining the entire family system and child language and/or communication development from a purely systemic standpoint were located. McCabe (1989) has proposed a systemic model encompassing both child and parent influences on each other in the content and form of communication. Included are numerous parent, child, and environmental factors (e.g., family socioeconomic status). Although promising, McCabe's model remains just that—a model—at this time.

A child is bathed in a language environment; some language is directed toward the child, whereas some of it simply flows about the child (Horowitz & Sullivan, 1981). Even in the United States, where one-to-one interaction with the child is considered optimal, most speech occurs around the infant rather than directly to the infant. Phenomena such as the presence of two parents and/or siblings, indirect or overheard speech, and other systemic influences remain largely neglected in Western research.

Generalizations

The movement toward systems studies allows some generalizations to be forwarded. First, there is little strong evidence of sex differences in regard to mother versus father interaction with the children. Differences that have emerged are likely due to the typical role of the mother as primary caregiver and to the qualitative difference in activities mothers and fathers engage in with children. Mothers seem to focus more on verbal interaction, even in play, whereas fathers are more nonverbally play oriented. Both types of interaction have been associated with language and communication development, but usually in different realms.

The presence of both spouses changes the nature of individual parent-child interaction. It is not clear how such triadic conversations interplay with child language and communication development.

Generally, harmonious marriages provide more communicative-enhancing opportunities than conflictual ones. Furthermore, both parental conflict and involvement of children in parental disputes have ramifications on the child's communicative responses. A key finding is that the child withdraws from interaction. To the extent that such withdrawal limits exposure to, or practice in verbal interaction, it is possible that the development of communication skills may be impaired. As such, this is a special concern for communication scholars.

The adolescent's normal developmental of autonomy results in decreased self-disclosure to parents. This is related to a strain in the parent-child relationship and likely to strain in the marital relationship.

Mother-children communication is significantly different from mother-child communication. One stance is that triadic interactions are less communicatively enhancing for both children and especially the second born child. This stance has, however, been challenged.

In sum, in middle-class Western cultural settings, direct one-to-one focused interaction is the sine qua non of language and communication enhancement (see e.g., Wells, 1986). Nonetheless, it is clear from a systems view that such a stance is too narrow. Admittedly, some researchers have studied factors other than the child's mother in association with language (e.g., the presence of both parents, marital harmony, siblings). In addition, factors beyond the present scope have also sometimes been examined (e.g., socioeconomic status, cultural values, beliefs, and norms). Yet these are still generally studied in a unidirectional manner, as opposed to a systemic one. But there is good reason to move to systems perspectives. Evidence from cross-cultural studies suggests that children do learn language proficiently in cultures in which mutually exclusive and responsive parent-child interaction is not emphasized (Schieffelin & Ochs, 1986). As for the question raised previously, "Is this evidence of innate language devices or is the culture simply different so that elements other than the mother are more relevant to communication learning?" Systems perspectives merit the attention of social interactionists who emphasize the environment as an important role in language learning. Many paths to optimal communication development may exist, most of which have been overlooked to date by Western researchers (Dunn & Shatz, 1989).

SUMMARY AND CONCLUSIONS

This chapter has highlighted the implications of family systems for child consequences. Despite the number of generalizations offered, more systems research is needed (recall these generalizations are from quasi-systemic research at best).

The focal point here has been the nuclear family. Similar generalizations run through all three of the exemplar variables in regard to the nuclear family. However, research on communication competencies has been extended beyond the mother less often than work on self-regulation or self-concept. Therefore, systemic claims about the development of communicative competence are highly speculative.

Findings on sex differences are inconsistent across all three variables. Overall though, both mothers' and fathers' characteristics and relationships influence, and are influenced by, both sons' and daughters' level of compliance, self-concept, and language abilities.

The quality of the marital relationship is intertwined with all three socialization variables. Spousal conflict is associated with noncompliance, lower self-concept, and lower overall social communication competencies. Alternatively, more harmonious and satisfying marriages coincide with more optimal child achievements on all three variables.

Moreover, higher-quality marriages are connected to positive relationships between parents and children. This is not to imply that harmonious marriages are void of conflict. It is the duration, intensity, and the manner in which conflict is handled that seems to be relevant to child consequences. Inconsistency in the system, within the same parent, or between parents seems to coexist with child problems. Parental disagreement specifically about compliance attempts and discipline policies as well as inconsistent application of such policies coincide with less child compliance, lowered self-esteem, and child withdrawal from communication.

Perceptions and beliefs serve important functions in family relationships. The level of satisfaction in a marriage may color the parental image of the child. A negative distortion is proposed to be linked not only to child problems in virtually any domain but also to problematic parent-child interaction as well. Children seem to operate in a similar manner with respect to their worldviews of the family.

Permeable parent-child boundaries are found in dysfunctional systems; parentification is seldom manifested in functional families. Inappropriate coalition of a parent and a child corresponds with discordant marital relationships, lower child obedience, and lowered child self-esteem. Although less direct evidence is available, such dysfunctional systems likely do not provide optimal language learning environments either.

The presence of siblings in the family, children's relationships with siblings and parental interaction with children's siblings are intertwined with a child's self-esteem, difficulties in using fair compliance-gaining techniques, and unquestionably, with the language learning environment of the child.

An overall warm family system coincides with optimal levels of all the variables: a good self-concept, self-regulation, and language and communication skills. Due to the interdependence of families, children operating at such optimal levels contribute to maintenance of the warm environment. An overall warm environment interrelates with parent-child relationships, spousal relationships, and sibling relationships. Pessimistically, a negative family system can also be maintained. Systems characterized by negative patterns lacking warmth also act to maintain homeostasis through their interrelated consequences and antecedents as well. Such associations co-occur in mutually reinforcing and multidirectional ways. In conclusion, evidence to date supports family systems theories (Easterbrooks & Emde, 1988). In other words, there is general agreement concerning the notion of interdependence between marriage, parenting, parent-child relationships, and child consequences.

Relationships and factors outside of the immediate family should also be considered. For example, the construct of intergenerational transmission is considered crucial by many systems researchers. Basically, interactions in family of origin are proposed to impact the communicative behaviors and beliefs of children to the extent that when grown up, these people will replicate the communication patterns in their family of procreation. Support for intergenerational transmission has been mixed; even integrative reviews of studies on intergenerational transmission arrive at different conclusions (cf., Belsky & Pensky, 1988; Kaufman & Zigler, 1989). Obviously, this is salient to the controversy over the formativeness of early experience.

In closing, from a systems view, the birth of a child resounds through the entire system. The family is re-created, and the question is, "How do parents and their offspring create new modes of interaction, while maintaining the social and emotional bonds between them?" (Collins, 1990, p. 103).

How this creation is accomplished is not easily discerned from the current literature. Even when agreement exists that families need to change interaction patterns, notions of in what way(s) the family system should change and how to go about invoking change are seldom agreed on (Combrinck-Graham, 1990). For example, the pragmatic perspective focuses only on changing patterns of communicative behavior, whereas other perspectives encourage modification of individuals' and family belief systems, which in turn should result in the change in interaction patterns. Cappella (1987) has observed that our knowledge is insufficient as to whether intervention should be directed toward behavior or belief systems. A prime opportunity exists for scholars interested in the communication between parents and children for further theoretical development, research, and the integration of theory, research, and practice.

10

Epilogue: Conclusions, Concomitant Concerns, and Closing

INTRODUCTION

In closing, a quick recap of the unidirectional, bidirectional, and systems perspectives is given. A synthesis of major points of convergence follows. Next, potential concerns raised by the exclusion of certain topic areas are addressed. Limitations of work on parent-child and family communication are noted. In closing, the goals of this book are restated.

RECAP OF THE THREE FRAMEWORKS

Before the social mold era, the predominant force in social psychology was psychoanalytic theory. Although Freudian theory is unidirectional, primary focus was on the internal drives of the child, not the molding of the child by parents. Given the failure to find much empirical support for psychoanalytic tenets, attention was turned directly to the inquiry of how the characteristics of the parent or parenting impacted the child. The basic question asked from such a social mold approach is, "How does the communication of the parent affect the child?" This approach has functioned as the cornerstone of research for the past several decades.

Bidirectional models were spurred by widespread disillusionment with the view of the child as merely an outcome variable. After decades of work, few generalizations could be forwarded in answer to the unidirectional researchers' question (Clarke-Stewart, 1988). Bidirectional researchers ask, "Who influences whom?" In essence, recognition of children's roles in their own socialization and development re-emerged as well as awareness that children socialize their parents. Unquestionably, adults react to children. The decade of the 1980s was characterized by the recognition of reciprocal causality between children and parents (Belsky, 1990).

Systemic models emerged in the study of parent-child interaction as researchers began to consider catalysts of child socialization other than the mother. At last, the family was considered as more than two distinct dyads. The fundamental premise is that parents, children, and all other systemic components jointly affect each other. The central question is, "What are the patterns or cycles of interactions?" Hence, systemic models shift from linear to circular thinking, with special attention given to process. Furthermore, child development researchers have used systemic approaches to address the question, "What are the consequences of these family communication patterns for the child?" The answer is where one finds a disturbed child, one finds a disturbed marriage, and vice versa. In the 1990s systems models are taking hold.

CONVERGING CONCLUSIONS

Scholars using all three frameworks express interest in socialization processes and the consequences for the child. The selection of the exemplar variables was driven, in part, by their foundational roles in socialization. Hence, the first point of convergence is that scholars concerned with communication between children and parents have as an implicit or explicit focal point the socialization of the child, regardless of the overarching perspective.

It should be evident by now that many of the same issues concerning the nature of children and the role of parenting have been debated for centuries. Nonetheless, even the most fundamental debates, like that of nature versus nurture, have not been resolved. Furthermore, resolution any time soon is unlikely.

Third, quite different styles or modes of parent-child interaction may lead to optimal outcomes for the child. The Hindus have a saying that "all roads that lead to God are good." This philosophy reflects the findings in regard to parent-child communication thus far and illuminates a path for future research. There are numerous routes a parent and child may take; as of yet it remains unclear that any single route is universally best or even best in given contexts. Furthermore, it seems doubtful that any one ideal way to parent will be unearthed soon. If one puts any credence in individual temperaments, the active nature of the child, and so forth, it seems unlikely that "10 easy steps to communication with your child" will be found. Still, not all researchers give credence to factors such as temperament or active natures (e.g., behaviorism) and do look for this Holy Grail.

Undaunted, social scientists continue on their quests striving to account for the most variance possible. This does not mean that social scientists believe that lawlike principles necessarily will be discovered. Rather, most take interactionist vantage points, exploring, for example, the combined effects of nature and nurture, the active will of the child, child behaviors, and parental control. The only generalization, tentatively offered, is that in all the variables studied, from all frames and theories, the expression of interpersonal warmth and responsiveness appears beneficial to the child and the family. This seems to hold regardless of mode of study, theory, or concept (e.g., nurturance, support, acceptance, and confirmation). It is hoped that as interdisciplinary integration occurs, more robust generalizations will be ascertained.

The crux of this book has been on communication between parents and children. Yet it is true that such interaction takes place in the context of the entire family environment. Given this, interpersonal communication within the family is the obvious place to begin to understand socialization in general. The family is the child's first introduction to self and to interpersonal relationships (Goodman, 1985b). Hence, as a final point of convergence, all three frameworks, in some way or another, concur that the family is the Mesopotamia in which self and relationships are first formed.

CONCERNS AND CAUTIONS

The exclusion of several topic areas as distinct domains of inquiry could lead the reader to draw unintended inferences. In particular, we refer to nonverbal behavior, emotions, co-cultures and alternative family structures, and sex differences research.

Nonverbal behavior was not specifically considered. Hence, one could incorrectly assume that we consider nonverbal behavior an unimportant aspect of the communication between children and adults. When nonverbal behavior was mentioned, it was within the context of prelinguistic interactions: turn-taking routines, JIEs, and infant-parent synchronization. Nonverbal communication is part of the development of family relationships that, unfortunately, is often overlooked in parent-child interaction beyond the prelinguistic stage (but see Callan & Noller, 1986, and Noller & Callan, 1989, on nonverbal communication between adolescents and parents). It is certainly not as if the moment the child shifts to verbal speech that nonverbal cues became superfluous. Numerous studies document the development of nonverbal cues in children as well as the role of nonverbal behavior in parent-child interaction (see e.g., Feldman, 1982, for a review). Another facet of parent-child communication not singled out for inspection is that of emotions. In no way should the reader infer that emotions are unimportant for understanding interaction. The role of emotions in interpersonal interaction is one of the most overlooked aspects of communication within relationships (Bowers, Metts, & Duncanson, 1985). Obviously, parent-child bonds are easily seen as multifaceted constructs that include emotions. Because the topic of emotions has not been specifically discussed in this book, one could infer that parents and children engage in only rational, nonemotional communication with each other. In other words, the supposition could be drawn that parents or children rationally decide to be warm, logically decide to adapt to stress, and so forth. Contrariwise, the notion that interactions are nonrational, illogical, and are often driven by emotional responses is certainly plausible. Indeed, it has been argued that emotions are central to all human behavior and cognition (Lazarus, 1991).

We have said little about Western alternative family structures or co-cultures. No bias is intended. Our purpose has been to offer the most robust conclusions of the extant research. The summaries simply reflect the fact that to date researchers have primarily selected as their subjects white middle-class traditional families. Two intertwined topics are present. One is family structure and alternative forms to the two-parent nuclear family (e.g., divorced, single-parent, step-, and blended families). The other is co-cultures, which, of course, also exhibit variation in family structures. Biases are similar in regard to these alternatives to the mainstream in that any variation from this mainstream has historically been considered suboptimal.

In regard to nonwhites and other co-cultures, research has been dominated by a deficit model as opposed to a model of difference, otherwise known as *pluralistic* models. Debates over which model constitutes a better representation of co-cultures have not been that far in the past (see e.g., Blank, 1982). The reality of positive aspects of parent-child interaction in any culture other than the white middle-class one has been largely overlooked, even though social scientists (at least those of a positivistic bent) claim to be objective and value neutral. There are numerous problems when researchers implicitly impose the values of such families on alternative family structures or families of various co-cultures. Some conclude that the traditional nuclear white middle-class American family remains the standard against which other family forms are judged (see e.g., Ganong, Coleman, & Mapes, 1990). Consider this introductory sentence to a recent article: "Children raised by single parents or in stepfamilies are disadvantaged on several indicators, compared to children raised by both original parents" (Thomson, McLanahan, & Curtin, 1992). Attitudes held by many clinicians and researchers that an "intact family structure is an essential criterion for the healthy development and functioning of members . . . has demoralized many single-parent family members" (Phelps, Huntley, Valdes, & Tompson, 1987, p. 158). The same basic idea holds true for co-cultural family members. Such individuals often internalize the values of the white middle-class ideal and evaluate their own families as lacking (Adams, 1988).

Considering any variation from the traditional nuclear white middle-class family as different, rather than deviant, is relatively new. Efforts have been made to discredit the "given fact" of difference as dysfunctional. Various models of family functioning are being developed based on features of parent-child interaction within given cultures or structures. Relatively recently, different structures and co-cultural interaction patterns have received acknowledgment (see McKenry, Everett, Ramseur, & Carter, 1989). There is now, supposedly, "recognition and acceptance of the diversity of American families and their lifestyles" (Berardo, 1990, p. 817). Despite scholarly awareness and an emerging body of literature on the nonwhite, the nonmiddle class, and structures other than the traditional form, the literature base at this point in time is not extensive enough to allow the derivation of strong generalizations (Berardo, 1990).

However, are researchers really viewing alternative family cultures and structures as alternative? Or is the long-held bias that deviations are not healthy still present? Recall the 1992 quote above concerning the advantage of the intact nuclear family. Hence, despite the scholarly recognition of this issue by some, it remains questionable as to the extent to which it is being embraced.

Furthermore, a word of caution may be in order. The reader should not leap to the conclusion that within-group variance is not present. It would be extremely biased to see all families in co-cultural groups as the same. Diversity exists within any group, traditional white middle-class families included.

In addition, intercultural concerns were mentioned only occasionally. Even if there were agreement as to what prompts optimal development in Western white middle-class culture, these conclusions in all likelihood would not generalize to other cultural groups. "We must be careful in the application of models derived in one culture when attempting to export them to others. What will prove to be universal to the species will be determined by evidence yet to be collected and theories yet to be created" (Robinson &

Giles, 1990b, p. 4). Recall Bronfenbrenner's model includes culture as a prime influence on interaction. Investigations of cultural and structural differences represent third-order questions (Cappella, 1987). To what extent are interactions influenced by culture and society at large? Furthermore, to what extent does interpersonal interaction shape culture? Given our focus on second-order questions of interactions, these queries have not been addressed herein (but see Wertsch, 1985).

Finally, although differences and similarities in mother versus father interaction were discussed at length, recall the conclusion was that more similarities than differences exist. Little attention was devoted to potential differences in children due to sex of parent, sex of child, or to sex of parent by sex of child interaction effects. This is because caution is advised in conducting and interpreting sex differences research. Most studies employing biological sex are actually exploring typical gender-linked roles. That is, roles and situations associated with roles may play more of a part in parent-child interaction than biological sex of the parent or the child. Examining only biological sex confounds potential sex differences with potential role-linked differences. Also, sex role expectations of the researcher often cloud research designs and the interpretations of findings. Present research designs and biases often lead to conflicting findings and muddling of sex differences and role differences.

Fitzpatrick's (1991) stance on the interplay between biological sex and socialization is relevant here. In weaving her own arguments with evidence provided by others, she asserted that differences between the sexes are not simply creations of socialization. There are obviously biological differences between the sexes. Yet, sociobiologists who adopt unidirectional perspectives stressing biological differences to the exclusion of the numerous facets of socialization are admonished. "Many feminists [who] categorically object to any theory arguing for a biological component in human behavior" (Fitzpatrick, 1991, p. 72) are equally criticized. Fitzpatrick urged scholars to keep open minds to the integration of biological and social variables: "As more knowledge becomes available concerning the neurological, hormonal, and physiological differences between males and females, theories of marriage and the family will suffer if they fail to include these factors" (p. 72).

LIMITATIONS

There are many limitations of parent-child research across frameworks and disciplines. Sadly, many handicaps are beginning to sound trite despite their importance. This is perhaps due to the frequency with which such limitations are pointed out and the infrequency with which they are actually taken into account. The purpose here is to portray plights that plague parent-child interaction research as well as inhibit interdisciplinary collaboration. Attention is centered on numerous problems, including (1) the role of theory, (2) methodology and methods, (3) studying interaction, (4) longitudinal studies, (5) developmental concerns, (6) conceptual ambiguity, and (7) the lack of integration of theory and research.

Poole and McPhee (1985) discussed theory as the supposed driving force in both methodology and method. Theory, methodology, and methods are intertwined constructs, and *theory* is the god-term of social science (Cappella, 1977). Thus theory determines method; it indicates what data are appropriate and places limits on how these data may be best obtained. In other words, "an emphasis on method apart from theory is misguided and may be downright misleading" (Poole & McPhee, 1985, p. 101). Accordingly, methods employed without clear theoretical guidance are condemned as mindless research. The truth in this stance is that often whatever methods are in vogue tend to be used, even if not the best at hand. Without considering the method, question, and theory link, and given the availability of statistical packages, the danger is "the substitution of method for thinking" (Poole & McPhee, 1985, p. 160).

For all the importance of theory, at the outset we observed that theories have apparently run rampant. According to some, the proliferation of theoretical positions and issues has been "based upon weak methodology and come to premature, and probably incorrect conclusions" (Moerk, 1992, p. 1). A great deal of vigorous theoretical and ideological discourse has taken place in the last few decades (Moerk, 1992). This discourse has illuminated at least one obstacle to collaborative effort: "Different researchers accept different criteria for proof of the validity of an inference, and different theorists accept different criteria for the adequacy of a theory" (Waterhouse, 1986, p. 155).

Nonetheless, it is not necessarily problematic that numerous views thrive at this point in time. Some contend it is the lack of dialogue between scholars of different positions that is problematic:

> Although competition between paradigms may be healthy and may stimulate research, problems arise when proponents of different paradigms are unable to communicate effectively with each other or when each group insists that only its view is correct. Divergent paradigms offer a splendid opportunity for people to talk past each other, even about the most obvious things. . . . Further divisions of a discipline, or a subject area, such as parent-child interaction across disciplines and across paradigms within disciplines makes the accumulation of

research findings difficult, for there is no common language for discussing research findings. (Bailey, 1987, p. 26)

Another interesting standpoint has been proposed. Regardless of method or theory, data are sometimes congruent, sometimes conflicting. At times, the same data have been reinterpreted and reanalyzed from several different theoretical perspectives. It simply depends on how good one's power of persuasion is to convince the reader of "proof" of a particular theory (Bohannon & Warren-Leubecker, 1989; see also Bochner, 1985). Perhaps this is the reason that some researchers have chosen to focus more on problems than to take theoretical stances.

Method is not the same as methodology, although they are often used interchangeably. *Methodology* refers to the philosophy of the research processes: the assumptions and values of the rationale, the method, the data collected and the interpretation, the conclusions drawn, and so forth. One is generally taught that certain paradigmatic beliefs (i.e., ideologies) guide methodology, which then guides the selection of method. *Method* is the technique, tool, or mode of data collection employed. Despite the reason scholars make choices—whether due to methodology, theoretical beliefs, practicality, or trendiness—each method has advantages and drawbacks.

All too often the supremacy of one method over another is touted. Logical positivist traditions aside, objectivity is a myth. Every method is subject to some problems with reliability, validity, generalizability, subjectivity, and the like. "That is a reason for need of a variety of methods, not a reason for rejecting all but one technique!" (Robinson & Giles, 1990a, p. 585). Methods pitted against methods

> have been axes of dispute in the last 20 years, but perhaps our academic culture is becoming better informed and perhaps our . . . courses are now beginning to encourage a diversity of approaches to problems, thereby reducing the time wasted in sterile argumentation. (Robinson & Giles, 1990a, p. 585)

Indeed, fastidious adherence to a particular stance results in a tendency to overlook the meaning of the issues under study (Miller, 1990).

Deciding on the best method is not an easy task. As Huston and Robins (1982) noted, there are many practical considerations. Human, financial, and temporal resources often limit researchers to methods that they are highly aware are not ideal. Often awareness of problems with a choice of method can correct some of the problems due to selection based, in part, on expediency. A more grave concern is an unawareness of the limitations of various methods (Huston & Robins, 1982).

A common problem in many studies of parent-child interaction is that interaction is not studied. That is, research on communication frequently relies on self-report questionnaire data instead of observational interactive data. This is appropriate when subjects' perceptions of communication are desired data to study questions concerning beliefs, perceptions, temperament, and so forth that clearly are related to interaction. But too often claims are made concerning the communication behavior between parents and children, when in reality the *perceptions* of said communication have been examined. "Most importantly, perhaps, we believe that investigators often have inappropriately used the argument that the actor's perception is what ultimately matters when their real interest has been in what people do" (Huston & Robins, 1982, p. 907).

But what constitutes data about interaction? Writing about talk and conversation generally, McLaughlin (1984) outlined primary sources of data. These are naturalistic conversations in everyday, ordinary settings; natural speech obtained in laboratory or other controlled environments; samples of specific speech behaviors that are elicited as the result of a direct request from the researcher; samples of spoken discourse taken from literary and/or historical sources; and examples of spoken interaction constructed by the researcher. This laundry list illustrates that there is little consensus as to which data are most appropriate for studying interaction (McLaughlin, 1984).

Intriguingly, scholars even disagree as to whether or not diversity is useful. Spirited battles are waged over the superiority of one approach over another. There is a debate over which of the two general types of analysis, conversational analysis or discourse analysis, yields better results. Generally, discourse analysis aims to assess how conversation functions, whereas conversational analysis is more focused on structure (J. Edwards, 1990). (And this is not even to mention other approaches such as content analysis and time series analysis.)

While some are engaged in such disputes, others seem content with multiple methods of interaction analysis; all methods complement all others. Most language and developmental scholars are "forgivingly catholic in their own choice of methods and in their acceptance of others' methods" (Conti-Ramsden & Snow, 1990, p. 4). Unlike those engaged in polemic debates, Conti-Ramsden and Snow (1990) "stress the importance . . . of maintaining an openness to a variety of research methods, of disciplinary inclinations, and intellectual traditions" (p. 6). They call for a new era characterized by collaboration between disciplines and researchers around the world from various intellectual heritages and various methodologies. The key lies in "maintaining an openness to a variety of research methods, of disciplinary inclinations, and of intellectual traditions" (p. 6).

The general dearth of longitudinal studies is problematic. Cross-sectional studies are often used in place of longitudinal studies. Longitudinal studies are difficult, expensive, and have high dropout rates. Yet they are advantageous in that changes over time truly can be examined. Cross-sectional studies are more practical. However, then other problems arise, such as cohort effects. When samples are studied at only one point in time, cross-sectionally, developmental processes are difficult to ascertain. Issues such as the interactive nature of children's, parents', and the family's life cycles in regard to the changing nature of interpersonal interaction and interpersonal relationships are likewise difficult to capture via cross-sectional designs. Such designs also do not allow assessment of communicative changes, or lack thereof, within the family system across time. For example, homeostasis could not be assessed. Also, cross-sectional studies provide little evidence of causal relationships within the family system.

Developmental issues must be brought into research for the simple reason that children change. Often, in developmental studies, chronological age and level of development have been confounded. In addition, long time intervals between data collection are likely to miss small incremental changes in the child. Characteristic interactions at one point in the child's development may be different from another. Moreover, family events such as conflict or parental separation may have different consequences at different times in the child's life (Hinde & Stevenson-Hinde, 1988a).

Not only are there problems and debates over methods but there are hindrances to collaboration in the conceptual realm. These concern a lack of clarity in constructs as well as ambiguity in terms, especially when used differently across disciplines. Clearly operationalizations will suffer when the constructs themselves are soft, fuzzy, and/or muddled. Recall from the Overview the difficulty in even defining *communication*. The point was also made when discussing self-concept and self-control. Similarly, difficulty persists in translating many theoretical and/or clinical concepts into research designs. Recall the various operationalizations of love withdrawal. Systemic concepts are especially problematic. To conceptualize and measure the joint influence of parents or a general family style are somewhat mind-boggling. In other words, the unit of analysis is a major concern. Although statistical advances are being made, such tools generally have cumbersome problems and complexities and still fail to capture the essence of the entire system (see e.g., Kenny, 1988; Montgomery & Duck, 1991).

Blame for the slow progress in comprehending systems does not rest entirely with the lack of tools. Rather what is needed is more researchers dedicated to tackling longitudinal, time-consuming observational analysis, and to learning more complex statistical procedures necessary to capture interactive communication dynamics.

A last limitation that plagues most fields is the lack of integration of theory and research. Schumm (1982) described how in many disciplines students are educated about various components separately. Theory, measurement and design, statistical procedures, and application are taught as isolated features. Seldom is the integration of these components taught or practiced.

CLOSING

Communication, it seems, should concentrate on social interaction between persons and this should lead to appropriate conceptualizations and operationalizations. Just mentioned was the unit of analysis as a major statistical concern. However, the unit of analysis is perhaps more importantly a conceptual concern. Communication studies cannot rely on the individual as the unit of analysis. Lannamann (1991) built the argument, however, that the ideology of individualism has taken root. By continuing to select one person as the unit of analysis, scant attention has been given to the reciprocal processes of communication. Hence, although interaction by definition should look beyond the individual, communication research has too frequently rested its sights on individuals rather than on interaction between individuals.

Not all communication research employs only individual level analyses, but certainly too much does. In addition, communication scholars seldom explore issues of parent-child interaction, family interaction, or for that matter communication concerning anyone under the age of 18. Obviously, no discipline is without its weak spots. For example, sociologists have tended to study only the husband and wife pair of the family. Language scholars have emphasized the mother-child dyad, to the relative exclusion of the father. Psychologists and psycholinguists generally narrow their scope to the individual to the neglect of interactive processes between individuals. But in recent years many fields have also made significant progress in moving beyond their traditional limits.

Nevertheless, a lack of collaborative dialogue is prevalent. It is no wonder that "knowledge of a truly cumulative nature is scarce" (Rommetveit, 1988, p. ix). Furthermore, "no one current theoretical approach is likely to prove adequate . . . [there is] value of theoretical eclecticism. A multimethod approach, with measures, including 'outcome' measures relevant to the problem at hand, should lead to more complete understanding than any single line of attack" (Hinde & Stevenson-Hinde, 1988a, p. 383). Thus the goal of this book has not been merely to summarize work on the exemplar variables but rather to capture the essence of the diverse orientations, issues, and results in regard to interpersonal interactions between parents and children. Desire has been in prompting interest in this area of inquiry in dire need of theoretical and interdisciplinary integration.

In closing, we repeat Huston and Robins (1982): "Our goal has been to provide a general conceptual context that would serve to encourage communication among researchers trained in diverse disciplines" (p. 923). This has been our goal too. The ultimate objective of this book is to serve as a heuristic device for interdisciplinary collaboration into what is a critical area begging for attention by those interested in communication processes.

It seems likely that the reader will conclude, as we have, that the study of parent-child communication is rich with potential. Enhanced understanding of the interaction between parents and children would benefit from interdisciplinary integration and theoretical development; collective contributions from various methodologies; and increased dialogue between theoreticians, researchers, and practitioners. In sum, the subject of parent-child communication is ripe for the application of communication perspectives, regardless of discipline.

References

Adams, B. N. (1988). Fifty years of family research: What does it mean? *Journal of Marriage and the Family, 50,* 5-17.

Adler, A. (1927). *Understanding human nature* (W. B. Wolfe, Trans.). Garden City, NY: Garden City.

Adler, A. (1955). *The practice and theory of individual psychology* (P. Radin, Trans.). London: Routledge & Kegan Paul. (Original work published 1923)

Adler, F., & Furman, W. (1988). A model for children's relationships and relationship dysfunction. In S. W. Duck (Ed.), *Handbook of personal relationships* (pp. 211-232). New York: Wiley.

Ainsworth, M. D. S., & Bell, S. M. (1970). Attachment, exploration, and separation: Illustrated by the behavior of one-year-olds in a strange situation. *Child Development, 41,* 49-67.

Akhtar, N., Dunham, F., & Dunham, P. J. (1991). Directive interactions and early vocabulary development: The role of joint attentional focus. *Journal of Child Language, 18,* 41-49.

Allport, G. W. (1961). *Pattern and growth in personality.* New York: Holt, Rinehart, & Winston.

Amato, P. R. (1986). Marital conflict, the parent-child relationship and child self-esteem. *Family Relations, 35,* 403-410.

Anastasi, A. (1958). Heredity, environment, and the question "how?" *Psychological Review, 65,* 197-208.

Andersen, E. S. (1990). *Speaking with style: The sociolinguistic skills of children.* New York: Routledge.

Anderson, B. J., Vietze, P., & Dokecki, P. R. (1977). Reciprocity in vocal interactions of mothers and infants. *Child Development, 48,* 1676-1681.

Anderson, K. A., & King, H. E. (1974). Time-out reconsidered. *Instructional Psychology, 1,* 11-17.

Anderson, K. E., Lytton, H., & Romney, D. M. (1986). Mothers' interactions with normal and conduct-disorded boys: Who affects whom? *Developmental Psychology, 22,* 604-609.

Applegate, J. L. (1990). Constructs and communication: A pragmatic integration. In G. J. Neimeyer and R. A. Neimeyer (Eds.), *Advances in personal construct psychology* (Vol. 1, pp. 203-230). Greenwich, CT: JAI.

Applegate, J. L., Burke, J. A., Burleson, B. R., Delia, J. G., & Kline, S. L. (1985). Reflection-enhancing parental communication. In I. E. Sigel (Ed.), *Parental belief systems: The psychological consequences for children* (pp. 107-142). Hillsdale, NJ: Erlbaum.

Applegate, J. L., Burleson, B. R., & Delia, J. G. (1992). Reflection-enhancing parenting as an antecedent to children's social-cognitive and communicative development. In I. E. Sigel, A. V. McGillicuddy-DeLisi, & J. J. Goodnow (Eds.), *Parental belief systems: The psychological consequences for children* (Vol. 2., pp. 3-39). Hillsdale, NJ: Erlbaum.

Aronfreed, J. (1969). The concept of internalization. In D. A. Goslin (Ed.), *Handbook of socialization theory and research* (pp. 263-322). Chicago: Rand McNally.

Bachman, J. B. (1970). *Youth in transition: Vol. 2. The impact of family background and intelligence on tenth grade boys.* Ann Arbor, MI: Survey Research Center, Institute for Social Research.

Bailey, K. D. (1987). *Methods of social science research* (3rd ed.). New York: Free Press.

Baldwin, A. L. (1948). Socialization and the parent-child relationship. *Child Development, 19,* 127-136.

Baldwin, J. D. (1986). *George Herbert Mead: A unifying theory for sociology.* Beverly Hills, CA: Sage.

Bandura, A. (1969). Social learning theory of identificatory processes. In D. A. Goslin (Ed.), *Handbook of socialization theory and research* (pp. 216-262). Chicago: Rand McNally.

Bandura, A. (1977). *Social learning theory.* Englewood Cliffs, NJ: Prentice-Hall.

Bandura, A. (1978). The self system in reciprocal determinism. *American Psychologist, 33,* 344-358.

Bandura, A. (1986). *Social foundations of thought and action: A social cognitive theory.* Englewood Cliffs, NJ: Prentice-Hall.

Bank, S. P., & Kahn, M. D. (1982). *The sibling bond.* New York: Basic.

Barrett, M., Harris, M., & Chasin, J. (1991). Early lexical development and maternal speech: A comparison of children's initial and subsequent uses of words. *Journal of Child Language, 18,* 21-40.

Bartle, S. E., Anderson, S. A., & Sabatelli, R. M. (1989). A model of parenting style, adolescent individuation and adolescent self-esteem: Preliminary findings. *Journal of Adolescent Research, 4,* 283-298.

Bateson, G., Jackson, D. D., Haley, J., & Weakland, J. (1956). Toward a theory of schizophrenia. *Behavioral Science, 1,* 251-264.

Baumrind, D. (1966). Effects of authoritative parental control on child behavior. *Child Development, 37,* 887-907.

Baumrind, D. (1967). Child care practices anteceding three patterns of preschool behavior. *Genetic Psychology Monographs, 75,* 43-83.

Baumrind, D. (1968). Authoritarian vs. authoritative parental control. *Adolescence, 3,* 255-272.

Baumrind, D. (1971). Current patterns of parental authority. *Developmental Psychology Monographs, 4,* 1-101.

Baumrind, D. (1980). New directions in socialization research. *American Psychologist, 35,* 639-652.

Baumrind, D. (1991). The influence of parenting style on adolescent competence and substance use. *Journal of Early Adolescence, 11,* 56-95.

Baumrind, D., & Black, A. E. (1967). Socialization practices associated with dimensions of competence in preschool boys and girls. *Child Development, 38,* 291-327.

Bavelas, J. B., & Segal, L. (1982). Family systems theory: Background and implications. *Journal of Communication, 32,* 99-107.

Becker, W. C. (1964). Consequences of different kinds of parental discipline. In M. L. Hoffman & L. W. Hoffman (Eds.), Review of child development research (Vol. 1, pp. 169-208). New York: Russell Sage Foundation.

Bell, R. Q. (1968). A reinterpretation of the direction of effects in studies of socialization. Psychological Review, 75, 81-95.

Bell, R. Q., & Chapman, M. (1986). Child effects in studies using experimental or brief longitudinal approaches to socialization. Developmental Psychology, 22, 595-603.

Bell, R. Q., & Harper, L. V. (1977). Child effects on adults. Hillsdale, NJ: Erlbaum.

Belsky, J. (1979). Mother-father-infant interaction: A naturalistic observational study. Developmental Psychology, 15, 601-607.

Belsky, J. (1981). Early human experience: A family perspective. Developmental Psychology, 17, 3-23.

Belsky, J. (1984). The determinants of parenting: A process model. Child Development, 55, 83-96.

Belsky, J. (1990). Parental and nonparental child care and children's socioemotional development: A decade in review. Journal of Marriage and the Family, 53, 885-903.

Belsky, J., Gilstrap, B., & Rovine, M. (1984). The Pennsylvania Infant Development Project, I: Stability and change in mother-infant and father-infant interaction in a family setting at one, three and nine months. Child Development, 55, 692-795.

Belsky, J., & Pensky, E. (1988). Developmental history, personality, and family relationships: Toward an emergent family system. In R. A. Hinde & J. Stevenson-Hinde (Eds.), Relationships within families: Mutual influences (pp. 193-217). New York: Oxford University Press.

Belsky, J., & Rovine, M. (1990). Patterns of marital change across the transition to parenthood: Pregnancy to three years postpartum. Journal of Marriage and the Family, 52, 5-19.

Belsky, J., Rovine, M., & Fish, M. (1989). The developing family system. In M. R. Gunnar (Ed.), Minnesota symposia on child psychology: Vol. 22. Systems and development (pp. 119-166). Hillsdale, NJ: Erlbaum.

Belsky, J., & Volling, B. (1987). Mothering, fathering, and marital interaction in the family triad during early infancy: Exploring family system's processes. In P. W. Berman & F. A. Pedersen (Eds.), Men's transition to parenthood: Longitudinal studies of early family experience (pp. 37-63). Hillsdale, NJ: Erlbaum.

Belsky, J., & Vondra, J. (1985). Characteristics, consequences, and determinants of parenting. In L. L'Abate (Ed.), Handbook of family psychology and therapy (Vol. 1, pp. 523-556). Homewood, IL: Dorsey.

Belsky, J., Youngblade, L., Rovine, M., & Volling, B. (1991). Patterns of marital change and parent-child interaction. Journal of Marriage and Family, 53, 487-498.

Berardo, F. M. (1990). Trends and directions in family research in the 1980s. Journal of Marriage and the Family, 52, 809-817.

Berger, C. R. (1973). Task performance and attributional communication as determinants of interpersonal attraction. Speech Monographs, 40, 280-286.

Berger, C. R. (1985). Social power and interpersonal communication. In M. L. Knapp & G. R. Miller (Eds.), Handbook of interpersonal communication (pp. 439-499). Beverly Hills, CA: Sage.

Berger, C. R., & Metzger, N. J. (1984). The functions of human communication in developing, maintaining, and altering self-image. In C. C. Arnold & J. W. Bowers (Eds.), Handbook of rhetorical and communication theory (pp. 273-337). Boston: Allyn & Bacon.

Berghout-Austin, A. M., & Peery, J. C. (1983). Analysis of adult-neonate synchrony during speech and nonspeech. Perceptual and Motor Skills, 57, 455-459.

Berk, L. E. (1991). *Child development* (2nd ed.). Boston: Allyn & Bacon.

Bernstein, B. (1974). *Class, codes, and control: Theoretical studies toward a sociology of language* (rev. ed.). New York: Schocken.

Betton, J. P., & Koester, L. S. (1983). The impact of twinship: Observed and perceived differences in mothers and twins. *Child Study Journal, 13,* 85-93.

Blank, M. (1982). Moving beyond the difference-deficit debate. In L. Feagans & D. C. Farran (Eds.), *The language of children reared in poverty: Implications for evaluation and intervention* (pp. 245-250). New York: Academic.

Block, J. H., Block, J., & Gjerde, P. F. (1986). The personality of children prior to divorce: A prospective study. *Child Development, 57,* 827-840.

Blumer, H. (1969). *Symbolic interactionism: Perspective and methods.* Englewood Cliffs, NJ: Prentice-Hall.

Bochner, A. P. (1985). Perspectives on inquiry: Representation, conversation, and reflection. In M. L. Knapp & G. R. Miller (Eds.), *Handbook of interpersonal communication* (pp. 27-58). Beverly Hills, CA: Sage.

Bochner, A. P., & Eisenberg, E. M. (1987). Family process: Systems perspectives. In C. R. Berger & S. H. Chaffee (Eds.), *Handbook of communication science* (pp. 540-563). Newbury Park, CA: Sage.

Bohannon, J. N., & Warren-Leubecker, A. (1989). Theoretical approaches to language acquisition. In J. B. Gleason (Ed.), *The development of language* (pp. 167-225). Columbus, OH: Merrill.

Borstelmann, L. J. (1983). Children before psychology: Ideas about children from antiquity to the late 1800s. In W. Kessen (Ed.), *Handbook of child psychology: Vol. 1. History, theory and methods* (pp. 1-40). New York: Wiley.

Bowers, J. W., Metts, S. M., & Duncanson, W. T. (1985). Emotion and interpersonal communication. In M. L. Knapp & G. R. Miller (Eds.), *Handbook of interpersonal communication* (pp. 500-550). Beverly Hills, CA: Sage.

Brazelton, T. B., Koslowski, B , & Main, M. (1974). The early mother-infant interaction. In M. Lewis & L. A Rosenblum (Eds.), *The effect of the infant on its caregiver* (pp. 49-76). New York: Wiley.

Bretherton, I. (1984). Social referencing and the interfacing of minds: A commentary on the views of Feinman and Campos. *Merrill-Palmer Quarterly, 30,* 419-427.

Brody, G. H., Pellegrini, A., & Sigel, I. (1986). Marital quality and mother-child and father-child interactions with school aged children. *Developmental Psychology, 22,* 291-296.

Brody, G. H., & Shaffer, D. R. (1982). Contributions of parents and peers to children's moral socialization. *Developmental Review, 2,* 31-75.

Brody, G. H., Stoneman, Z., & Burke, M. (1987). Child temperaments, maternal differential behavior, and sibling relationships. *Developmental Psychology, 23,* 354-362.

Brody, G. H., Stoneman, Z., & McCoy, J. K. (1992). Parental differential treatment of siblings and sibling differences in negative emotionality. *Journal of Marriage and the Family, 54,* 643-651.

Bronfenbrenner, U. (1979). *The ecology of human development: Experiments by nature and design.* Cambridge, MA: Harvard University Press.

Bronfenbrenner, U. (1986). Ecology of the family as a context for human development: Research perspectives. *Developmental Psychology, 22,* 723-742.

Bronfenbrenner, U. (1989). Ecological systems theory. In R. Vasta (Ed.), *Annals of child development* (Vol. 6, pp. 187-250). Greenwich, CT: JAI.

Bronstein-Burrows, P. (1981). Patterns of parent behavior: A cross-cultural study. *Merrill-Palmer Quarterly, 27,* 129-143.

Brown, R. (1973). *A first language: The early stages.* Cambridge, MA: Harvard University Press.

Bruner, J. S. (1981). The pragmatics of acquisition. In W. Deutsch (Ed.), *The child's construction of language* (pp. 39-55). New York: Academic.

Bruner, J. S. (1983). *Child's talk: Learning to use language.* New York: Norton.

Burgess, E. W. (1926). The family as a unit of interacting personalities. *The Family, 7,* 3-9.

Buri, J. R., Kirchner, P. A., & Walsh, J. M. (1987). Familial correlates of self-esteem in young American adults. *Journal of Social Psychology, 127,* 583-588.

Buri, J. R., Louiselle, P. A., Misukanis, T. M., & Mueller, R. A. (1988). Effects of parental authoritarianism and authoritativeness on self-esteem. *Personality and Social Psychology Bulletin, 14,* 271-282.

Burleson, B. R. (1983). Interactional antecedents of social reasoning development: Interpreting the effects of parent discipline on children. In D. Zarefsky, M. O. Sillars, & J. R. Rhodes (Eds.), *Argument in transition: Proceedings of the third summer conference on argumentation* (pp. 597-610). Annandale, VA: Speech Communication Association.

Burleson, B. R. (1987). Cognitive complexity. In J. C. McCroskey & J. A. Daly (Eds.), *Personality and interpersonal communication* (pp. 305-349). Newbury Park, CA: Sage.

Burleson, B. R., Delia, J. G., & Applegate, J. L. (1990, June). *Effects of mothers' disciplinary and comforting strategies on children's communication skills and acceptance by the peer group.* Paper presented at the meeting of the International Communication Association, Dublin, Ireland.

Burman, B., John, R. S., & Margolin, G. (1987). Effects of marital and parent-child relations on children's adjustment. *Journal of Family Psychology, 1,* 91-108.

Burr, W. R., Leigh, G. W., Day, R. D., & Constantine, J. (1979). Symbolic interaction and the family. In W. R. Burr, R. Hill, F. I. Nye, & I. L. Reiss (Eds.), *Contemporary theories about the family: Vol. 2. General theories/theoretical orientations* (pp. 42-129). New York: Free Press.

Buss, A. H., & Plomin, R. (1984). *Temperament: Early developing personality traits.* Hillsdale, NJ: Erlbaum.

Callan, V. J., & Noller, P. (1986). Perceptions of communicative relationships in families with adolescents. *Journal of Marriage and the Family, 48,* 813-820.

Campos, J. J. (1983). The importance of affective communication in social referencing: A commentary on Feinman. *Merrill-Palmer Quarterly, 29,* 83-87.

Campos, J. J., & Stenberg, C. R. (1981). Perception, appraisal and emotion: The onset of social referencing. In M. E. Lamb & L. R. Sherrod (Eds.), *Infant social cognition: Empirical and theoretical considerations* (pp. 273-314). Hillsdale, NJ: Erlbaum.

Cappella, J. N. (1977). Research methodology in communication: Review and commentary. In B. D. Ruben (Ed.), *Communication yearbook 1* (pp. 37-53). New Brunswick, NJ: Transaction.

Cappella, J. N. (1981). Mutual influences in expressive behavior: Adult-adult and infant-adult dyadic interaction. *Psychological Bulletin, 89,* 101-132.

Cappella, J. N. (1987). Interpersonal communication: Fundamental questions and issues. In C. R. Berger & S. H. Chaffee (Eds.), *Handbook of communication science* (pp. 184-238). Newbury Park, CA: Sage.

Cappella, J. N. (1991). The biological origins of automated patterns of human interaction. *Communication Theory, 1,* 4-35.

Carey, S., & Gelman, R. (Eds.). (1991). *The epigenesis of mind: Essays on biology and cognition.* Hillsdale, NJ: Erlbaum.

Carlton-Ford, S., & Collins, W. A. (1988). *Family conflict: Dimensions, differential reporting, and developmental differences.* Paper presented at the annual meeting of the American Sociological Association, Chicago, IL.

Cath, S. H., Gurwitt, A., & Gunsberg, L. (Eds.). (1989). *Fathers and their families.* Hillsdale, NJ: Analytic.

Chance, J. E. (1972). Academic correlates and maternal antecedents of children's belief of internal control of reinforcement. In J. B. Rotter, J. E. Chance, & E. J. Phares (Eds.), *Applications of a social learning theory of personality* (pp. 168-179). New York: Holt, Rinehart, & Winston.

Chandler, T. A., Wolf, F. M., Cook, B., & Dugovics, D. A. (1980). Parental correlates of locus of control in fifth graders: An attempt at experimentation in the home. *Merrill-Palmer Quarterly, 26,* 183-195.

Chapman, M., Skinner, E. A., & Baltes, P. B. (1990). Interpreting correlations between children's perceived control and cognitive performance: Control, agency, or means-ends beliefs? *Developmental Psychology, 26,* 246-253.

Chapman, M., & Zahn-Waxler, C. (1982). Young children's compliance and noncompliance to parental discipline in a natural setting. *International Journal of Behavioral Development, 5,* 81-94.

Chien, I. (1944). The awareness of self and the structure of the ego. *Psychological Review, 52,* 304-414.

Chomsky, N. (1957). *Syntactic structures.* The Hague: Mouton.

Chomsky, N. (1965). *Aspects of the theory of syntax.* Cambridge, MA: MIT Press.

Christensen, A., & Margolin, G. (1988). Conflict and alliance in distressed and non-distressed families. In R. A. Hinde & J. Stevenson-Hinde (Eds.), *Relationships within families: Mutual influences* (pp. 263-282). New York: Oxford University Press.

Christensen, A., Phillips, S., Glasgow, R. E., & Johnson, S. M. (1983). Parental characteristics and interactional dysfunction in families with child behavior problems: A preliminary investigation. *Journal of Abnormal Child Psychology, 11,* 153-166.

Cicirelli, V. G. (1985). Sibling relationships throughout the life cycle. In L. L'Abate (Ed.), *Handbook of family psychology and therapy* (Vol. 1, pp. 177-214). Homewood, IL: Dorsey.

Cicirelli, V. G., & Nussbaum, J. F. (1989). Relationships with siblings in later life. In J. F. Nussbaum (Ed.), *Life-span communication: Normative processes* (pp. 225-254). Hillsdale, NJ: Erlbaum.

Clark, R. A., & Delia, J. G. (1977). Cognitive complexity, social perspective-taking, and functional persuasive skills in second- to ninth-grade children. *Human Communication Research, 3,* 128-134.

Clarke-Stewart, K. A. (1973). Interactions between mothers and their young children: Characteristics and consequences. *Monographs of the Society for Research in Child Development, 38*(Ser. No. 153), 6 7.

Clarke-Stewart, K. A. (1978). And daddy makes three: The father's impact on mother and young child. *Child Development, 49,* 466-478.

Clarke-Stewart, K. A. (1988). Parents' effects on children's development: A decade of progress? *Journal of Applied Developmental Psychology, 9,* 41-84.

Collins, W. A. (1990). Parent-child relationships in the transition to adolescence: Continuity and change in interaction, affect, and cognition. In R. Montemayor, G. R. Adams, & T. P. Gullotta (Eds.), *From childhood to adolescence: A transitional period* (pp. 85-106). Newbury Park, CA: Sage.

Collins, W. A., & Gunnar, M. R. (1990). Social and personality development. *Annual Review of Psychology, 41,* 387-416.

Collins, W. A., & Russell, G. (1991). Mother-child and father-child relationships in middle childhood and adolescence: A developmental analysis. *Developmental Review, 11,* 99-136.

Combrinck-Graham, L. (1990). Developments in family systems theory and research. *Journal of the American Academy of Child Adolescent Psychiatry, 29,* 501-512.

Connell, J. P., & Wellborn, J. G. (1991). Competence, autonomy, and relatedness: A motivational analysis of self-system processes. In M. R. Gunnar & L. A. Sroufe (Eds.), *The Minnesota symposia on child development: Vol. 23. Self processes and development* (pp. 43-77). Hillsdale, NJ: Erlbaum.

Conti-Ramsden, G., & Snow, C. E. (1990). Children's language: How it develops and how it is used. In G. Conti-Ramsden & C. E. Snow (Eds.), *Children's language* (Vol. 7, pp. 1-6). Hillsdale, NJ: Erlbaum.

Cooley, C. H. (1902). *Human nature and the social order.* New York: Scribner's.

Cooley, C. H. (1909). *Social organization.* New York: Scribner's.

Cooper, C., Grotevant, H., & Condon, S. (1983). Individuality and connectedness in the family as a context for adolescent identity formation and role-taking. In H. D. Grotevant & C. R. Cooper (Eds.), *Adolescent development and the family* (pp. 42-49). San Francisco: Jossey-Bass.

Coopersmith, S. (1967). *The antecedents of self-esteem.* San Francisco: Freeman.

Crandall, V. C., & Crandall, B. W. (1983). Maternal and childhood behaviors as antecedents of internal-external control perceptions in young adulthood. In H. M. Lefcourt (Ed.), *Research with the locus of control construct: Vol. 2. Developments and social problems* (pp. 53-103). New York: Academic.

Crandall, V. C., Katkovsky, W., & Crandall, V. J. (1965). Children's beliefs in their own control of reinforcements in intellectual academic achievement situations. *Child Development, 36,* 91-109.

Crnic, K., & Booth, C. L. (1991). Mothers' and fathers' perceptions of daily hassles of parenting across early childhood. *Journal of Marriage and the Family, 53,* 1042-1050.

Crockenberg, S. (1985). Toddlers' reactions to maternal anger. *Merrill-Palmer Quarterly, 31,* 361-373.

Crockenberg, S. (1987). Predictors and correlates of anger toward and punitive control of toddlers by adolescent mothers. *Child Development, 58,* 964-975.

Crockenberg, S., & Litman, C. (1990). Autonomy as competence in 2-year-olds: Maternal correlates of child defiance, compliance, and self assertion. *Developmental Psychology, 26,* 961-971.

Cross, T. G. (1977). Mothers' speech adjustments: The contribution of selected child listener variables. In C. E. Snow & C. A. Ferguson (Eds.), *Talking to children: Language input and acquisition* (pp. 151-188). New York: Cambridge University Press.

Cross, T. G. (1978). Mothers' speech and its association with rate of linguistic development in young children. In N. Waterson & C. E. Snow (Eds.), *The development of communication* (pp. 199-217). New York: Wiley.

Crouter, A. C., & Crowley, M. S. (1990). School-age children's time alone with fathers in single-and dual-earner families: Implications for the father-child relationship. *Journal of Early Adolescence, 10,* 296-312.

Crowell, J. A., & Feldman, S. S. (1988). Mothers' internal models of relationships and children's behavioral and developmental status: A study of mother-child interaction. *Child Development, 59,* 1273-1285.

Cummings, E. M. (1987). Coping with background anger in early childhood. *Child Development, 58,* 976-984.

Cummings, E. M., Zahn-Waxler, C., & Radke-Yarrow, M. (1981). Young children's responses to expressions of anger and affection by others in the family. *Child Development, 52,* 1274-1282.

Cummings, E. M., Zahn-Waxler, C., & Radke-Yarrow, M. (1984). Developmental changes in children's reactions to anger in the home. *Journal of Child Psychology and Psychiatry, 25,* 63-74.

Cummings, J. S., Pellegrini, D. S., Notarius, C. I., & Cummings, E. M. (1989). Children's responses to angry adult behavior as a function of marital distress and history of interparent hostility. *Child Development, 60,* 1035-1043.

Damon, W. (1983). *Social and personality development.* New York: Norton.

Damon, W. (1988). *The moral child: Nurturing children's natural moral growth.* New York: Free Press.

Darling-Fisher, C. S., & Tiedje, B. (1990). The impact of maternal employment characteristics on fathers' participation in child care. *Journal of Applied Family and Child Studies, 39,* 20-26.

Darwin, C. (1859). *On the origin of species.* New York: Hurst.

Day, E. J. (1932). The development of language in twins: I A comparison of twins and single children. *Child Development, 3,* 179-199.

Deal, J. E., Halverson, C. F., Jr., & Wampler, K. S. (1989). Parental agreement on child-rearing orientations: Relations to parental, marital, family, and child characteristics. *Child Development, 60,* 1025-1034.

Delia, J. G., Kline, S. L., & Burleson, B. R. (1979). The development of persuasive communication strategies in kindergartners through twelfth graders. *Communication Monographs, 46,* 241-256.

Delia, J. G., O'Keefe, B. J., & O'Keefe, D. J. (1982). The constructivist approach to communication. In F. E. X. Dance (Ed.), *Human communication theory: Comparative essays* (pp. 147-191). New York: Harper & Row.

Demo, D. H., Small, S. A., & Savin-Williams, R. C. (1987). Family relations and the self-esteem of adolescents and their parents. *Journal of Marriage and the Family, 49,* 705-715.

Demuth, K. (1986). Prompting routines in the language socialization of Basotho children. In B. Schieffelin & E. Ochs (Eds.), *Language socialization across cultures* (pp. 51-79). New York: Cambridge University Press.

Denham, S. A., & Couchard, E. A. (1991). Social-emotional predictors of preschoolers' responses to adult negative emotion. *Journal of Child Psychology and Psychiatry, 32,* 595-608.

Dewey, J. (1922). *Human nature and conduct: An introduction to social psychology.* New York: H. Holt.

Dickstein, S., & Parke, R. D. (1988). Social referencing in infancy: A glance at fathers and marriage. *Child Development, 59,* 506-511.

Dimitracopoulou, I. (1990). *Conversational competence and social development.* New York: Cambridge University Press.

Dore, J. (1978). Conditions for the acquisition of speech acts. In I. Markova (Ed.), *The social context of language* (pp. 87-112). New York: Wiley.

Dornbusch, S. M., Ritter, P. L., Leiderman, P. H., Roberts, D. F., & Fraleigh, M. J. (1987). The relation of parenting styles to adolescent school performance. *Child Development, 58,* 1244-1257.

Dunn, J. (1983). Sibling relationships in early childhood. *Child Development, 54,* 787-811.

Dunn, J. (1985). *Sisters and brothers.* Cambridge, MA: Harvard University Press.

Dunn, J. (1988a). Connections between relationships: Implications of research on mothers and siblings. In R. A. Hinde & J. Stevenson-Hinde (Eds.), *Relationships within families: Mutual influences* (pp. 168-180). New York: Oxford University Press.

Dunn, J. (1988b). Relations among relationships. In S. W. Duck (Ed.), *Handbook of personal relationships* (pp. 193-209). New York: Wiley.

Dunn, J., & Kendrick, C. (1982a). *Siblings: Love, envy, and understanding*. Cambridge, MA: Harvard University Press.

Dunn, J., & Kendrick, C. (1982b). The speech of two- and three-year-olds to infant siblings: "Baby talk" and the context of communication. *Journal of Child Language, 9*, 579-595.

Dunn, J., & Munn, P. (1985). Becoming a family member: Family conflict and the development of social understanding in the second year. *Child Development, 56*, 480-492.

Dunn, J., & Munn, P. (1986). Siblings and the development of prosocial behaviour. *International Journal of Behavioral Development, 9*, 265-284.

Dunn, J., & Shatz, M. (1989). Becoming a conversationalist despite (or because of) having an older sibling. *Child Development, 60*, 399-410.

Dunn, J., & Stocker, C. (1989). The significance of differences in siblings' experiences within the family. In K. Kreppner & M. Lerner (Eds.), *Family systems and life-span development: Issues and perspectives* (pp. 289-302). Hillsdale, NJ: Erlbaum.

Dunn, J., Stocker, C., & Plomin, R. (1990). Nonshared experiences within the family: Correlates of behavior problems in middle childhood. *Developmental Psychopathology, 2*, 113-126.

Easterbrooks, M. A., & Emde, R. N. (1988). Marital and parent-child relationships: The role of affect in the family system. In R. A. Hinde & J. Stevenson-Hinde (Eds.), *Relationships within families: Mutual influences* (pp. 83-103). New York: Oxford University Press.

Eder, R. A. (1988). The self conceived in memory. *Early Child Development and Care, 40*, 25-51.

Edwards, J. (1990). Language in education. In H. Giles & W. P. Robinson (Eds.), *Handbook of language and social psychology* (pp. 475-494). Chichester, UK: Wiley.

Edwards, R. (1990). Sensitivity to feedback and the development of self. *Communication Quarterly, 38*, 101-111.

Eisenberg, A. R. (1992). Conflicts between mothers and their young children. *Merrill-Palmer Quarterly, 38*, 21-43.

Eisenberg, N., Cialdini, R. B., McCreath, H., & Shell, R. (1987). Consistency-based compliance: When and why do children become vulnerable? *Journal of Personality and Social Psychology, 52*, 1174-1181.

Ekman, P. (1972). Universals and cultural differences in facial expression of emotion. In J. K. Cole (Ed.), *Nebraska symposium on motivation, 1971* (pp. 207-283). Lincoln: University of Nebraska Press.

Ellis, R., & Wells, C. G. (1980). Enabling factors in adult-child discourse. *First Language, 1*, 46-62.

Emery, R. E. (1982). Interparental conflict and the children of discord and divorce. *Psychological Bulletin, 92*, 310-330.

Emery, R. E., & O'Leary, K. D. (1984). Marital discord and child behavior problems in a non-clinic sample. *Journal of Abnormal Child Psychology, 12*, 411-420.

Engfer, A. (1988). The interrelatedness of marriage and the mother-child relationship. In R. A. Hinde & J. Stevenson-Hinde (Eds.), *Relationships within families: Mutual influences* (pp. 104-118). New York: Oxford University Press.

Entwisle, D. R. (1985). Becoming a parent. In L. L'Abate (Ed.), *Handbook of family psychology and therapy* (Vol. 1, pp. 557-585). Homewood, IL: Dorsey.

Epstein, S. (1981). The unity principle versus the reality and pleasure principles, or the tale of the scorpion and the frog. In M. D. Lynch, A. A. Norem-Hebeisen, & K. J. Gergen (Eds.), *Self-concept: Advances in theory and research* (pp. 27-37). Cambridge, MA: Ballinger.

Erikson, E. H. (1950). *Childhood and society.* New York: Norton.

Erikson, E. H. (1959). Identity and the life cycle. *Psychological Issues, 1,* 1-171.

Feinman, S. (1982). Social referencing in infancy. *Merill-Palmer Quarterly, 28,* 445-470.

Feinman, S. (1983). How does a baby socially refer? Two views of social referencing: A reply to Campos. *Merrill-Palmer Quarterly, 29,* 467-471.

Feinman, S. (1985). Emotional expression, social referencing, and preparedness for learning in infancy—Mother knows best, but sometimes I know better. In G. Zivin (Ed.), *The development of expressive behavior: Biology-environment interactions* (pp. 291-318). New York: Academic.

Feinman, S., & Lewis, M. (1983). Social referencing at ten months: A second-order effect on infants' responses to strangers. *Child Development, 54,* 878-887.

Feldman, R. S. (Ed.). (1982). *Development of nonverbal behavior in children.* New York: Springer-Verlag

Felson, R. B., & Reed, M. (1986). The effect of parents on the self-appraisals of children. *Social Psychology Quarterly, 49,* 302 308.

Felson, R. B., & Zielinski, M. A. (1989). Children's self-esteem and parental support. *Journal of Marriage and the Family, 51,* 727-735.

Ferguson, C. A. (1977). Baby talk as a simplified register. In C. E. Snow & C. A. Ferguson (Eds.), *Talking to children: Language input and acquisition* (pp. 219-236). New York: Cambridge University Press.

Field, T. (1990). *Infancy.* Cambridge, MA: Harvard University Press.

Findley, M. J., & Cooper, H. M. (1983). Locus of control and academic achievement: A literature review. *Journal of Personality and Social Psychology, 44,* 419-427.

Fisher, B. A. (1978). *Perspectives on human communication.* New York: Macmillan.

Fitzpatrick, M. A. (1987). Marital interaction. In C. R. Berger & S. H. Chaffee (Eds.), *Handbook of communication science* (pp. 564-618). Newbury Park, CA: Sage.

Fitzpatrick, M. A. (1991). A microsocietal approach to marital communication. In B. Dervin & M. J. Voigt (Eds.), *Progress in communication sciences* (Vol. 10, pp. 67-101). Norwood, NJ: Ablex.

Fitzpatrick, M. A., & Badzinski, D. M. (1985). All in the family: Interpersonal communication in kin relationships. In M. L. Knapp & G. R. Miller (Eds.), *Handbook of interpersonal communication* (pp. 687-736). Beverly Hills, CA: Sage.

Flavell, J. H. (1982). Structures, stages, and sequences in cognitive development. In W. A. Collins (Ed.), *Minnesota symposia on child development: Vol. 15. The concept of child development* (pp. 1-28). Hillsdale, NJ: Erlbaum.

Flavell, J. H. (1985). *Cognitive development* (2nd ed.). Englewood Cliffs, NJ: Prentice-Hall.

Forehand, R. (1977). Child noncompliance to parental requests: Behavior analysis and treatment. In M. Hersen, R. M. Eisler, & P. M. Miller (Eds.), *Progress in behavior modification* (Vol. 5, pp. 111-247). New York: Academic.

Foster, S. H. (1990). *The communicative competence of young children: A modular approach.* London: Longman.

Franks, D. (1985). The self in evolutionary perspective. In H. H. Farberman & R. S. Perinbanayagam (Eds.), *Foundations of interpretive sociology: Original essays in symbolic interaction. Studies in symbolic interaction* (Suppl. 1, pp. 29-63). Greenwich, CT: JAI.

Freud, S. (1938). *The basic writings of Sigmund Freud* (A. A. Brill, Trans.). New York: The Modern Library.

Frey, J. R., III, & Wendorf, D. J. (1985). Families of gifted children. In L. L'Abate (Ed.), *Handbook of family psychology and therapy* (Vol. 2, pp. 781-809). Homewood, IL: Dorsey.

Furrow, D., Nelson, K., & Benedict, H. (1979). Mothers' speech to children and syntactic development: Some simple relationships. *Journal of Child Language, 6,* 423-442.

Ganong, L. H., Coleman, M., & Mapes, D. (1990). A meta-analytic review of family structure and stereotypes. *Journal of Marriage and the Family, 52,* 287-297.

Garko, M. G. (1990). Perspectives on conceptualizations of compliance and compliance-gaining. *Communication Quarterly, 38,* 138-157.

Gaul, R., Simon, L., Friedlander, M. L., Cutler, C., & Heatherington, L. (1991). Correspondence of family therapists' perceptions with FRCCS coding rules for triadic interactions. *Journal of Marital and Family Therapy, 17,* 379-393.

Gecas, V. (1971). Parental behavior and dimensions of adolescent self-evaluation. *Sociometry, 34,* 466-482.

Gecas, V. (1989). The social psychology of self-efficacy. *Annual Review of Sociology, 15,* 291-316.

Gecas, V., & Schwalbe, M. L. (1986). Parental behavior and adolescent self-esteem. *Journal of Marriage and the Family, 48,* 37-46.

Gergen, K. J. (1973). Social psychology as history. *Journal of Personality and Social Psychology, 26,* 309-320.

Gesell, A. L. (1928). *Growth and personality.* New York: Macmillan.

Gleason, J. B. (1975). Fathers and other strangers: Men's speech to young children. In D. P. Dato (Ed.), *Developmental psycholinguistics: Theory and application. Georgetown University Round Table on Languages and Linguistics* (pp. 289-297). Washington, DC: Georgetown University Press.

Gleitman, L. R., Newport, E. L., & Gleitman, H. (1984). The current status of the motherese hypothesis. *Journal of Child Language, 11,* 43-79.

Goldberg, W. A., & Easterbrooks, M. A. (1984). Role of marital quality in toddler development. *Developmental Psychology, 20,* 504-514.

Goodman, N. (1985a). Introduction. In H. A. Farberman & R. S. Perinbanayagam (Eds.), *Foundations of interpretive sociology: Original essays in symbolic interaction. Studies in symbolic interaction* (Suppl. 1, pp. 65-72). Greenwich, CT: JAI.

Goodman, N. (1985b). Socialization I: A sociological overview. In H. A. Farberman & R. S. Perinbanayagam (Eds.), *Foundations of interpretive sociology: Original essays in symbolic interaction. Studies in symbolic interaction* (Suppl. 1, pp. 73-94). Greenwich, CT: JAI.

Gordon, D., Nowicki, S., Jr., & Wichern, F. (1981). Observed maternal and child behaviors in a dependency producing task as a function of children's locus of control orientation. *Merrill-Palmer Quarterly, 27,* 43-51.

Gordon, T. (1970). *P.E.T.: Parent effectiveness training: The tested new way to raise responsible children.* New York: Plume.

Goswick, R. A., & Jones, W. H. (1982). Components of loneliness during adolescence. *Journal of Youth and Adolescence, 11,* 373-383.

Gottlieb, G. (1983). The psychobiological approach to developmental issues. In J. J. Campos & M. M. Haith (Eds.), *Handbook of child psychology: Vol. 2. Infancy and developmental psychobiology* (pp. 1-26). New York: Wiley.

Greenberger, E., & Goldberg, W. A. (1989). Work, parenting, and the socialization of children. *Developmental Psychology, 25,* 22-35.

Grolnick, W. S., & Ryan, R. M. (1989). Parent styles associated with children's self-regulation and competence in school. *Journal of Educational Psychology, 81,* 143-154.

Grotevant, H. D., & Cooper, C. R. (1985). Patterns of interaction in family relationships and the development of identity exploration in adolescence. *Child Development, 56,* 415-428.

Grotevant, H. D., & Cooper, C. R. (1986). Individuation in family relationships: A perspective on the individual differences in the development of identity and role-taking skill in adolescence. *Human Development, 29,* 82-100.

Growe, G. A. (1980). Parental behavior and self-esteem in children. *Psychological Reports, 47,* 499-502.

Grusec, J. E., & Lytton, H. (1988). *Social development: History, theory, and research.* New York: Springer-Verlag.

Grych, J. H., & Fincham, F. D. (1990). Marital conflict and children's adjustment: A cognitive-contextual framework. *Psychological Bulletin, 108,* 267-290.

Gunnar, M. R., & Sroufe, L. A. (Eds.). (1991). *The Minnesota symposia on child development: Vol. 23. Self processes and development.* Hillsdale, NJ: Erlbaum.

Gunnar, M. R., & Stone, C. (1984). The effects of positive maternal affect on infant responses to pleasant, ambiguous, and fear-provoking toys. *Child Development, 55,* 1231-1236.

Gurin, P., & Brim, O. G., Jr. (1984). Change in self in adulthood: The example of sense of control. In P. B. Baltes, & O. G. Brim, Jr. (Eds.), *Life-span development and behavior* (Vol. 6, pp. 281-334). New York: Academic.

Haley, J. (1959). The family of the schizophrenic: A model system. *American Journal of Nervous and Mental Disorders, 129, 357-374.*

Haley, J. (1963). *Strategies of psychotherapy.* New York: Grune & Stratton.

Halliday, M. A. K. (1973). *Explorations in the functions of language.* London: Edward Arnold.

Halverson, C. F., Jr. (1988). Remembering your parents: Reflections on the retrospective method. *Journal of Personality, 56,* 435-443.

Hanson, N. R. (1955). Causal chains. *Mind, 255,* 289-311

Harris, K. M., & Morgan, S. P. (1991). Fathers, sons, and daughters: Differential paternal involvement in parenting. *Journal of Marriage and the Family, 53,* 531-544.

Harris, M., Jones, D., Brookes, S., & Grant, J. (1986). Relations between the nonverbal context of maternal speech and rate of language development. *British Journal of Development Psychology, 4,* 261-268.

Harter, S. (1983). Developmental perspectives on the self-system. In E. M. Hetherington (Ed.), *Handbook of child psychology: Vol. 4. Socialization, personality, and social development* (pp. 275-385). New York: Wiley.

Haslett, B. (1987). *Communication: Strategic action in context.* Hillsdale, NJ: Erlbaum.

Haslett, B. (1990). Developing strategic communication. In J. P. Dillard (Ed.), *Seeking compliance: The production of interpersonal influence messages* (pp. 143-160). Scottsdale, AZ: Gorsuch Scarisbrick.

Hauser, S. T., Houlihan, J., Powers, S. I., Jacobson, A. M., Noam, G. G., Weiss-Perry, B., Follansbee, D., & Book, B. K. (1991). Adolescent ego development within the family: Family styles and family sequences. *International Journal of Behavioral Development, 14,* 165-193.

Heatherington, L., & Friedlander, M. L. (1990). Complementarity and symmetry in family therapy communication. *Journal of Counseling Psychology, 36,* 261-268.

Hess, R. D., & Shipman, V. C. (1965). Early experience and the socialization of cognitive modes in children. *Child Development, 36,* 869-886.

Hetherington, E. M., Cox, M., & Cox, R. (1978). The aftermath of divorce. In J. H. Stevens, Jr., & M. Matthews (Eds.), *Mother-child, father-child relations* (pp. 110-155). Washington: NAEYC.

Higgins, E. T. (1991). Development of self-regulatory and self-evaluative processes: Costs, benefits, and tradeoffs. In M. R. Gunnar & L. A. Sroufe (Eds.), *The Minnesota symposia on child development: Vol. 23. Self processes and development* (pp. 125-165). Hillsdale, NJ: Erlbaum.

Hill, R. (1949). *Families under stress.* New York: Harper.

Hinde, R. A. (1979). *Towards understanding relationships.* New York: Academic.

Hinde, R. A. (1984). Why do the sexes behave differently in close relationships? *Journal of Social and Personal Relationships, 1,* 471-501.

Hinde, R. A. (1988). Introduction. In R. A. Hinde & J. Stevenson-Hinde (Eds.), *Relationships within families: Mutual influences* (pp. 1-4). New York: Oxford University Press.

Hinde, R. A. (1989). Reconciling the family systems and the relationship approaches to child development. In K. Kreppner & R. M. Lerner (Eds.), *Family systems and life-span development* (pp. 149-164). Hillsdale, NJ: Erlbaum.

Hinde, R. A., & Stevenson-Hinde, J. (1986). Relating childhood relationships to individual characteristics. In W. W. Hartup & Z. Rubin (Eds.), *Relationships and development* (pp. 27-50). Hillsdale, NJ: Erlbaum.

Hinde, R. A., & Stevenson-Hinde, J. (1987). Interpersonal relationships and child development. *Developmental Review, 7,* 1-21.

Hinde, R. A., & Stevenson-Hinde, J. (1988a). Epilogue. In R. A. Hinde & J. Stevenson-Hinde (Eds.), *Relationships within families: Mutual influences* (pp. 365-385). New York: Oxford University Press.

Hinde, R. A., & Stevenson-Hinde, J. (Eds.). (1988b). *Relationships within families: Mutual influences.* New York: Oxford University Press.

Hoff-Ginsberg, E. (1985). Some contributions of mothers' speech to their children's syntax growth. *Journal of Child Language, 12,* 367-385.

Hoff-Ginsberg, E. (1987). Topic relations in mother-child conversation. *First Language, 7,* 145-158.

Hoff-Ginsberg, E. (1990). Maternal speech and the child's development of syntax: A further look. *Journal of Child Language, 17,* 85-99.

Hoff-Ginsberg, E., & Krueger, W. M. (1991). Older siblings as conversational partners. *Merrill-Palmer Quarterly, 37,* 465-482.

Hoffman, M. L. (1960). Power assertion by the parent and its impact on the child. *Child Development, 31,* 129-143.

Hoffman, M. L. (1970). Moral development. In P. H. Mussen (Ed.), *Carmichael's manual of child psychology* (3rd ed., Vol. 2, pp. 261-360). New York: Wiley.

Hoffman, M. L. (1975). Moral internalization, parental power, and the nature of parent-child interaction. *Developmental Psychology, 11,* 228-239.

Hoffman, M. L. (1983). Affective and cognitive processes in moral internalization. In E. T. Higgins, D. N. Ruble, & W. W. Hartup (Eds.), *Social cognition and social development: A sociocultural perspective* (pp. 236-274). Cambridge, UK: Cambridge University Press.

Holden, G. W., & West, M. J. (1989). Proximate regulation by mothers: A demonstration of how differing styles affect young children's behavior. *Child Development, 60,* 64-69.

Honig, A. S. (1985). Compliance, control, and discipline. *Young Children, 40,* 50-58.

Honig, A. S. (1991). Parent-child couples are the key: A review of Sameroff and Emde's relationship disturbances in early childhood. *Merrill-Palmer Quarterly, 37,* 519-522.

Horowitz, F. D., & Sullivan, J. W. (1981). Mother-child interaction issues. In R. L. Schiefelbusch & D. D. Bricker (Eds.), *Early language: Acquisition and intervention* (pp. 253-256). Baltimore: University Park Press.

Howe, C. (1981). *Acquiring language in a conversational context.* New York: Academic.

Huber, J., & Spitze, G. (1988). Trends in family sociology. In N. J. Smelser (Ed.), *Handbook of sociology* (pp. 425-448). Newbury Park, CA: Sage.

Huston, T. L., & Robins, E. (1982). Conceptual and methodological issues in studying close relationships. *Journal of Marriage and the Family, 44,* 901-925.

Hutter, M. (1985). Symbolic interaction and the study of the family. In H. A. Farberman & R. S. Perinbanayagam (Eds.), *Foundations of interpretive sociology: Original essays in symbolic interaction. Studies in symbolic interaction* (Suppl. 1, pp. 117-152). Greenwich, CT: JAI.

Hymes, D. (1972). On communicative competence. In J. Pride & J. Holmes (Eds.), *Sociolinguistics* (pp. 269-293). London: Penguin.

Ingram, D. (1991). Toward a theory of phonological acquisition. In J. F. Miller (Ed.), *Research on child language disorders: A decade of progress* (pp. 55-72). Austin, TX: Pro-Ed.

Isberg, R. S., Hauser, S. T., Jacobson, A. M., Powers, S. I., Noam, G., Weiss-Perry, B., & Follansbee, D. (1989). Parental contexts of adolescent self-esteem: A developmental perspective. *Journal of Youth and Adolescence, 18,* 1-23.

Izard, C. E., & Malatesta, C. Z. (1987). Perspectives on emotional development, I: Differential emotions theory of early emotional development. In J. D. Osofsky (Ed.), *Handbook of infant development* (2nd ed., pp. 494-554). New York: Wiley.

Jackson, D. D. (1957). The question of family homeostasis. *Psychiatric Quarterly Supplement, 31,* 79-90.

Jackson, D. D. (1959). Family interaction, family homeostasis and some implications for conjoint family psychotherapy. In J. H. Masserman (Ed.), *Individual and familial dynamics* (pp. 122-141). New York: Grune & Stratton.

Jacobs, S. (1985). Language. In M. L. Knapp & G. R. Miller (Eds.), *Handbook of interpersonal communication* (pp. 205-262). Beverly Hills, CA: Sage.

Jacobs, S. (1986). How to make an argument from example in discourse analysis. In D. G. Ellis & W. A. Donohue (Eds.), *Contemporary issues in language and discourse processes* (pp. 313-343). Hillsdale, NJ: Erlbaum.

James, W. (1890). *Principles of psychology.* New York: Holt.

Jensen, L. C., & Kingston, M. (1986). *Parenting.* New York: Holt, Rinehart, and Winston.

Johnston, J. R., Gonzalez, R., & Campbell, L. E. G. (1987). Ongoing postdivorce conflict and child disturbance. *Journal of Abnormal Child Psychology, 15,* 493-509.

Jones, C. P., & Adamson, L. B. (1987). Language use in mother-child and mother-child-sibling interactions. *Child Development, 58,* 356-366.

Jouriles, E. N., Bourg, W. J., & Farris, A. M. (1991). Marital adjustment and child conduct problems: A comparison of the correlation across subsamples. *Journal of Consulting and Clinical Psychology, 59,* 354-357.

Jouriles, E. N., Pfiffner, L. J., & O'Leary, K. D. (1988). Marital conflict, parenting, and toddler conduct problems. *Journal of Abnormal Child Psychology, 16,* 197-206.

Kagan, J. (1971). *Change and continuity in infancy.* New York: Wiley.

Kaler, S. R., & Kopp, C. B. (1990). Compliance and comprehension in very young toddlers. *Child Development, 61,* 1997-2003.

Kaufman, J., & Zigler, E. (1989). The intergenerational transmission of child abuse. In D. Cicchetti & V. Carlson (Eds.), *Child maltreatment: Theory and research on the causes and consequences of child abuse and neglect* (pp. 129-150). New York: Cambridge University Press.

Kavanaugh, R. D., & Jen, M. (1981). Some relationships between parental speech and children's object language development. *First Language, 2,* 103-115.

Kawash, G., & Kozeluk, L. (1990). Self-esteem in early adolescence as a function of position within Olson's circumplex model of marital and family systems. *Social Behavior and Personality, 18,* 189-196.

Kaye, K. (1977). Toward the origin of dialogue. In H. R. Schaffer (Ed.), *Studies in mother-infant interaction* (pp. 89-117). New York: Academic.

Kaye, K., & Charney, R. (1980). How mothers maintain "dialogue" with two-year-olds. In D. Olson (Ed.), *The social foundations of language and thought* (pp. 211-230). New York: Norton.

Kelly, G. A. (1955). *The psychology of personal constructs.* New York: Norton.

Kelman, H. C. (1958). Compliance, identification and internalization: Three processes of opinion change. *Journal of Conflict Resolution, 2,* 51-60.

Kenny, D. A. (1988). The analysis of data from two-person relationships. In S. Duck (Ed.), *Handbook of personal relationships* (pp. 57-78). New York: Wiley.

Kent, R. D., & Hodge, M. (1991). The biogenesis of speech: Continuity and process in early speech and language development. In J. F. Miller (Ed.), *Research on child language disorders: A decade of progress* (pp. 25-54). Austin, TX: Pro-Ed.

Kessen, W. (1965). *The child.* New York: Wiley.

Kochanska, G. (1991). Socialization and temperament in the development of guilt and conscience. *Child Development, 62,* 1379-1392.

Kochanska, G., & Kuczynski, L. (1991). Maternal autonomy granting: Predictors of normal and depressed mothers' compliance and noncompliance with the requests of five-year-olds. *Child Development, 62,* 1449-1459.

Kochanska, G., Kuczynski, L., & Radke-Yarrow, M. (1989). Correspondence between mothers' self-reported and observed child-rearing practices. *Child Development, 60,* 50-63.

Kohlberg, L. (1969). Stage and sequence: The cognitive-developmental approach to socialization. In D. A. Goslin (Ed.), *Handbook of socialization theory and research* (pp. 347-480). Chicago: Rand McNally.

Kohlberg, L. (1976). Moral stages and moralization. In T. Lickona (Ed.), *Moral development and behavior: Theory of research and social issues* (pp. 31-53). New York: Holt, Rinehart, & Winston.

Kohlberg, L., Ricks, D., & Snarey, J. (1984). Childhood development as a predictor of adaptation in adulthood. *Genetic Psychology Monographs, 110,* 91-172.

Kopp, C. B. (1982). Antecedents of self-regulation: A developmental perspective. *Developmental Psychology, 18,* 199-214.

Krampen, G. (1989). Perceived childrearing practices and the development of locus of control in early adolescence. *International Journal of Behavioral Development, 12,* 177-193.

Kreppner, K. (1988). Changes in dyadic relationships within a family after the arrival of a second child. In R. A. Hinde & J. Stevenson-Hinde (Eds.), *Relationships within families: Mutual influences* (pp. 143-167). New York: Oxford University Press.

Kuczynski, L. (1983). Reasoning, prohibitions and motivations for compliance. *Developmental Psychology, 19,* 126-134.

Kuczynski, L. (1984). Socialization goals and mother-child interaction: Strategies for long-term and short-term compliance. *Developmental Psychology, 20,* 1061-1073.

Kuczynski, L., & Kochanska, G. (1990). Development of children's noncompliance strategies from toddlerhood to age 5. *Developmental Psychology, 26,* 398-408.

Kuczynski, L., Kochanska, G., Radke-Yarrow, M., & Girnius-Brown, O. (1987). A developmental interpretation of young children's noncompliance. *Developmental Psychology, 23,* 799-806.

Labouvie-Vief, G., Hakim-Larson, J., DeVoe, M., & Schoeberlein, S. (1989). Emotions and self-regulation: A life span view. *Human Development, 32,* 279-299.

Lamb, M. E. (1977a). The development of mother-infant and father-infant attachments in the second year of life. *Developmental Psychology, 13,* 637-648.

Lamb, M. E. (1977b). Father-infant and mother-infant interaction in the first year of life. *Child Development, 48,* 167-181.

Lamb, M. E. (Ed.). (1981). *The role of the father in child development* (2nd ed.). New York: Wiley.

Lamb, M. E., & Easterbrooks, M. A. (1981). Individual differences in parental sensitivity: Some thoughts about origins, components, and consequences. In M. E. Lamb & L. R. Sherrod (Eds.), *Infant social cognition: Empirical and theoretical considerations* (pp. 127-153). Hillsdale, NJ: Erlbaum.

Landauer, T. K., Carlsmith, J. M., & Lepper, M. (1970). Experimental analysis of the factors determining obedience of four-year-old children to adult females. *Child Development, 41,* 601-611.

Lannamann, J. W. (1991). Interpersonal communication research as ideological practice. *Communication Theory, 1,* 179-203.

La Voie, J. C. (1974). Cognitive determinants of resistance to deviation in seven-, nine-, and eleven-year-old children of low and high maturity of moral judgement. *Developmental Psychology, 10,* 393-403.

Lazarus, R. S. (1991). *Emotion and adaptation.* New York: Oxford University Press.

Leaper, C., Hauser, S. T., Kremen, A., Powers, S. I., Jacobson, A. M., Noam, G. G., Weiss-Perry, B., & Follansbee, D. (1989). Adolescent parent interactions in relation to adolescents' gender and ego development pathway: A longitudinal study. *Journal of Early Adolescence, 9,* 335-361.

Lefcourt, H. M. (1976). *Locus of control: Current trends in theory and research.* Hillsdale, NJ: Erlbaum.

Lepper, M. R. (1973). Dissonance, self-perception, and honesty in children. *Journal of Personality and Social Psychology, 25,* 65-74.

Lepper, M. R. (1983). Social-control processes and the internalization of social values: An attributional perspective. In E. T. Higgins, D. N. Ruble, & W. W. Hartup (Eds.), *Social cognition and social development: A sociocultural perspective* (pp. 294-330). Cambridge, UK: Cambridge University Press.

Lewis, C. C. (1981). Effects of parental firm control: A reinterpretation of findings. *Psychological Bulletin, 90,* 547-563.

Lewis, C., & Gregory, S. (1987). Parents' talk to their infants: The importance of context. *First Language, 7,* 201-216.

Lewis, M. (1987). Social development in infancy and early childhood. In J. D. Osofsky (Ed.), *Handbook of infant development* (2nd ed., pp. 419-493). New York: Wiley.

Lewis, M. (1988a). The transition to parenthood: I. *Family Process, 27,* 149-165.

Lewis, M. (1988b). The transition to parenthood: II. *Family Process, 27,* 273-278.

Liem, J. H. (1980). Family studies of schizophrenia: An update and commentary. *Schizophrenia Bulletin, 6,* 429-475.

Lindfors, J. W. (1987). *Children's language and learning.* Englewood Cliffs, NJ: Prentice-Hall.

Litovsky, V. G., & Dusek, J. B. (1985). Perceptions of child rearing and self-concept development during the early adolescent years. *Journal of Youth and Adolescence, 14,* 373-387.

Locke, J. (1959). *An essay concerning human understanding.* New York: Dover. (Original work published 1690)

Locke, J. (1964). *Some thoughts concerning education* (F. W. Garforth, Ed.). Woodbury, NY: Barron's. (Original work published 1693)

Loeb, R. C. (1975). Concomitants of boys' locus of control examined in parent-child interactions. *Developmental Psychology, 11,* 353-358.

Loeb, R. C., Horst, L., & Horton, P. J. (1980). Family interaction patterns associated with self-esteem in preadolescent girls and boys. *Merrill-Palmer Quarterly, 26,* 205-217.

Loevinger, J. (1966). The meaning and measurement of ego development. *American Psychologist, 21,* 195-206.

Loevinger, J. (1976). *Ego development conceptions and theories.* San Francisco: Jossey-Bass.

Lytton, H. (1979). Disciplinary encounters between young boys and their mothers and fathers: Is there a contingency system? *Developmental Psychology, 15,* 256-268.

Lytton, H. (1980). *Parent-child interaction: The socialization process observed in twin and singleton families.* New York: Plenum.

Lytton, H., Watts, D., & Dunn, B. E. (1988). Continuity and change in child characteristics and maternal practices between ages 2 and 9: An analysis of interview responses. *Child Study Journal, 18,* 1-15.

Lytton, H., & Zwirner, W. (1975). Compliance and its controlling stimuli observed in a natural setting. *Developmental Psychology, 11,* 769-779.

Maccoby, E. E. (1980). *Social development: Psychological growth and the parent-child relationship.* New York: Harcourt Brace Jovanovich.

Maccoby, E. E. (1984). Middle childhood in the context of the family. In W. A. Collins (Ed.), *Development during middle childhood: The years from six to twelve* (pp. 184-239). Washington, DC: National Academy.

Maccoby, E. E., & Martin, J. A. (1983). Socialization in the context of the family: Parent-child interaction. In E. M. Hetherington (Ed.), *Handbook of child psychology: Vol. 4. Socialization, personality, and social development* (pp. 1-101). New York: Wiley.

MacDonald, K., & Parke, R. D. (1984). Bridging the gap: Parent-child play interaction and peer interactive competence. *Child Development, 55,* 1265-1277.

Mannle, S., & Tomasello, M. (1987). Fathers, siblings, and the bridge hypothesis. In K. E. Nelson & A. Van Kleek (Eds.), *Children's language* (Vol. 6, pp. 23-42). Hillsdale, NJ: Erlbaum.

Margolin, G. (1981). The reciprocal relationship between marital and child problems. In J. P. Vincent (Ed.), *Advances in family intervention, assessment, and theory* (Vol. 2, pp. 131-182). Greenwich, CT: JAI.

Margolin, G. (1988). Marital conflict is not marital conflict is not marital conflict. In R. D. Peters & R. J. McMahon (Eds.), *Social learning and systems approaches to marriage and the family* (pp. 193-216). New York: Brunner/Mazel.

Margolin, L., Blyth, D. A., & Carbone, D. (1988). The family as a looking glass: Interpreting family influences on adolescent self-esteem from a symbolic interaction perspective. *Journal of Early Adolescence, 8,* 211-224.

Marion, M. (1983). Child compliance: A review of the literature with implications for family life education. *Family Relations, 32,* 545-555.

Markus, H. (1977). Self-schemata and processing information about the self. *Personality and Social Psychology, 35,* 63-78.

Markus, H. J., & Nurius, P. S. (1984). Self-understanding and self-regulation in middle childhood. In W. A. Collins (Ed.), *Development during middle childhood* (pp. 147-183). Washington, DC: National Academy.

Maslow, A. H. (1954). *Motivation and personality.* New York: Harper & Row.

Matteson, R. (1974). Adolescent self-esteem, family communication, and marital satisfaction. *Journal of Psychology, 86*, 35-47.

McCabe, A. E. (1989). Differential language learning styles in young children: The importance of context. *Developmental Review, 9*, 1-20.

McClearn, G. E. (1964). Genetics and behavior development. In M. L. Hoffman & L. W. Hoffman (Eds.), *Review of child development research* (Vol. 1, pp. 433-480). New York: Russell Sage Foundation.

McConnell, J. V. (1989). *Understanding human behavior* (6th ed.). New York: Holt, Rinehart, and Winston.

McCrae, R. R., & Costa, P. T., Jr. (1988a). Do parental influences matter? A reply to Halverson. *Journal of Personality, 56*, 446-449.

McCrae, R. R., & Costa, P. T., Jr. (1988b). Recalled parent-child relations and adult personality. *Journal of Personality, 56*, 417-434.

McDonald, L., & Pien, D. (1982). Mother conversational behaviour as a function of interactional intent. *Journal of Child Language, 9*, 337-358.

McHale, S. M., & Pawletko, T. M. (1992). Differential treatment of siblings in two family contexts. *Child Development, 63*, 68-81.

McKenry, P. C., Everett, J. E., Ramseur, H. P., & Carter, C. J. (1989). Research on black adolescents: A legacy of cultural bias. *Journal of Adolescent Research, 4*, 254-264.

McKinney, B., & Peterson, R. A. (1987). Predictors of stress in parents of developmentally disabled children. *Journal of Pediatric Psychology, 12*, 133-150.

McLaughlin, B. (1983). Child compliance to parental control techniques. *Developmental Psychology, 19*, 667-673.

McLaughlin, M. L. (1984). *Conversation: How talk is organized*. Beverly Hills, CA: Sage.

Mead, G. H. (1934). *Mind, self and society: From the standpoint of a social behavioralist*. Chicago: University of Chicago Press.

Miller, G. A. (1990). The place of language in a scientific psychology. *Psychological Science, 1*, 7-14.

Miller, N. E., & Dollard, J. (1962). *Social learning and imitation*. New Haven, CT: Yale University Press.

Miller, P., & Garvey, C. (1984). Mother-baby role play: Its origins in social support. In I. Bretherton (Ed.), *Symbolic play: The development of social understanding* (pp. 101-130). Orlando, FL: Academic.

Miller, P. C., Lefcourt, H. M., Holmes, J. G., Ware, E. E., & Saleh, W. E. (1986). Marital locus of control and marital problem solving. *Journal of Personality and Social Psychology, 51*, 161-169.

Mills, R. S., & Grusec, J. E. (1988). Socialization from the perspective of the parent-child relationship. In S. W. Duck (Ed.), *Handbook of personal relationships: Theory, research and interventions* (pp. 177-191). New York: Wiley.

Minuchin, P. (1985). Families and individual development: Provocations from the field of family therapy. *Child Development, 56*, 289-302.

Minuchin, P. (1988). Relationships within the family: A systems perspective on development. In R. A. Hinde & J. Stevenson-Hinde (Eds.), *Relationships within families: Mutual influences* (pp. 7-26). New York: Oxford University Press.

Minuchin, S. (1974). *Families and family therapy*. Cambridge, MA: Harvard University Press.

Minuchin, S., & Fishman, H. C. (1981). *Family therapy techniques*. Cambridge, MA: Harvard University Press.

Minuchin, S., Rosman, B., & Baker, L. (1978). *Psychosomatic families: Anorexia nervosa in context.* Cambridge, MA: Harvard University Press.

Moerk, E. L. (1989). The LAD was a lady and the tasks were ill-defined. *Developmental Review, 9,* 21-57.

Moerk, E. L. (1992). *A first language: Taught and learned.* Baltimore: Paul H. Brookes.

Monge, P. R. (1977). The systems perspective as a theoretical basis for the study of human communication. *Communication Quarterly, 25,* 19-29.

Montemayor, R., & Brownlee, J. R. (1987). Fathers, mothers, and adolescents: Gender-based differences in parental roles during adolescence. *Journal of Youth and Adolescence, 16,* 281-291.

Montgomery, B. M., & Duck, S. (Eds.). (1991). *Studying interpersonal interaction.* New York: Guilford.

Moore, J. J., Mullis, R. L., & Mullis, A. K. (1986). Examining metamemory within the context of parent-child interactions. *Psychological Reports, 59,* 39-47.

Murphey, D. A. (1992). Constructing the child: Relations between parents' beliefs and child outcomes. *Developmental Review, 12,* 199-232.

Murray, A. D., Johnson, J., & Peters, J. (1990). Fine-tuning of utterance length to preverbal infants: Effects on later language development. *Journal of Child Language, 17,* 511-525.

Murray, L., & Trevarthen, C. (1986). The infant's role in mother-infant communications. *Journal of Child Language, 13,* 15-29.

Neimeyer, G. J., & Neimeyer, R. A. (Eds.). (1990). *Advances in personal construct psychology* (Vol. 1). Greenwich, CT: JAI.

Nelson, D. G. K., Hirsh-Pasek, K., Jusczyk, P. W., & Cassidy, K. W. (1989). How the prosodic cues in motherese might assist language learning. *Journal of Child Language, 16,* 55-68.

Nelson, K. E. (1977). Facilitating children's syntax acquisition. *Developmental Psychology, 13,* 101-107.

Newport, E. L., Gleitman, H., & Gleitman, L. R. (1977). Mother, I'd rather do it myself: Some effects and non-effects of maternal speech style. In C. E. Snow & C. A Ferguson (Eds.), *Talking to children: Language input and acquisition* (pp. 109-151). New York: Cambridge University Press.

Noller, P., & Callan, V. J. (1989). Nonverbal behavior in families with adolescents. *Journal of Nonverbal Behavior, 13,* 47-64.

Norton, R. (1983). Measuring marital quality: A critical look at the dependent variable. *Journal of Marriage and the Family, 5,* 141-151.

Nussbaum, J. F. (Ed.). (1989). *Life-span communication: Normative processes.* Hillsdale, NJ: Erlbaum.

Ochs, E. (1988). *Culture and language development: Language acquisition and language socialization in a Samoan village.* New York: Cambridge University Press.

Ochs, E., & Schieffelin, B. (1984). Language acquisition and socialization: Three developmental stories and their implications. In R. A. Shweder & R. LeVine (Eds.), *Culture theory: Essays on mind, self and emotion* (pp. 276-320). New York: Cambridge University Press.

Ochs, E., & Schieffelin, B. B. (Eds.). (1986). *Socialization across cultures.* New York: Cambridge University Press.

O'Donnell, W. J. (1976). Adolescent self-esteem related to feelings toward parents and friends. *Journal of Youth and Adolescence, 5,* 179-185.

Offer, D., & Sabshin, M. (1974). *Normality: Theoretical and clinical concepts of mental health* (2nd ed.). New York: Basic.

O'Keefe, B. J. (1988). The logic of message design: Individual differences in reasoning about communication. *Communication Monographs, 55,* 80-103.

O'Leary, K. D. (1984). Marital discord and children: Problems, strategies, methodologies, and results. In A. Doyle, D. Gold, & D. S. Moskowitz (Eds.), *Children in families under stress* (pp. 35-47). San Francisco: Jossey-Bass.

Olson, D. H. (1991). Commentary: Three-dimensional (3-D) circumplex model and revised scoring of FACES III. *Family Process, 30,* 74-79.

Olson, D. H., McCubbin, H. I., Barnes, H. L., Larsen, A. S., Muxen, M. J., & Wilson, M. A. (1983). *Families: What makes them work.* Beverly Hills, CA: Sage.

Olson, S. L., Bates, J. E., & Bayles, K. (1984). Mother-infant interaction and the development of individual differences in children's cognitive competence. *Developmental Psychology, 20,* 166-179.

Olson, S. L., Bayles, K., & Bates, J. E. (1986). Mother-child interaction and children's speech progress: A longitudinal study of the first two years. *Merrill-Palmer Quarterly, 32,* 1-20.

Papini, D. R., & Sebby, R. A. (1987). Adolescent pubertal status and affective family relationships: A multivariate assessment. *Journal of Youth and Adolescence, 16,* 1-15.

Parisi, T. (1987). Why Freud failed: Some implications for neurophysiology and sociobiology. *American Psychologist, 42,* 235-245.

Park, K. A., & Waters, E. (1988). Traits and relationships in developmental perspective. In S. W. Duck (Ed.), *Handbook of personal relationships: Theory, research and interventions* (pp. 177-191). New York: Wiley.

Parke, R. D. (1978). Children's home environments: Social and cognitive effects. In I. Altman & J. F. Wohlwill (Eds.), *Children and the environment* (pp. 33-81). New York: Plenum.

Parke, R. D. (1981). *Fathers.* Cambridge, MA: Harvard University Press.

Parke, R. D., & Asher, S. R. (1983). Social and personality development. *Annual Review of Psychology, 34,* 465-509.

Parke, R. D., & Tinsley, B. J. (1987). Family interaction in infancy. In J. D. Osofsky (Ed.), *Handbook of infant development* (2nd ed., pp. 579-641). New York: Wiley.

Parpal, M., & Maccoby, E. E. (1985). Maternal responsiveness and subsequent child compliance. *Child Development, 56,* 1326-1334.

Patterson, G. R. (1982). *Coercive family processes.* Eugene, OR: Castalia.

Patterson, G. R. (1986). Performance models for antisocial boys. *American Psychologist, 41,* 432-444.

Pavlov, I. P. (1927). *Conditioned reflexes.* London: Claredon.

Peterson, G. W., & Rollins, B. C. (1987). Parent-child socialization. In M. B. Sussman & S. K. Steinmetz (Eds.), *Handbook of marriage and the family* (pp. 471-506). New York: Plenum.

Peterson, G. W., Rollins, B. C., & Thomas, D. L. (1985). Parental influence and adolescent conformity: Compliance and internalization. *Youth and Society, 16,* 397-420.

Peterson, J. L., & Zill, N. (1986). Marital disruption, parent-child relationships, and behavior problems in children. *Journal of Marriage and the Family, 48,* 295-307.

Phares, E. J. (1976). *Locus of control in personality.* Morristown, NJ: General Learning.

Phelps, R. E., Huntley, D. K., Valdes, L. A., & Tompson, M. C. (1987). Parent-child interactions and child social networks in one parent families. In J. P. Vincent (Ed.), *Advances in family intervention, assessment, and theory* (Vol. 4, pp. 143-163). Greenwich, CT: JAI.

Piaget, J. (1959). *The language and thought of the child* (3rd ed.). London: Routledge & Kegan Paul.

Piaget, J. (1983). Piaget's theory. In W. Kessen (Ed.), *Handbook of child psychology: Vol. 1. History, theory and methods* (pp. 103-128). New York: Wiley.

Pleck, J. H. (1985). *Working wives, working husbands.* Beverly Hills, CA: Sage.

Poole, M. S., & McPhee, R. D. (1985). Methodology in interpersonal communication research. In M. L. Knapp & G. R. Miller (Eds.), *Handbook of interpersonal communication* (pp. 100-170). Beverly Hills, CA: Sage.

Porter, B., & O'Leary, K. D. (1980). Marital discord and childhood behavior problems. *Journal of Abnormal Child Psychology, 8,* 287-295.

Pratt, M. W., Kerig, P. K., Cowan, P. A., & Cowan, C. P. (1992). Family worlds: Couple satisfaction, parenting style, and mothers' and fathers' speech to young children. *Merrill-Palmer Quarterly, 38,* 245-262.

Putallaz, M., & Heflin, A. H. (1990). Parent-child interaction. In S. R. Asher & J. D. Coie (Eds.), *Peer rejection in childhood* (pp. 189-216). Cambridge, MA: Cambridge University Press.

Quinn, R. H. (1987). The humanistic conscience: An inquiry into the development of principled moral character. *Journal of Humanistic Psychology, 27,* 69-92.

Rathus, S. A. (1990). *Psychology* (4th ed). Chicago: Holt, Rinehart, & Winston.

Rice, M. L. (1989). Children's language acquisition. *American Psychologist, 44,* 149-156.

Rizzo, T. A., Corsaro, W. A., & Bates, J. E. (1992). Ethnographic methods and interpretive analysis: Expanding the methodological options of psychologists. *Developmental Review, 12,* 101-123.

Roberts, G. C., Block, J. H., & Block, J. (1984). Continuity and change in parents' child-rearing practices. *Child Development, 55,* 586-597.

Robinson, W. P., & Giles, H. (1990a). Epilogue. In H. Giles & W. P. Robinson (Eds.), *Handbook of language and social psychology* (pp. 583-588). Chichester, UK: Wiley.

Robinson, W. P., & Giles, H. (1990b). Prologue. In H. Giles & W. P. Robinson (Eds.), *Handbook of language and social psychology* (pp. 1-8). Chichester, UK: Wiley.

Rocissano, L., Slade, A., & Lynch, V. (1987). Dyadic synchrony and toddler compliance. *Developmental Psychology, 23,* 698-704.

Rogers, C. (1961). *On becoming a person: A therapist's view of psychotherapy.* Boston: Houghton-Mifflin.

Rogers, L. E., & Farace, R. (1975). Analysis of relational communication dyads. *Human Communication Research, 1,* 222-239.

Rollins, B. C., & Thomas, D. L. (1979). Parental support, power, and control techniques in the socialization of children. In W. R. Burr, R. Hill, F. I. Nye, & I. L. Reiss (Eds.), *Contemporary theories about the family: Vol. 1. Research-based theories* (pp. 317-362). New York: Free Press.

Rommetveit, R. (1988). Foreword. In D. C. O'Connell (Ed.), *Critical essays on language use and psychology* (pp. v-xii). New York: Springer-Verlag.

Rosaldo, M. Z. (1984). Toward an anthropology of self and feeling. In R. Shweder & R. A. LeVine (Eds.), *Culture theory: Essays on mind, self, and emotions* (pp. 138-158). New York: Cambridge University Press.

Rosenberg, M. (1965). *Society and the adolescent self-image.* Princeton, NJ: Princeton University Press.

Rosenberg, M. (1979). *Conceiving the self.* New York: Basic.

Rosenberg, M. (1985). Self-concept and psychological well-being in adolescence. In R. L. Leaky (Ed.), *The development of self* (pp. 205-246). Orlando, FL: Academic.

Rotter, J. (1966). Generalized expectancies for internal versus external control of reinforcement. *Psychological Monographs, 80,* 1-28.

Rousseau, J-J. (1911). *Emile, or on education* (B. Foxley, Trans.). London: Dent. (Original work published 1762)

Rowe, D. C. (1990). As the twig is bent? The myth of child-rearing influences on personality development. *Journal of Counseling and Development, 68,* 606-611.

Russell, A., & Russell, G. (1988). Mothers' and fathers' explanations of observed interactions with their children. *Journal of Applied Developmental Psychology, 9,* 421-440.

Russell, A., & Russell, G. (1989). Warmth in mother-child and father-child relationships in middle childhood. *British Journal of Developmental Psychology, 7,* 219-235.

Russell, G., & Russell, A. (1987). Mother-child and father-child relationships in middle childhood. *Child Development, 58,* 1573-1585.

Rutter, M. (1974). *The qualities of mothering: Maternal deprivation reassessed.* New York: Aronson.

Rutter, M. (1981). Stress, coping, and development: Some issues and some questions. *Journal of Child Psychology and Psychiatry, 22,* 233-260.

Ryan, R. M., & Lynch, J. H. (1989). Emotional autonomy versus detachment: Revisiting the vicissitudes of adolescence and young adulthood. *Child Development, 60,* 340-356.

Salkind, N. J. (1985). *Theories of human development* (2nd ed.). New York: Wiley.

Sameroff, A. J. (1975). Transaction models in early social relations. *Human Development, 18,* 65-79.

Sameroff, A. J., & Emde, R. N. (Eds.). (1989). *Relationship disturbances in early childhood: A developmental approach.* New York: Basic.

Sanders, M. R., Dadds, M. R., & Bor, W. (1989). Contextual analysis of child oppositional and maternal aversive behaviors in families of conduct-disordered and nonproblem children. *Journal of Clinical Child Psychology, 18,* 72-83.

Santrock, J. W., Warshak, R., Lindbergh, C., & Meadows, L. (1982). Children's and parents' observed social behavior in stepfather families. *Child Development, 53,* 472-480.

Satir, V. (1983). *Conjoint family therapy* (3rd ed). Palo Alto, CA: Science & Behavior Books.

Satir, V. (1988). *The new peoplemaking.* Mountain View, CA: Science & Behavior Books.

Savic, S. (1980). *How twins learn to talk.* New York: Academic.

Schachter, F. (1982). Sibling deidentification and split-parent interaction: A family tetrad. In M. E. Lamb & B. Sutton-Smith (Eds.), *Sibling relationships: Their nature and significance across the life-span* (pp. 123-154). Hillsdale, NJ: Erlbaum.

Schaefer, E. S. (1959). A circumplex model for maternal behavior. *Journal of Abnormal and Social Psychology, 59,* 226-235.

Schaefer, E. S. (1989). Dimensions of mother-infant interaction: Measurement, stability, and predictive validity. *Infant Behavior and Development, 12,* 379-393.

Schaffer, H. R. (1984). *The child's entry into a social world.* London: Academic.

Schaffer, H. R. (1989). Language development in context. In S. von Tetzchner, L. S. Siegel, & L. Smith (Eds.), *The social and cognitive aspects of normal and atypical language development* (pp. 1-22). New York: Springer-Verlag.

Schaffer, H. R., & Collis, G. M. (1986). Parental responsiveness and child behavior. In W. Sluckin & M. Herbert (Eds.), *Parental behavior in animals and humans* (pp. 283-315). Oxford, UK: Blackwell.

Schaffer, H. R., & Crook, C. K. (1979). Maternal control techniques in a directed play situation. *Child Development, 50,* 989-996.

Scheck, D. C., Emerick, R., & El-Assal, M. M. (1973). Adolescents' perceptions of parent-child relations and the development of internal-external control orientation. *Journal of Marriage and the Family, 33,* 643-654.

Schieffelin, B., & Ochs, E. (1983). A cultural perspective on the transition from prelinguistic to linguistic communication. In R. M. Golinkoff (Ed.), *The transition from prelinguistic to linguisitic communication* (pp. 115-132). Hillsdale, NJ: Erlbaum.

Schieffelin, B., & Ochs, E. (1986). *Language socialization across cultures.* New York: Cambridge University Press.

Schrauger, J. S., & Schoeneman, T. J. (1979). Symbolic interactionist view of self: Through the looking glass darkly. *Psychological Bulletin, 86,* 549-573.

Schumm, W. R. (1982). Integrating theory, measurement and data analysis in family studies survey research. *Journal of Marriage and the Family, 44*, 983-998.

Schvaneveldt, J. D., & Ihinger, M. (1979). Sibling relationships in the family. In W. R. Burr, R. Hill, F. I. Nye, & I. L. Reiss (Eds.), *Contemporary theories about the family: Vol. 1. Research-based theories* (pp. 453-467). New York: Free Press.

Searle, J. R. (1969). *Speech acts: An essay in the philosophy of language.* New York: Cambridge University Press.

Sears, R. R. (1951). A theoretical framework for personality and social behavior. *American Psychologist, 6,* 476-483.

Sears, R. R. (1970). Relation of early socialization experiences to self-concept and gender role in middle childhood. *Child Development, 41,* 267-289.

Sears, R. R., Maccoby, E. E., & Levin, H. (1957). *Patterns of child rearing.* Evanston, IL: Row, Peterson.

Shatz, M. (1981). Learning the rules of the game: Four views of the relation between social interaction and syntax acquisition. In W. Deutsch (Ed), *The child's construction of language* (pp. 17-38). New York: Academic.

Shatz, M. (1982). On mechanisms of language acquisition: Can features of the communicative environment account for development? In E. Wanner & L. R. Gleitman (Eds.), *Language acquisition: The state of the art* (pp. 102-127). New York: Cambridge University Press.

Shatz, M. (1983). Communication. In J. H. Flavell & E. M. Markman (Eds.), *Handbook of child psychology: Vol. 3. Cognitive development* (pp. 841-889). New York: Wiley.

Shatz, M., & O'Reilly, A. W. (1990). Conversational or communicative skill? A reassessment of two-year-olds' behaviour in miscommunication episodes. *Journal of Child Language, 17,* 131-146.

Shweder, R., & LeVine, R. (1984). *Culture theory: Essays on mind, self, and emotion.* New York: Cambridge University Press.

Sigel, I. E. (Ed.). (1985). *Parental belief systems: The psychological consequences for children.* Hillsdale, NJ: Erlbaum.

Sillars, A. L., & Wilmot, W. W. (1989). Marital communication across the life-span. In. J. F. Nussbaum (Ed.), *Life-span communication: Normative processes* (pp. 225-254). Hillsdale, NJ: Erlbaum.

Silverstein, M. (1991). A funny thing happened on the way to the form: A functionalist critique of functionalist developmentalism. *First Language, 11,* 143-179.

Skinner, B. F. (1957). *Verbal behavior.* New York: Appleton-Century-Crofts.

Skinner, B. F. (1963). Behaviorism at fifty. *Science, 140,* 951-958.

Skinner, B. F. (1987). Whatever happened to psychology as the science of behavior? *American Psychologist, 42,* 780-786.

Skinner, E. A. (1986). The origins of young children's perceived control: Mother contingent and sensitive behavior. *International Journal of Behavioral Development, 9,* 359-382.

Skinner, E. A. (1991). Development and perceived control: A dynamic model of action in context. In M. R. Gunnar & L. A. Sroufe (Eds.), *The Minnesota symposia on child development: Vol. 23. Self processes and development* (pp. 79-124). Hillsdale, NJ: Erlbaum.

Sluzki, C. E., & Ransom, D. C. (1976). *Double bind: The foundation of the communicational approach to the family.* New York: Grune & Stratton.

Smetana, J. G. (1983). Social-cognitive development: Domain distinctions and coordinations. *Developmental Review, 3,* 131-147.

Smetana, J. G. (1989). Toddlers' social interactions in the context of moral and conventional transgressions in the home. *Developmental Psychology, 25,* 499-508.

Smith, T. E. (1988). Parental control techniques: Relative frequencies and relationships with situational factors. *Journal of Family Issues, 9,* 155-176.

Smolak, L. (1987). Child characteristics and maternal speech. *Journal of Child Language, 14,* 481 492.

Snow, C. E. (1977a). The development of conversation between mothers and babies. *Journal of Child Language, 4,* 1-22.

Snow, C. E. (1977b). Mothers' speech research: From input to interaction. In C. E. Snow & C. A. Ferguson (Eds.), *Talking to children: Language input and acquisition* (pp. 31-50). New York: Cambridge University Press.

Snow, C. E. (1979). The role of social interaction in language acquisition. In W. A. Collins (Ed.), *The Minnesota Symposium on Child Development: Vol. 12. Children's language and communication* (pp. 157-182). Hillsdale, NJ: Erlbaum.

Snow, C. E. (1984). Parent child interaction and the development of communicative ability. In R. L. Schiefelbusch & J. Pickar (Eds.), *The acquisition of communicative competence* (pp. 69-108). Baltimore: University Park Press.

Snow, C. E. (1991). Diverse conversational contexts for the acquisition of various language skills. In J. F. Miller (Ed.), *Research on child language disorders: A decade of progress* (pp. 105-124). Austin, TX: Pro-Ed.

Snow, C. E., Dubber, C., & De Blauw, A. (1982). Routines in parent-child interaction. In L. Feagans & D. C. Farran (Eds.), *The language of children reared in poverty: Implications for evaluation and intervention* (pp. 53-72). New York: Academic.

Snow, C. E., & Ferguson, C. A. (Eds.). (1977). *Talking to children: Language input and acquisition.* New York: Cambridge University Press.

Snow, C. E., Perlmann, R., & Nathan, D. (1987). Why routines are different: Toward a multiple-factors model of the relation between input and language acquisition. In K. E. Nelson & A. Van Kleeck (Eds.), *Children's language* (Vol. 6, pp. 65-98). Hillsdale, NJ: Erlbaum.

Sorce, J. F., Emde, R. N., Campos, J., & Klinnert, M. D. (1985). Maternal emotional signaling: Its effect on the visual cliff behavior of 1-year-olds. *Developmental Psychology, 21,* 195-200.

Stafford, L. (1986). A comparison of maternal conversational interaction with twin and singleton children: Implications for language acquisition (Doctoral dissertation, The University of Texas at Austin, 1985). *Dissertation Abstracts International, 47,* 346A.

Stafford, L. (1987). Maternal input to twin and singleton children: Implications for language acquisition. *Human Communication Research, 14,* 429-462.

Steinmetz, S. K. (1979). Disciplinary techniques and their relationship to aggressiveness, dependency, and conscience. In W. R. Burr, R. Hill, F. I. Nye, & I. L. Reiss (Eds.), *Contemporary theories about the family: Vol. 1. Research-based theories* (pp. 405-438). New York: Free Press.

Stern, D. N. (1974). Mother and infant play: The dyadic interaction involving facial, vocal and gaze behaviors. In M. Lewis & L. A. Rosenblum (Eds.), *The effect of the infant on its caregiver* (pp. 188-214). New York: Wiley.

Stern, D. N (1985). *The interpersonal world of the infant: A view from psychoanalysis and development psychology.* New York: Basic.

Stern, D. N., Hofer, L., Haft, W., & Dore, J. (1985). Affect attunement: The sharing of feeling states between mother and infant by means of intermodal fluency. In T. M. Field & N. A. Fox (Eds.), *Social perception in infants* (pp. 249-268). Norwood, NJ: Ablex.

Stevenson-Hinde, J. (1988). Individuals in relationships. In R. A. Hinde & J. Stevenson-Hinde (Eds.), *Relationships within families: Mutual influences* (pp. 68-82). New York: Oxford University Press.

Stocker, M. C., & McHale, S. M. (1992). The nature and family correlates of preadolescents' perceptions of their sibling relationships. *Journal of Social and Personal Relationships, 9,* 179-195.

Stoneman, Z., Brody, G. H., & Burke, M. (1989a). Marital quality, depression, and inconsistent parenting: Relationship with observed mother-child conflict. *American Journal of Orthopsychiatry, 59,* 105-117.

Stoneman, Z., Brody, G. H., & Burke, M. (1989b). Sibling temperaments and maternal and paternal perceptions of marital, family, and personal functioning. *Journal of Marriage and the Family, 51,* 99-113.

Street, R. L., Jr. (1982). Evaluation of noncontent speech accommodation. *Language and Communication, 2,* 13-31.

Street, R. L., Jr., & Cappella, J. N. (1989). Social and linguistic factors influencing adaptation in children's speech. *Journal of Psycholinguistic Research, 18,* 497-519.

Stryker, S., & Statham, A. (1985). Symbolic interaction and role theory. In G. Lindzey & E. Aronson (Eds.), *The handbook of social psychology* (3rd ed., Vol. 1, pp. 311-378). New York: Random House/Erlbaum.

Symonds, P. (1939). *The psychology of parent-child relationships.* New York: Appleton-Century-Crofts.

Tesser, A. (1980). Self-esteem maintenance in family dynamics. *Journal of Personality and Social Psychology, 39,* 77-91.

Thoman, E. B. (1981). Affective communication as the prelude and context for language learning. In R. L. Schiefelbusch & D. D. Bricker (Eds.), *Early language: Acquisition and intervention* (pp. 183-199). Baltimore: University Park Press.

Thompson, L. A., & Plomin, R. (1988). The sequenced inventory of communication development: An adoption study of two- and three-year olds. *International Journal of Behavioral Development, 11,* 219-231.

Thomson, E., McLanahan, S. S., & Curtin, R. B. (1992). Family structure, gender and parental socialization. *Journal of Marriage and the Family, 54,* 368-378.

Toda, S., Fogel, A., & Kawai, M. (1990). Maternal speech to three-month-old infants in the United States and Japan. *Journal of Child Language, 17,* 279-294.

Tomasello, M., Conti-Ramsden, G., & Ewert, B. (1990). Young children's conversations with their mothers and fathers: Differences in breakdown and repair. *Journal of Child Language, 17,* 115-130.

Tomasello, M., & Farrar, M. J. (1986). Joint attention and early language. *Child Development, 57,* 1454-1463.

Tomasello, M., & Mannle, S. (1985). Pragmatics of sibling speech to one year olds. *Child Development, 56,* 911-917.

Tomasello, M., Maulle, S., & Kruger, A. C. (1986). Linguistic environment of 1- to 2-year-old twins. *Developmental Psychology, 22,* 169-176.

Trevarthen, C. (1977). Descriptive analyses of infant communicative behaviour. In H. R. Schaffer (Ed.), *Studies in mother-infant interaction* (pp. 227-270). New York: Academic.

Van Kleeck, A., & Carpenter, R. L. (1980). The effects of children's language comprehension level on adults' child-directed talk. *Journal of Speech and Hearing Research, 23,* 546-569.

Volling, B. L., & Belsky, J. (1991). Multiple determinants of father involvement during infancy in dual-earner and single-earner families. *Journal of Marriage and Family, 53,* 461-474.

von Bertalanffy, L. (1962). General systems theory: A critical review. *General Systems: Yearbook of the Society for General Systems Research, 7,* 1-20.

Vuchinich, S., Vuchinich, R., & Coughlin, C. (1992). Family talk and parent-child relationships: Toward integrating deductive and inductive paradigms. *Merrill-Palmer Quarterly, 38,* 69-93.

Walsh, F. (1982). Conceptualizations of normal family functioning. In F. Walsh (Ed.), *Normal family process* (pp. 3-42). New York: Guilford.

Waterhouse, L. H. (1986). Problems in framing the nature/nurture question in child language acquisition: A review. *Language Sciences, 8,* 153-168.

Watson, J. B. (1924). *Behavorism.* New York: Norton.

Watzlawick, P., Beavin, J. H., & Jackson, D. D. (1967). *Pragmatics of human communication.* New York: Norton.

Weber-Olsen, M. (1984). Motherese: The language of parent to child. *Texas Tech Journal of Education, 11,* 123-141.

Webster-Stratton, C. (1989). The relationship of marital support, conflict, and divorce to parent perceptions, behaviors, and childhood conduct problems. *Journal of Marriage and the Family, 51,* 417-430.

Welkowitz, J., Bond, R. N., Feldman, L., & Tota, M. E. (1990). Conversational time patterns and mutual influences in parent-child interactions: A time series approach. *Journal of Psycholinguistic Research, 19,* 221-243.

Wells, C. G. (1985a). *Language at home and at school: Vol. 1. Language development in the pre-school years.* New York: Cambridge University Press.

Wells, C. G. (1985b). *Language, learning and education* (2nd ed.). Philadelphia: Nfer-Nelson.

Wells, C. G. (1986). *The meaning makers.* London: Heinmann.

Wells, C. G., & Gutfreund, M. (1987). The development of conversation. In R. Steele & T. Threadgold (Eds.), *Language topics: Essays in honour of Michael Halliday* (Vol. 1, pp. 206-225). Amsterdam: Benjamins.

Wernar, C. (1982). On negativism. *Human Development, 25,* 1-23.

Werner, H. (1957). The concept of development from a comparative and organismic point of view. In D. B. Harris (Ed.), *The concept of development* (pp. 125-146). Minneapolis: University of Minnesota Press.

Werner, H., & Kaplan, B. (1963). *Symbol formation.* New York: Wiley.

Wertsch, J. V. (Ed.). (1985). *Culture, communication, and cognition: Vygotskian perspectives.* Cambridge, UK: Cambridge University Press.

Wilkie, C., & Ames, E. W. (1986). The relationship of infant crying to parental stress in the transition to parenthood. *Journal of Marriage and the Family, 48,* 545-550.

Wilks, J. (1986). The relative importance of parents and friends in adolescent decision making. *Journal of Youth and Adolescence, 15,* 323-334.

Williamson, J. A., & Campbell, L. P. (1985). Parents and their children comment on adolescence. *Adolescence, 20,* 745-748.

Wolman, B. B. (1989). *Dictionary of behavioral science* (2nd ed.). New York: Academic.

Wood, D. J. (1980). Teaching the young child: Some relationships between social interaction, language, and thought. In D. R. Olson (Ed.), *The social foundations of language and thought: Essays in honor of Jerome S. Bruner* (pp. 280-296). New York: Norton.

Wood, D. J., Bruner, J. S., & Ross, G. (1976). The role of tutoring in problem solving. *Journal of Child Psychology and Psychiatry, 17,* 89-100.

Worobey, J. (1989). Mother-infant interaction: Protocommunication in the developing dyad. In J. F. Nussbaum (Ed.), *Life-span communication: Normative processes* (pp. 7-26). Hillsdale, NJ: Erlbaum.

Wundt, W. M. (1902). *Outlines of psychology* (C. H. Judd, Trans.). Leipzig: Engleman. (Original work published 1897)

Yerby, J., Buerkel-Rothfuss, N., & Bochner, A. P. (1990). *Understanding family communication.* Scottsdale, AZ: Gorsuch Scarisbrick.

Yoder, P. J., & Kaiser, A. P. (1989). Alternative explanations for the relationship between maternal verbal interaction style and child language development. *Journal of Child Language, 16,* 141-160.

Zamanou, S. (November, 1985). *A study of teenagers' perceptions of topic appropriateness for discussion with parents.* Paper presented at the annual meeting of the Speech Communication Association, Denver.

Zarbatany, L., & Lamb, M. E. (1985). Social referencing as a function of information source: Mothers versus strangers. *Infant Behavior and Development, 8,* 25-33.

Zilbach, J. J. (1986). *Young children in family therapy.* New York: Brunner/Mazel.

Zukow, P. G. (1989). Communicating across disciplines: On integrating psychological and ethnographic approaches to sibling research. In P. G. Zukow (Ed.), *Sibling interaction across cultures* (pp. 1-6). New York: Springer-Verlag.

Name Index

Meadows, L., 158
Mendel, G., 10
Metgzer, N. J., 42
Metts, S. M., 169
Miller, G. A., 48, 82, 173
Miller, N. E., xiii
Miller, P. C., 42
Mills, R. S., 74, 106
Minuchin, P., 31, 32, 123, 139, 140, 141, 146
Minuchin, S., 31, 134, 144, 147
Misukanis, T. M., 59
Moerk, E. L., 47, 172
Monge, P. R., 30
Montemayor, R., 129
Montgomery, B. M., 175
Moore, J. J., 66
Morgan, S. P., 128, 129, 133, 136
Mueller, R. A., 59
Mullis, A. K., 66
Mullis, R. L., 66
Munn, P., 146
Murphey, D. A., 7
Murray, A. D., 113, 114, 117

Nathan, D., 48, 82
Neimeyer, G. J., 25
Neimeyer, R. A., 25
Nelson, D. G. K., 82, 84, 86
Nelson, K. E., 81, 116
Newport, E. L., 81, 82, 113
Norton, R., 13, 131
Notarius, C. I., 133
Nowicki, S., 44
Nurius, P. S., xv1, 34, 143
Nussbaum, J. F., 12, 136, 149

Ochs, E., 81, 82, 83, 163
O'Donnell, W. J., 80
Offer, D., 13
O'Keefe, B. J., 24, 64, 97
O'Keefe, D. J., 24
O'Leary, K. D., 132, 143, 145, 152
Olson, D. H., 138, 159
Olson, S. L., 85, 86, 87
O'Reilly, A. A., 156

Papini, D. R., 130
Parisi, T., 19
Park, K. A., 24, 139
Parke, R. D, 14, 99, 123, 129, 130, 131, 133, 135, 137, 157, 157
Parpal, M., 105, 106, 107
Patterson, G. R., 103, 108
Pavlov, I. P, 21
Pawletko, T. M., 38, 146
Peery, J. C., 97
Pellegrini, D. S., 133, 158
Pensky, E., 165
Perlman, C. E., 48
Perlmann, R., 82
Peters, J., 113
Peterson, G. W., xi, xiii, xiv, xv, 6, 29, 32, 36, 49, 51, 54, 67, 68, 71, 73, 91, 92, 96, 105, 120, 126
Peterson, J. L., 132, 133
Peterson, R. A., 39, 95
Pfinner, L. J., 143
Phares, E. J., 75
Phelps, R. E., 170
Phillips, S., 144
Piaget, J., 26, 27, 35, 47, 61, 62, 97
Pien, D., 85, 86
Plato, 4, 5, 35
Pleck, J. H., 10, 129
Plomin, R., 9, 21, 94, 146
Poole, M. S., 8, 172
Porter, B., 5
Pratt, M. W., 86, 157, 158
Putallaz, M., 67, 68, 72, 89, 107

Quinn, R. H., 36, 72

Radke-Yarrow, M., 59, 103, 132
Ramseur, H. P., 170
Ransom, D. C., 94
Rathus, S. A., xiii
Reed, M., 76, 77, 110
Rice, M. L., 45, 46
Ricks, B, 16
Ritter, P. L., 59
Rizzo, T. A., 13

About the Authors

Laura Stafford (Ph.D., The University of Texas at Austin, 1985) is Associate Professor in the Communication Department at The Ohio State University. Her research interests include relationship maintenance, conversational memory, and family communication. Recent publications appear in *Communication Monographs, Human Communication Research, Family Relations,* and the *Journal of Social and Personal Relationships.* Current research interests are reflected in forthcoming book chapters on the topics of family communication and relational maintenance. She has served on the editorial boards of *Human Communication Research* and *Communication Research Reports.*

Cherie L. Bayer (M.A., The Ohio State University, 1990) is a doctoral student in Communication at The Ohio State University. Within the area of interpersonal communication, her specific interests include social cognition and communication, the development of communication competence, and children's social development. Her current research includes a longitudinal study of children's interactions with peers and teachers in group settings. The initial phase of this work is focused on argumentative discourse, including social influence and social problem solving. Other interests include children's indirect and direct experience of adult communication in the home as related to children's social competence in other settings.